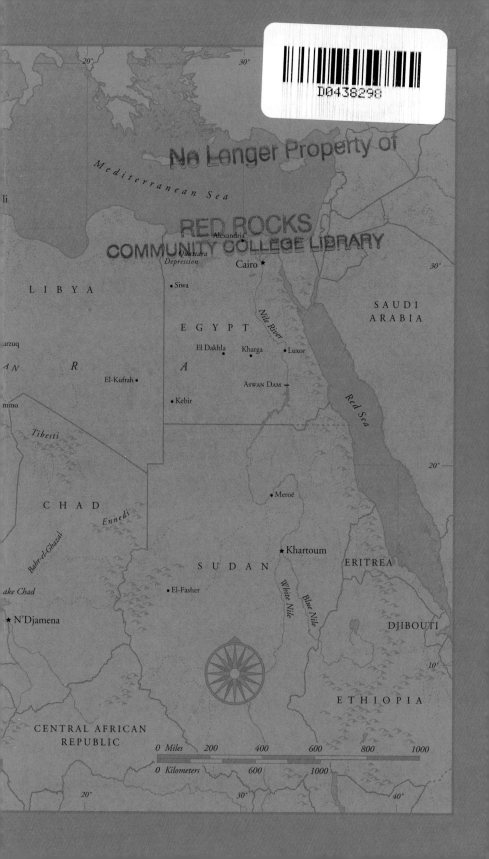

Mediterranean Sea

L I B Y A

E G Y P T

Nile River

SAUDI
ARABIA

Alexandria

*Qattara
Depression*

Cairo ★

Siwa

El Dakhla   Kharga   Luxor

El-Kufrah

A

Red Sea

ASWAN DAM

Kebir

li

rzuq

A N

R

mmo

Tibesti

C H A D

Ennedi

Bahr-el-Ghazal

ake Chad

★ N'Djamena

Meroë

★ Khartoum

S U D A N

El-Fasher

ERITREA

White Nile

Blue Nile

DJIBOUTI

E T H I O P I A

CENTRAL AFRICAN
REPUBLIC

20°   30°

30°

30°

20°

10°

20°   30°   40°

0 *Miles*   200   400   600   800   1000

0 *Kilometers*   600   1000

Sahara

ও

❧

Marq de Villiers

and

Sheila Hirtle

❧

Sahara

A Natural History

Walker & Company
New York

First published in the United States of America in 2002 by
Walker Publishing Company, Inc.

For information about permission to reproduce selections from
this book, write to Permissions, Walker & Company, 435 Hudson
Street, New York, New York 10014

The author has been granted permission to quote material from the
following sources: *The Conquest of the Sahara* by Douglas Porch, reprinted
by permission of Don Congdon Associates, Inc., copyright 1984 by
Douglas Porch. *The Desert Realm: Lands of Majesty and Mystery* (Tor
Eigeland, et al.) and *National Geographic* magazine, reprinted by
permission of the National Geographic Society. *Encyclopedia Britannica*
(on-line). *General History of Africa Vol. 3: Africa from the Seventh to the
Eleventh Century*, I. Hrbek, editor; published by the University of
California Press (Berkeley) and UNESCO (Paris), 1991. Reprinted by
permission of the publishers. *The Golden Trade of the Moors* by E. Bovill,
courtesy of the Bovill family, owners of the Bovill Estate. *The Peopling of
Africa* by James L. Newman (Yale University Press, 1995), reprinted by
permission of Yale University Press. *Saharan Myth and Saga* by H.T. Norris
(© Oxford University Press, 1972), reprinted by permission of
Oxford University Press.

Title page illustration used by permission of Fuoristrada.

Library of Congress Cataloging-in-Publication Data

De Villiers, Marq.
Sahara : a natural history / Marq de Villiers and Sheila Hirtle.
p.   cm.
Includes bibliographical references (p.   ).
ISBN 0-8027-1372-6 (alk. paper)
1. Natural history—Sahara.   I. Hirtle, Sheila.   II. Title.
QH195.S3 D4   2002
508.66—dc21   2002071391

Visit Walker & Company's Web site at www.walkerbooks.com

Book design by Katy Riegel

Printed in the United States of America

2   4   6   8   10   9   7   5   3   1

To Boubacar al-Moctar dit Wantam,
Tuareg of Agadez,
who lives in both worlds
and taught us to love the desert as he does,
unreservedly.

Contents

Sahara

❧

INTRODUCTION

✧

The Idea of the Desert

A GROUP OF MEN, half a dozen in all, are lounging in the meager shade of an acacia in the Sahara Desert somewhere east of Agadez, on the fringe of the sand sea called the Erg de Ténéré, in Niger. Sweet tea is brewing on a twig fire, to accompany a modest midday meal of couscous pressed into small cakes, and dates. It's just after noon. Overhead is the glaring Saharan sun, and the heat is like an iron weight, radiating back from the ground, creating little eddies of convection turbulence, something like sitting on a grill beneath a toaster. An hour earlier the thermometer had climbed past 105 degrees to 115 and then 120, and the steel of the battered Toyota Landcruiser is too hot to touch, the metal pinging in protest.

The men had set out early that morning to look for a petrified forest, now smothered in sand, and for cave paintings. The conversation about these things has wound down, and they are sitting in silence, all talk dried up in the superheated and desiccated air. The breeze is far from a gale, but enough to stir the desert sand, fine as flour. It drifts through the camp and overhead, turning the sky a hazy yellow and blurring the inescapable sun. They have parked their vehicle to windward, but it does nothing to hinder the sand; a tin plate placed on the ground is covered in seconds with a thin gritty film. Sand fills the ears and the nose and the reddening eyes and infiltrates the clothing, drifting sand in every crack and crevice: sand in the tea glasses, sand in the food, a dismaying grit on the teeth. Visibility is minimal, perhaps thirty feet. They sit hunched, merely waiting. Wantam, the leader, has his head on his knees; he seems to be barely breathing.

Out of this sulfurous, swirling obscurity loom three men on camels, plodding steadily through the veil of sand. They pass within a few yards of the camp, but no one says anything, or raises a hand in greeting. The camels are very tall, with impossibly long and knobby legs and an imperious look, snorting and humphing as they move, like old men with heartburn. The three nomads are robed in blue, and veiled, only their eyes showing. Each carries a long staff, pointed downward at an angle past his mount's neck. They are wearing broadswords in leather scabbards, and one has a rifle slung over his shoulder. Water in goatskin bags called *guerbas* bump against the animals' sides.

They move through the camp silently, the camels' feet making no sound on the soft sand. A brief creaking of leather, the breathy burping of the animals, and then they are gone, vanishing into the shroud of sand, heading out into the desert, nothing to mark their passing, as elusive and mysterious as wraiths. Where are they going, these three deep-desert Tuareg? Where have they come from? On what errand? And how, in this trackless land of no horizons, in this minuscule visible universe of maybe twenty paces, do they know their path? They are heading north, but north is nothing but weeks of difficult traveling to nowhere. To the west is the stony massif called Aïr, but to the north and east—nothing.

℘

THE SAHARA, the largest and most austere desert on earth, is indeed the Great Nothing, the Endless Emptiness, land of terrible thirst, a sea without water, a place of fear, of sandblasted bones on the desert floor, a wilderness of sand and stone and barren rock. It's also true that in Saharan travel many, many days pass with no landmarks at all, nothing to mark progress, only a slow plodding in the shimmering heat from sunrise to sunset, over a landscape of numberless stony valleys and plains, of slabs of rock and sheets of gravel, each as featureless as the last. You can plod through the Sahara apparently forever, and all that remains in the memory after a long day's journey are meaningless snapshots: a broken ravine, a line of flat-topped blackened hills, a solitary tree in a tongue of sand where no water has run for years. But all those snapshots blur into those of days previous and days to come, and in a journey's timeline nothing really remains but the heat.

In the Saharan noon it feels as though the temples had been bound with wire pulled tight; the head feels both too large and too light, as though it might crack open like an eggshell in boiling water. A fever of imbalance overtakes the body and the limbs feel disconnected, strange. All motion is painful. Sweat pours out but the skin is dry. It's almost impossible to think clearly, because you can't escape the heat that seems to pierce the center of the skull.

Outsiders who have penetrated this terrible wilderness have struggled to convey their despair. "Parched and lonely wanderers, tormented by the wind and the sand and the sun, cruelly deceived by mirages"[1]; "the silence broken only by the weird unaccountable droning to be heard on a still night"[2]; "the ground and the air melt to a kind of infernal liquid that scorches with every breath."[3] One such wanderer, fallen into the melancholy and contemplative air that the deep desert inserts into travelers' minds, recorded in his journal: "In its grandiose uniformity [it] surpassed any [other] plain of this kind. There was nothing on which the eye could fasten, not the slightest sign of life, a complete picture of emptiness and infinity. Nowhere else does man feel himself so insignificant and forlorn as he struggles with this loneliness, devoid of all resources in a lifeless space apparently without limits. Journeys in the desert make men serious and reflective; the Tuareg and the Tubu, the most gen-

uine sons of the desert, who spend their lives in the lonely struggle
have an almost sinister air, with which no innocent cheerfulness
seems any longer to harmonize."[4]

No European or American who wandered the Sahara in the nineteenth century, not even the grizzled veterans of exploration, lived
to an old age. Those who weren't killed by the nomads for a fancied
slight or for being an infidel or for no other reason but that they had
something a nomad wanted died in the end of exhaustion and wast-
ing and mucky water and bad food and the dreadful sense of
the very flesh under the skin being grilled by the glaring and ever-
present sun.

However, all this is outsider thinking, the more or less romantic
notions of people who have "plunged into the Sahara only to plunge
out of it again," in the phrase of one of them,[5] people who have
gone into the desert as a challenge or an adventure, or as prospectors, or simply to seek solace in a place as remote and empty and
perilous as it is possible to be, hoping to find their center by becoming lost in the eternal, hoping, perhaps, that the soul can be
healed there, in a place where it must perforce contemplate only the
starkest of choices.

It's also outsider thinking to talk of the "pitiless sun of the Sahara," to impute malevolence to the waves of heat that burn down
through the thin air and radiate up from the desiccated oven of the
soil. The sun will turn you into a husk, will shrivel you up, will kill
you if you're careless, but it's not pitiless, it just *is*, as unremarkable
as ice in the Arctic. It's as though a Tuareg nomad of the deep desert
came to New York and on the way into town from La Guardia Air-
port remarked on the "pitiless traffic," for so it would seem, alien,
hostile, life-threatening. To the nomads of the desert, the Berbers
and the Moors and the Tuareg and the Tubu, the Sahara is not a
"howling wilderness," although it's often true that djinns live there,
the spirits who torment men's lives. It is merely the locus in which
they live their lives.

In the stony heart of the Sahara there are many places where no
life breathes. But even there the nomads don't see emptiness, only

openness. Bir-Lahlou, "a place of sweet water," in the austere plains of Western Sahara, was once an oasis for camel trains, but that's all gone. The whitewashed and drowsy buildings are now an outpost of the Polisario Front, whose soldiers have spent most of the past two decades idled in the desert, waiting out a cease-fire that ended sixteen years of war with Morocco. Ibrahim Salam Bouseif, a Polisario commander, explains why they're there: "This may seem like the end of the earth to you, but it is not for us. . . . In the desert we are free; there are no restrictions. We can see forever. We can cast our eyes to the horizon, and all we can see is sand and sky. In the desert our spirits can fly."[6] In this view, a native's view, the desert's austerity is merely a framework within which to imagine a larger life. As the desert saying goes, "Allah removed all surplus human and animal life from the desert so that there might be one place for him to walk in peace . . . and so the Great Sahara is called the Garden of Allah."[7]

But the desert is neither featureless, the endless dune of literary imagination, nor lifeless. Wild creatures live there, and nomads, who survive in the desert like sailors in a waterless sea; the Ahaggar or Tibesti or Aïr Massifs their refuges from the elements and their enemies, the oases knots in the string of caravan routes, places for rest and recuperation, gossip—and plunder. Not empty, but full— full of men and legends, full of sand and stone, full of wind that scours and sudden savage storms, full of relics from the dim recesses of the human imagination, full of creatures frequently deadly, full of refuges in secretive mountain fastnesses, full of traders and traffickers and travelers and trickery.

Full, in fact, of surprises. Water where no water should be expected. Immense reservoirs, deep underground. Lakes that change hue for reasons unknown. Lonely trees with roots a hundred yards long. Forest giants, toppled and turned to stone. Stone circles, older by far than Stonehenge. Emerald mountains, chalk mountains, mountains as black as a sinner's heart or a startling red. Dunes that move by hopping, not by drifting. Dunes the color of blood. Dunes forty miles long. Dunes a thousand feet tall. Sand as soft as talcum, treacherous to the traveler. Blind fish in deep wells. The pitted bones of prehistoric crocodiles the length of a bus. Live crocodiles in a tiny lake, five hundred miles from flowing water. Mummified birds. A raven that lives under a rock. Creatures that absorb the moisture in their own exhalations and don't need water. A place full of nature, endlessly persistent, magically inventive, astonishing in all its particulars. The Great Sahara, indeed.

PART ONE

❦

The Place Itself

CHAPTER ONE

❧

In a Geographer's Eye

FROM SPACE, the Sahara is a brilliant band of caramel and beige, stretching from the dried-blood-red cliffs of Mauritania on the Atlantic Ocean to the bleached bone of Egypt's Eastern Desert hard by the Red Sea. In the north, it laps up against the Atlas Mountains in Morocco, which the ancients thought held up the firmament itself; to the south it extends to the Sahel, the southern fringes of the desert on a line somewhere from the Niger River to Lake Chad, before it shades off into the *Bilad-as-Sudan*, the Land of the Blacks, and then into the savanna grasslands that in turn yield to the tropical forests. Apart from the polar caps, this is the most reflective piece of a planet otherwise made largely of softer blues and greens: an immense harsh glare, 3,320,000 square miles of aridity, stark and dangerous. If you traveled across the United States from Boston to San Diego, you still wouldn't have crossed the Sahara; if you started from Paris you'd be at the Urals, deep into Russia, long before you ran out of Sahara. Even from north to south, its shortest dimension, you'd travel for a thousand miles before you left its grip. In the Tanezrouft of southern Algeria, and in the

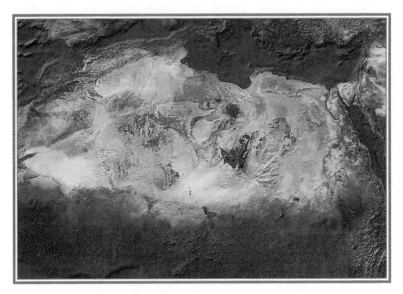

The Sahara from space. (NASA/Goddard Space Flight Center)

other great sand seas of the same country, wells with potable water can be 400 miles apart—from Los Angeles to San Francisco, from Paris across the Alps to Milan, with not a single drop.

What a satellite can see is the big picture, the most obvious features of the desert, though even those are not without their surprises: the great dune fields called *ergs*, which can stretch for hundreds of miles; the skein of wadis, watercourses and drainage basins that once were; the mountains and massifs with their exotic names—Adrar des Iforhas, Tassili n'Ajjer, Ahaggar, Aïr, Tibesti, and Ennedi, mountains that seem to have boiled out of the earth, great wounds, each more than 400 miles across. By contrast, in the northeast near the Egyptian border with Libya is the sunken bowl called the Qattara Depression, the deepest point of the Sahara, 436 feet below sea level, about 7,000 square miles of salt flats, dried-up marshes, and sand.

In closer focus the Sahara is so much more than trackless wastes, unseeable horizons, endless sand dunes, waterlessness, and mirages. Mountains are folded within the mountains, stripped by erosional forces into grotesque castles. Salt flats and smaller depressions were once lakes and are rich in relics of the stone age: pottery shards, tools, broken weapons, fish hooks. Gravel plains, grim and forbidding, are made of black stones. Petrified trees mark where forests used to stand. Secretive caves can be found in the massifs, shelter from the burning sun. And if you know where to look, there is more water than one might think: oases, swamps, artesian hot springs bubbling to the surface, and, in the Aïr and Ahaggar Mountains, a rare waterfall. Scattered here and there are "inselbergs," eroded pillars from a mountain's remnant bin, massive in size. You can climb some of these pillars, a thousand feet, fifteen hundred, but from their barren summits nothing can be seen but a tableau of jagged cliffs and tumbling scarps, stretching on forever.

&

THE SIMPLEST WAY to grasp the Saharan geography is to think of the desert in clusters of countries. Thus to the west, along the Atlantic coast, are Mauritania and Western Sahara (still sometimes called Spanish Sahara, for its status is disputed though the Spaniards are long gone—Morocco, provocatively, has been known to refer to it as "the western province"). Mauritania slides into Mali across an arbitrary straight-line border in the middle of a sea of sand, but Mali is best thought of as part of the southern, or Sahelian, cluster of countries. Counting from the west, these are Mali, Niger, and Chad. To the north of these, along the Atlantic and Mediterranean littoral, are, again from the west, Morocco, Algeria, Tunisia, and Libya. The Saharan heartland is where these northern countries shade into those to their south. The southern frontier of, say, Algeria and the northern one of Niger are the most remote and unchanged of Saharan landscapes. This is where the desert nomads, the Tuareg, the Moors, the Chaamba, and others, found a refuge after the Arab invasions of the seventh century, and it is where many of them still live: Tamanrasset, in Algeria, is often referred to as "the Tuareg capital." Finally, Egypt and Sudan complete the roster of modern Saharan countries. Egypt is ancient, venerable, and complicated enough to be a "cluster" of one, yet has long had its history tangled up with the territory that is now Sudan.

Many of these countries are, qua countries with national governments and seats in the United Nations, relatively new. Their modern frontiers are products of the colonial era, when most of Africa was carved into zones of influence by the imperial powers. But they are, nonetheless, ancient in their essence, with a long, occasionally glorious but oft-times melancholy history.

౯౨

THIS HISTORY is better known along the northern Sahara, where the most venerable of the kingdoms was that of the Pharaohs in Egypt, stretching southward along the Nile and into the larger oases of the Saharan hinterlands. After some three thousand years of continuous rule, the by then creaking edifice of the god-kings was overrun by the Persians in the fourth century B.C., and subsequently by the Macedonians, the Romans, and then—after the birth of Islam—by the Arabs. The rest of the north African littoral, the ancestral home of the Berber people—the modern countries of Libya, Tunisia, Algeria, and Morocco—was invaded by a similar succession of armed colonizers, the Phoenicians, the Carthaginians, the Romans again, and then the Vandals, who arrived in the fourth century, followed by the Byzantines. The Arabs, from their new base in Egypt, swept across the coast in the seventh and again in the eleventh centuries, causing havoc among the settled populations and driving many of them into the deep desert.

The early history of the southern Sahara is less well known. Sometime in the first centuries of the present era—even speculative dates are hard to come by—in what are now the modern countries of Mauritania, Mali, Niger, and Chad, indigenous kingdoms began to coalesce. What is known is that by the time the first Arab proselytizers of Islam crossed the desert, early in the eighth century, these kingdoms—some of them great enough to be styled empires and most of them virtually unknown in the West until recent times—were already well established. The earliest of these was Old Ghana, a trading culture founded on rich alluvial goldfields, and its contemporary and neighbor, Tekrur, followed in turn by Mali, the greatest empire of ancient Africa, and then by Songhai. Farther to the east, around Lake Chad, a kingdom formed around 900 that lasted a thousand years before it was broken up by the French colonialists: This was Kanem-Bornu, a great trading empire of the Middle Ages, well known to the merchants of Europe and the Levant.

In the time of the European Middle Ages, out of the swirling, restless politics of the Sahara, born of the fractiousness between the northern and southern Saharan powers, there emerged the militarized quasi-religious movements that came to be called the Almoravids and later the Almohads, Islamic tribal confederacies based in Morocco. They were born in bloodshed and chaos, but these were the same confederacies that governed Moorish Spain for several centuries, and left behind some of mankind's most perfect architectural monuments.

By the sixteenth century, the great empires of the southern Sahara had decayed, falling victim to internal decadence, or invasion, or jihad, disintegrating into small tribal kingdoms or sultanates of little consequence except to themselves. In the north, the caliphates and sultanates also fell into decay in their time, and for several centuries North Africa was the squabbling ground for a mess of empires and cultures—the Ottoman Turks, the Holy Romans, the Sicilians, the Spanish and Portuguese. In the sixteenth century Spain and Turkey fought a series of inconclusive wars there. In 1578, at the Battle of the Three Kings, Abd'al-Malik, the ruling sultan (and a poet of note), defeated a coalition of Portuguese forces and dissident Moroccans under a dethroned sultan, al-Mutawakkil, which led to a substantial decline in Portuguese influence in North Africa (and ended the dream of another crusade). In the seventeenth and eighteenth centuries the Barbary pirates, operating largely from Algiers, made commercial shipping in the Mediterranean almost impossible. The Americans, who were trying to build up their trade with Europe, reacted angrily. In 1803 George Washington made war against the beys. In one episode in 1805, American marines marched across the desert from Egypt into Tripolitania, giving rise to the famous line in the Marine anthem, "From the halls of Montezuma to the shores of Tripoli."[1]

From 1830, when the French overran Algeria, most of the Sahara was a European protectorate, a nice imperial euphemism, though formal occupation often came later. In 1881 the French occupied what is now Tunisia, and in 1911 the Italians expelled the Turkish government from Libya. The process was completed by the Franco-Spanish occupation of Morocco, which followed the signing of the Treaty of Fez in 1912. In the central and southern desert, the colonial powers—mostly France—simply moved into the power vacuum left by the decay of the old empires; much of their attention was devoted not to governance but to an attempt to subjugate the unruly nomads of the desert, whose politics were still fractious and quarrelsome almost a millennium after these people were driven into the desert by the invading Arabs.

෴

THE MOST WESTERLY CLUSTER of modern countries, Mauritania and Western Sahara, were neglected in the colonial era. Mauritania had been scooped up by the French in 1814, but they barely imposed themselves on the Moorish sultans of the Mauritanian desert until well into the twentieth century. The French rarely ventured into the northern interior, or even to what is now the capital, Nouakchott, and seem barely to have missed the country when it was granted independence in 1961.[2] Western Sahara, for its part, was disputed territory, although the disputes were not very energetic—it apparently had nothing anyone wanted, and it was mostly useful as a base for garrisons controlling the trans-Saharan trade. Spain acquired the land in the so-called Scramble for Africa in the nineteenth century, but did little with it; when they departed, it briefly became a French protectorate but after Morocco's independence both Morocco and Mauritania laid claim to the land, their desire no doubt fueled by the discovery of a huge phosphate deposit at a place called Bu Craa. These assertions were vigorously disputed by the liberationist fighters of the Polisario Front, which (with Algeria's covert backing) waged a guerrilla campaign against the Moroccan as well as Mauritanian authorities for almost two decades, a "war" that in theory was over with the signing of a cease-fire in 1991, though by most measures the ensuing peace has not yet begun.

Of the cluster along the northern Sahara—Morocco, Algeria, Tunisia, and Libya—Morocco is perhaps the best-known. This is partly for historical reasons—it was from Morocco, after all, that the Muslim invasion of Europe was launched, leading to the magnificent Andalusian civilization that bequeathed to posterity such monuments as the Alhambra in Granada. (The expulsion from Spain of the Islamic forces is still remembered as "the Andalusian tragedy" by zealots such as the terrorist Osama bin Laden.) The current king, Hassan, is the latest in an Arab dynasty, the Alawites, who have been at least nominally in charge since the seventeenth century, claiming descent directly from the Prophet himself, through his grandson, Al-Hassan bin Ali. The Treaty of Fez gave Morocco to France, though it took another twenty years for them to subdue the Berbers in the High Atlas Mountains and in the Rif, who waged typically ferocious battles against French units until well into the 1930s.

Algeria was until the middle of the nineteenth century at least nominally a province of the Ottoman Turkish Empire, and the beys or pashas were appointed by and responsible to the sultan in Constantinople. But Ottoman control was tenuous at best, and the pirates who used its ports paid little attention to edicts from the east. The French arrived in earnest in 1830, when they attacked Algiers in response to some fancied slight against a French consul—he apparently had his face slapped with a fan. The Algerian interior was for decades a military occupation zone, kept in check by *mehari* commandos (native troops mounted on swift camels) and the hard-bitten toughs of the Foreign Legion. In 1912 many of the Tuareg nomads of Algeria joined in the Senussi revolt, an Islamic revivalist crusade of Sufi origins whose intentions were to drive the Christians into the sea and free the land from their moral pollution. Nevertheless, France came to consider Algeria an integral part of metropolitan France, and governed it accordingly.

For most of the Islamic period, Tunisia was called Ifriqiyah, from the Roman word for Africa, and for centuries its politics had been bent on mediating between opposing bullying forces, the long-declining but still powerful Ottomans, and Europe resurgent. It was "independent," but only because neither of the two foreign powers was powerful enough to move in on the other, until the latter part of the nineteenth century. In 1881 the French sent in an army, ostensibly to control raids into neighboring French Algeria, and two years later the bey signed a convention acknowledging French "protection."

At the start of the nineteenth century, the territory now called Libya had been in the hands of quasi-independent rulers for several hundred years, most latterly the Karamnli dynasty, and had prospered by giving refuge to the Barbary pirates. In 1835 the Ottoman Turks sent a fleet to assert a rather more direct control. Still, all they managed was to dominate the coastal strip; in the interior, administration was in the hands of their surrogates, the Senussi movement, whose goal in Libya, as elsewhere along the northern littoral, was to restore the purity of society as they imagined it had been at the time of the Prophet. In 1911, though, Libyan self-rule was abruptly ended when the country was brutally invaded by the Italians. Under their tyrannical regime the Libyan population fell by 50 percent, through either extermination or forced exile. What there was of fertile land was expropriated and handed over to Sicilian peasants imported for the purpose.

In the southern Sahara, in what are now Mali, Niger, and Chad, the remnants of the old empires were from the sixteenth century nominally under the suzerainty of a series of regional sultanates and tribal chieftains, but for practical purposes the Tuareg and Tubu nomads of the deep desert were ungoverned and ungovernable. The ancient trading towns of Mali, Niger, and Chad were decaying, their populations static or shrinking. In the colonial era, under France, Chad was so isolated and of such fundamental unimportance that nearly half of all civil service positions were empty at any given time. Indeed, French officials were often assigned there as a punishment.

Egypt (and Sudan, with which its fortunes were entangled) had a succession of rulers who followed the Ptolemies—the Ottomans, the Mamelukes, and then Napoleon, who defeated the Mamelukes

by the simple expedient of rolling into town; after he went back to
France (where faux-Egyptian became the style of choice, feeding off
the treasures Napoleon looted) the British took over, and when they
left, the Ottomans returned, and one of their number, Mohammed
Ali, who came from Albania, set up a dictatorship uniquely pervasive for its time. After his death, control of southern Egypt and
northern Sudan became disorganized and corrupt. There were more
and more European intrusions; the British in particular were med-
dling in Egypt again and interfering in Sudan in a typically imperial
mix of profit-taking, high-mindedness, and an eye for the main
chance, which was control of the Nile. In 1881 the Sudanese finally
rebelled in a fervent religious and political uprising called Mahdism,
led by Mahdi Mohammed-Ahmed, who preached an ascetic version
of Sufism. After several disastrous attempts to defeat the Mahdi by
a succession of British generals had failed, Lord Kitchener finally
put paid to him, with immense slaughter and a considerable degree
of imperial callousness (it was later reported that he used the Mahdi's
skull as an inkstand, but the queen professed herself shocked and the
skull was decently buried at Wadi Halfa).

As for Sudan, it evolved from a number of small kingdoms along
the middle Nile, most of which had been converted to Christianity
somewhere around the sixth century. Increasing Arab immigration
made them unstable, and around 1500 they were absorbed by the
Egyptians, with one exception: In 1504 Amara Dunqas founded the
Funj kingdom in the area just to the south, an area called Gezira,
between the White and Blue Niles. The Funj people were neither
Arab nor Muslim, and except for the fact that they migrated down
the Blue Nile their origin is not known. At its peak in the seventeenth century, Funj, with its capital at Sennar, incorporated most
of Nubia and extended to the Ethiopian border in the southeast and
the semiarid steppes of Kordofan in the west. By the late seventeenth century a rival Islamic sultanate, Darfur, was able to exert
control over trade routes to Kanem-Bornu, and became the major
power in the western portion of present-day Sudan.[3] It covered considerable territory, between Kordofan in the east, Wadai in the west,

southward to the Bahr-el-Ghazal, and northward well into the Libyan desert.

ev

INDEPENDENCE FROM the European colonizers came to the Sahara as it did to the rest of Africa, after the chaos of World War II and the rebirth (or in some cases birth) of nationalism. Libya became an independent state in 1951, Morocco and Tunisia in 1956. Egypt became formally independent in 1952, Sudan in 1956. In 1960 a new country, Mauritania, was created to the south of Morocco and given its independence a year later; and in 1962 Algeria achieved independence in a bloody insurrection in which several millions were killed. The French departed from the Sahel in 1960, and all three Sahelian countries gained their independence that year: Mali, Niger, and Chad.

The colonial era did exert considerable influence on the great desert—European colonial administrators laid out boundaries with scant regard for nature or history, and thereby shaped the modern political map. But in the long Saharan timeline, all in all, the colonial era was a mere eyewink of time, after a single century just one more lot of sad-sack conquerors gone home, leaving the desert to its ancient devices.

ev

IN AFRICA, the notion of a fixed frontier, while cartographically and administratively useful, is a modern idea, a creature of the modern nation-state. For most of the precolonial period, boundaries in the Endless Desert were simply where a ruler's influence stopped. For the Egyptians, this meant the hinterlands of the Nile. For the Moroccan sultans, their "country" meant a huge band of the desert, ever flexible, yielding, and responding to threats and pressures from within and without. For the southern empires of old Africa, it meant they controlled what they could reach, and that was often a very long way—almost all the way across the desert at times.

Traders crossed the desert from antiquity, but they seemed incurious about the nature of the places to which they were going—the configuration of the lands beyond the Great Desert was for centuries a mystery. There were many lurid rumors, and fantastic tales of great wealth, but as a practical matter people north of the Sahara knew very little about those to the south. It really wasn't until later, when explorers such as the fourteenth-century Arab traveler Ibn Battuta were accompanying trading caravans across the desert "to see what was on the other side,"[4] as he blandly put it, that attempts were made to impose a more orderly pattern on the whole.

The first credible geography of the Saharan hinterlands was produced by the Moroccan Abu Abd' Allah Muhammad al-Idrisi, who traveled in North Africa during his youth (he was born in 1100) and then took up residence with Roger II of Sicily, his patron, beginning a lifetime's work of mapmaking and geographical writing. It is unclear how far into the desert Idrisi penetrated, and his main work, *The Pleasure Excursions of One Who Is Eager to Traverse the Regions of the World*, still found much of the land south of the Atlas Mountains a zone of mystery.

Abu l'Hasan Ali Ibn Said al-Gharnati, who was born in 1211, may well have been the first European (he was born in Granada, in Spain) to penetrate the Sahara, and possibly the first outsider to write about it ("may have been" and "possibly" because while he wrote a geographical treatise that included Africa south of the Sahara, much of it was based on the work of earlier writers, notably Idrisi, and it's uncertain whether he actually went anywhere).

For the next several hundred years, it was mostly Arabs who visited the deep desert and returned to write about it, among them Ibn Battuta, in the early 1300s, Ibn Khaldun (1380), and al-Makrizi (about 1400). The greatest of these, and the first to penetrate the Sahara and leave a detailed account of his journeys, was Ibn Battuta, or, as he's styled with admirable precision in a fifteenth-century Arabic dictionary of eminent persons, "Muhammad b. Abdullah b. Muhammad. b. Ibrahim b. Muhammad. b. Ibrahim b. Yusuf, of the tribe of Luwata and the city of Tanja, Abu Abdallah Ibn Battuta." He was born, we know, in Tangier in 1304 of a family of scholars

Ibn Battuta (Encyclopaedia Brittanica on-line)

and lawyers, and went to Mecca for his pilgrimage at the age of twenty-one. There he determined "to travel throughout the earth" and for the rest of his life he wandered about within the limits of his world, making it a basic rule "never, so far as is possible, to cover a second time any road" that he had once traveled, and marrying, on the way, countless wives. He visited Arabia, India, and China, and traveled down Africa's east coast, possibly as far as modern Mozambique. He twice crossed the Sahara to the Niger and beyond, and spent some time in the kingdom of Mali, then at the height of its power and affluence. His account constitutes a major source for a history of West Africa. He lived to the age of seventy, and died, as the dictionary put it laconically, "while holding the office of *qadi*, in some town or other."[5]

One of the earliest true geographies of the Sahara, and possibly the first to attempt a delineation of the natural boundaries within it, was that of the former slave and papal scribe called Leo Africanus, in the early 1500s. Leo, or "Giovanni Leone," born El-Hasan ben Muhammed el-Wazzan-ez-Zayyati in the Moorish city of Granada in 1485, was schooled in Fez, and as a teenager accompanied his uncle on diplomatic missions throughout North Africa and across the Sahara to the Sahelian kingdoms of Mali and Songhai. Leo was subsequently captured by European pirates and sold as "a very learned slave" to the pope in Rome, who promptly freed him and for whom he dutifully recounted what he had learned in an engaging work entitled *History and Description of Africa and the Curious Things Therein Contained.*

Leo's African travels, rendered into colorful English prose in the seventeenth century by one John Pory, were the only eyewitness accounts Europe had of the Sahara regions for several hundred years, and European mapmakers, in a frenzy of creative energy, imagined a place into being based on his sometimes erratic memories. Leo divided the whole Sahara into five different deserts, based on what he thought to be natural divisions, each distinct in the minds of the people who lived there. He called them Zanhaga, Zuenziga, Targa, Lemta, and Berdoa. On a modern atlas, each would cut across national frontiers but still make considerable geographical sense.

એ૭

EVENTUALLY, the urge to explore—essentially the urge to tidy up the chaotic unknown, to extend the borders of the known—came upon the European nations too. This urge was a combination of venal and not so venal motives, like colonialism itself. In the Renaissance the main impulse was avarice—traders followed the legends of the "rods of gold" in Ghana, and of cities whose minarets glittered gold in the desert sun. In the aftermath of the Enlightenment, knowledge was prized for its own sake, and that there should be large tracts still unknown was thought an affront to science. John Pory, Leo's seventeenth-century English translator, appended his own notions of the Great Unknown and what was lacking in our knowledge of it. The problem wasn't knowledge, he asserted, but the dearth of writers, thus proving himself the eternal editor: "In our times, when all Africke hath beene and is daily environed, there is sufficient knowledge had of the Marine parts thereof, but for the inland provinces there is not so much knowne as might be, rather through want of writers than for default of discoverie & trade."[6]

Among the most intrepid explorers of the colonial era were the Scotsman Mungo Park, the Frenchman René Caillié, and the Germans Heinrich Barth and Gustav Nachtigal, though there were many others. Many a curious traveler perished along the way: In the nineteenth century alone, some 150 European explorers lost their lives in the Sahara, a very high proportion of those who set out. Among them was the exotic young Dutchwoman Alexine Tinné, who had her arm hacked off by one of her Tuareg escorts and was left to bleed to death in the Libyan sand.

Mungo Park was one of the earliest European travelers to actually see the Niger and return (he was there in 1795). He became an instant celebrity when he got back to London, but like so many of his fellow explorers he couldn't stay away from the Sahara, and perished on a second expedition. Park's first appearance along the Niger caused a sensation among the isolated communities on the river's banks, which had heard of white people but had never seen one. Legends grew up around him in the southern Sahara—no doubt fueled by his dismaying penchant for pulling his pistol and firing on approaching strangers—and the superstitious Tuareg transformed him into something of a demon. His silver cane, lost when he was killed on his second visit, was said to be the badge of office of a local sultan for one hundred years afterward.

René Caillié is remembered in history not for being the first European to have visited Timbuktu but for being the first to visit the city and return more or less unscathed (Leo Africanus and the other Granadans aside, of course). Caillié was born near La Rochelle, in France, in 1799, the year Napoleon returned from Egypt, bringing with him a fashionable yearning for antiquity and a romantic identification with faraway places. In the introduction to his *Travels*, Caillié admitted he had absolutely no qualifications for exploring, but he always wanted to go to unknown Africa, "in particular, the City of Timbuktoo became the continual object of all my thoughts, the main goal of all my efforts, and I formed a resolution to reach it or perish."[7] When he returned to Paris, his reports were widely disbelieved, for his descriptions of a broken and decaying city were seriously at odds with the city's romantic reputation as a glorious metropolis lost in the desert.

Heinrich Barth was by contrast an academic, and inclined to pedantry, but he was a first-rate explorer, unfairly underestimated in his time. He had many attributes that perfectly suited him to exploration: He was very strong, for one thing; he was thorough and meticulous (his maps were models of their kind); he was a skilled linguist (fluent in Arabic, he later published vocabularies of eight African languages, including Tamashek and Hausa, and learned enough Hausa on a single journey from Ghat to Agadez to be able to converse freely). He stayed in the Sahara for six years, and returned with massive journals packed with priceless ethnographic and geographic information, only to find celebrity passing him by. His contemporary David Livingstone was much more suited than the stolid German to the life of a celebrity traveler, and spoke much more eloquently at revival meetings and at conventions of geographical societies. (Livingstone met Barth once, and gave him an inscribed copy of his *Missionary Travels*, which must have grated.) Barth's books were poorly reviewed and sold only two thousand copies. He died at the age of forty-four.

Gustav Nachtigal (Deutsche Kunstarchiv)

Gustav Nachtigal, who had met and was somewhat smitten with "Fraulein Tinné" in Libya, was not as scholarly as, say, Heinrich Barth, but his prose was more colorful and his journey through the desert lasted five and a half years and covered almost six thousand miles, taking him to parts where no European had yet been, into the secretive heart of Tibesti. His massive three-volume account of his travels makes riveting reading today.

❧

FROM THE NOTEBOOKS of all these travelers a picture slowly started to emerge of the Sahara-as-it-is, rather than the Sahara-of-legend that had dominated imaginations for so long. The desert's contours began to build up, and its natural boundaries to take shape. These were not the boundaries of politics, those imposed by the powers of princes or described in treaties signed in faraway places, but the shapes imposed by the place itself. Political cartographers have taken a ruler and slashed lines across the map, but in natural terms these are simply fictions: The forlorn landscape of Mauritania shades into that of Mali; Algeria and Niger have agreed, more or less, on where the frontier should be, but the desert itself is no different on either side.

Political boundaries aside, the Sahara is composed of distinct and separate parts, and Leo Africanus, despite his occasionally hazy memories, came close to grasping them—the five deserts he described do follow the natural contours of the desert. The huge sand seas of Mauritania, Mali, Algeria, Niger, and Libya are separated by the massifs of the central Sahara. There are mountains parallel to the north coast and in the center; the desert ends, west and east, in cliffs along the Atlantic and the Red Sea. Long-vanished watercourses lie in patterns like lace over the whole, and there are huge salt flats where lakes had once been. These are the boundaries that the nomads of the desert follow, boundaries imposed by nature, dictated by subterranean water and not by police posts, by passages through the massifs and not by national frontiers, by the endurance of camels and not by the edicts of parliaments.

In the far west, in Western Sahara and Mauritania, there are few harbors; the desert simply drops away in sheer cliffs to the Atlantic below. Ocean winds blow almost without letup, the air boiling, troubled, and unstable, stirred by the furnace of the desert intersecting with the cold Canary current coming down from the north Atlantic, hurricanes in waiting. On the ground, dune seas and immense gravel plains are the dominant reality. This was Leo Africanus's Zanhaga, a huge swath of Mauritania and Western Sahara and spilling over into Mali. "A drie and forlorne desert which bordereth westwards on the Ocean sea," he said of the place, and if he could be accused of exaggeration or misrepresentation elsewhere, here he was correct to the point of understatement: "Here are great store of creeping things. In this region there is a barren desert called Azaoad, wherein neither water nor any habitations are to be found in the space of an hundred miles, beginning from the well of Araoan [Arawan], which [itself] is distant from Tombuto [Timbuktu] about 150 miles. Here both for lacke of water and extremitie of heat, great numbers of men and beasts daily perish."[8]

Indeed, Zanhaga was "drie and forlorne," without doubt, in Leo's time as in the present. Archibald Robbins, an American mariner shipwrecked on the shore in the early years of the nineteenth century and enslaved by a ragtag band of Moorish nomads, later described his first sight of Cape Barbas, Western Sahara. After his party picked themselves up from the beach where their vessel had gone aground, "Captain Riley proposed that we should make our way to the land above, [by way of] this inaccessible precipice. We soon began to ascend, crawling up on our hands and knees, catching hold of every substance that would assist us in dragging our bodies forward. It was next to dragging ourselves to the scaffold. It was like becoming our own executioners. We at length ascended the top of the precipice, and, O merciful Heaven! What a prospect presented itself to our affrighted view! What despondency sunk into our hearts! Cast upon a barren heath, a boundless plain, made up of burning sand and flinty stones, producing neither a green vegetable, or refreshing; there to be famished with hunger, devoured by wild beasts, or become slaves to the most merciless of creatures that wear the form of man. Casting our eyes far to the southward, the plain, owing to the striking of the rays of the sun upon the dried sand, appeared like an immense lake. We moved off in a body, keeping in with the coast; and as we wandered near the end of the precipice, we were almost dizzied by the immense distance to the roaring surge at the base."[9] Robbins would see nothing to change his mind were he to reappear in the same spot now; if he were once again forced to clamber up that same great cliff, the same forlorn sight would confront him, causing just as much "affright" as before.

A few hundred miles inland, much too far for the bewildered and despondent castaways to have reached though still in modern Mauritania, are some of the most hauntingly beautiful Saharan landscapes, first massive dunes a startling red in color layered with honey, with a few rare green oases tucked into steep cliffs, and then vast stretches of stone and gravel awesome in their intimidating scale. The plains seem boundless, their surface unyielding, with stones apparently baked into it, as hard as pavement; the hoofs of camels or the tracks of trucks make no impression on it. For hundreds of miles the plain is as level as a lake, barren of shrub, plant, or weed.

These stony plains are called *regs*, or sometimes *hamada*, plains of pebbles and boulders. For the rest, the landscape is saline plains left over from what were once lakes, rare outcroppings of stony mountain, and, of course, dunes. Dunes cover almost half of Mauritania and most of Western Sahara, many of them a score of miles long, in long ridges, often three hundred or four hundred feet high. They butt and intersect and overlap in complex patterns, a network of ridges and dips, crescents and curls, that from above resemble the whorls of gigantic fingerprints. The central plateaus are cut by a network of wadis and drainage basins locally called *gueltas*. On the southern fringes of Mauritania are a few tributaries of the Senegal River, prone to flash floods in summer. The Senegal was once called the River of Gold, because much of the gold that reached Europe in the Middle Ages came down the river from the unknown and therefore mysterious countries in the interior, now known to be Old

Ghana and its neighbor, Tekrur (which today would spill over the Senegal-Mauritania frontier).

The Adrar and Tagant Plateaus are the heartland of Mauritania and home to a good proportion of its still-sparse population. They are jointly called the *Trab el-Hajra*, or country of stone, a rugged landscape of deep gorges and sheer cliff-edged mesas, softened by gently rolling dunes, scalloped and rippled, enfolding the upthrust spears of volcanic rock, a rich palette of golds and browns. Tucked up against these cliffs are oases that nourished the medieval trading cities of Chinguetti, Ouadane, Tichit, Tidjikdja, and Atar, most of them now just ghosts, faded and forgotten. Still, during the wetter part of the year, the few farmers who remain cultivate millet, sorghum, melons, and vegetables in these protected gorges. East of the Adrar are immense ledges of white marble, cut straight and square, as though ramparts for some immense castle, perhaps home to the giants of ancient legend.

North of Western Sahara, curving along the Atlantic coast and then the Mediterranean, and bumping up against Europe opposite Gibraltar, is Morocco. Most of Morocco is not really Sahara at all, but a benign version of the Sahel, cut off from the true desert by the North African coastal mountains, the Atlas ranges, and the Moroccan Rif. It's about twenty-five miles south from Marrakech to the foothills of the Atlas, then a steady climb, then another climb. At the top of the second ascent, and before the pass itself, the infamous Tizi-n-Tichka at better than seven thousand feet, snow frequently falls, and in modern times rows of truckers wait at the summit to descend the far side. *Insh'Allah*, they will say, God willing, we'll get over in safety, but their white knuckles and terrified expressions are not reassuring. On the other side the road drops down to Ouarzazate, there to face the second range, the craggy though less forbidding Anti Atlas. Once past that, the road descends to the Drâa valley, a series of oases with kasbahs and picturesque villages among the palms, on the borders of the desert itself. Zagora, at the end of the string of oases, is the last Moroccan outpost of upscale hostelries. On the outskirts of town is the famous sign, much beloved of tourists: "Tombouctou 52 jours"—Timbuktu fifty-two days. A few miles farther is the camel market town of Tagounite, and the first few shifting dune fields, and beyond that the dusty little town of M'Hamid. Then, over the still-vague border with Algeria, the real desert—nothing but sand, sere scrub, stones, and a few, perilously few, dank and musty wells.

In classical times, many of the northbound caravans coming in from the desert stopped at Zagora for a while to savor the waters before proceeding over the Anti Atlas Mountains and then over the High Atlas to the fleshpots of Marrakech. The Berber nomads still come in through the same dusty hamlet from the desert to Tagounite on market days to socialize, to find wives and husbands, to trade camels and goats and dates and tall tales.

℘

TWO CLUSTERS of countries, as we have seen, make up the Saharan heartland: Mali and Niger and Chad to the south, Algeria and Libya to the north. Tunisia, squeezed as it is on the Mediterranean coast between Algeria and Libya, is, like Morocco, not much of a Saharan presence.

Mali, in the Sahel and south of both Morocco and Algeria, contains fabled and fading Timbuktu, and is itself merely a ghost of the greatest empire of sub-Saharan antiquity. Mali's landscape is flat and monotonous to the north, riven with gullies and sandstone cliffs to the south, where the Dogon people a thousand years ago took refuge from the invading Berbers and Moors, developed their curiously intricate cosmology and buried their dead in high caves in the sheer cliffs (almost three thousand feet at Bandiagara) where they couldn't be disturbed by marauding armies.

Between Mali and Algeria to the north is Leo Africanus's second desert, Zuenziga, "a most barren and comfortlesse place"[10] in which many merchants are found "lying dead upon the same way in regard of extreme thirst." This was not the grimmest of Saharan crossings, but quite difficult enough. In modern days the only relief from the flatness is the Adrar des Iforhas Mountains, which in ancient days might have been an extension of the Ahaggar Plateau, a deeply eroded sandstone massif, barren and scrubbed by the wind, pressed in by the Tanezrouft and the Chech, great *ergs,* shifting seas of dunes.

To reach the Adrar des Iforhas on their way across the desert to the north, caravans set out from Gao, the ancient Songhai trading city on the Great Bend in the Niger River, where it turns southward from its probing of the desert and makes its run down to the fetid swamps of the Gulf of Guinea.

Once past the Adrar des Iforhas, and past its gateway town Tessalit, you are into the true desert, the Tanezrouft. And in the Tanezrouft, as in the deserts north of Timbuktu and Gao, Arawan and Taoudeni, Tamanrasset and dozens of other places in the central Sahara, the sun goes down in a flare like a star burst, and the temperature drops twenty, thirty degrees; a full moon throws the ripples in the dunes into sharp relief, etching the scrub thorns on the sand, indigo against sable. There is frost during the winter nights, but during the day the thermometer climbs again, eighty degrees, ninety degrees, or more. Even in the worst heat of summer, though, the Tuareg won't travel with the moon except in dire necessity; they pitch their tents in the moonlight, they make music against the malign spirits and demons of the night, and sometimes they dance, but often they withdraw into silence, goatskin cloaks wrapped around them, and wait for the dawn.

∾

THE TRUE HOME of these restless nomads, in Leo's view, was the desert he called Targa, and in this again he was accurate enough, for it still is. On a modern map, Targa is the heart of the Sahara: the eastern stretches of Mali, both great *ergs* of Algeria, the Grand Erg Oriental and the Grand Erg Occidental, the Ahaggar and Aïr Massifs of Algeria and Niger, and the venerable caravan routes from Agadez via Tamanrasset to In'Salah and the Algerian north.

Niger is the most dramatic and accessible of Saharan countries, much of it a world of smooth dunes and friendly, almost courtly, Tuareg.[11] Nomads still make their home in the Aïr Massif, where enough water still exists for them to nourish their herds. "The ayre," Leo wrote, "is [there] marvelous holesome, and the soyle aboundeth with all kinds of herbes."[12] Which is not to say that Niger is soft: Some travelers have called the Ténéré, in central Niger, the Land of Fear, though this is at best an uncertain translation from the Tamashek, the spoken language of the Tuareg. (Others have said Ténéré really means "nothing," but some suspect that it doesn't mean nothing—it just doesn't mean anything.) Nor are the Tuareg always as courtly as their reputation suggests. Many of them are in these parlous times just poverty-stricken goatherds, but their historic reputation as the desert's predators exists here too, and bandits still lurk in the high hills to the northeast.

Most of Algeria is desert, and all the flavors of the great desert can be savored there: In Morocco you can taste the desert, but Algeria is full immersion.

Both of Algeria's Great Ergs, the western and the eastern, have over the millennia been drifting slowly toward the Ahaggar Mountains, and both now slope gently downward from the foot of the Ahaggar in the south to the foot of the Massif de l'Aurès, below sea level in the north.

It has been dry here for a very long time, at least since the early Upper Pleistocene era, which ended about twelve thousand years ago, though there are elusive and uncertain signs that at times vegetation gained a foothold. But when the rest of the Sahara was verdant, these *ergs* remained arid; prehistoric man left no traces in this inhospitable wilderness. Today, the people are thinly spread, less than one person per square mile.[13]

In the center of the Great Sahara, Leo reported, was a benighted place he called Gogdem, "where for the space of nine daies journey not one drop of water is to the found." Gogdem has disappeared from modern maps, but was probably the plateau of Tademaït, between In'Salah and El-Goléa in Algeria (only one well, marked on the maps as "good enough water," for some four hundred miles, and in truth its water is usually brackish and smells strongly of rot).

And in the center of the center, on the Tropic of Cancer in southeastern Algeria, is the Ahaggar Plateau, sometimes called the Hoggar Mountains, a tableau of frozen violence, rocks stripped of any vegetation, vast slabs of slag, "a vision of Hell, a land that has incurred the wrath of God, an appropriate home for devils and spirits and for the black-clad men who served them."[14] Frozen violence, yes, but vegetation grows in the secretive valleys, and wild creatures live there, though scarce and wary, and water can be found, enough to make a life for those nomads who seek refuge there.

Ↄↄ

LEO AFRICANUS divided what he called the Libyan desert into two halves—Lemta in the west and Berdoa in the east. Both still make sense in geographical terms. Lemta is that part of the Sahara that stretches south from Tripoli and the province of Fezzan all the way to Lake Chad and the trading towns of the Hausa kingdoms in modern Nigeria, plus a small part of eastern Niger and a good slice of Chad, including the formidable Tibesti Massif. What is now called the Libyan desert would have been Leo's Berdoa. Somewhat confusingly, it includes only a slice of modern Libya, curving in a great arc down from Cyrenaica in Libya through western Egypt and into Sudan to Darfur.

Almost all of this "Libyan" desert was also "exceedingly drie," as Leo put it, "and verie dangerous for merchants." In the Lemta half, a grim if ancient and well-traveled road from Tripoli arrowed across the Hamada El-Homra to the Fezzan town of Murzuq, as indeed it still does, with a slightly less frightening one farther to the west, along the Libyan-Algerian border, through the towns of Ghadamès and Ghat. To the south is the wilderness area now called Addax Sanctuary, east of the Aïr Massif in Niger, and a series of high plateaus, Djado, Manguéni, and Tchigaï, which form a bridge between the Ahaggar and the Tibesti Mountains of Chad. By Sahara standards, though, these weren't difficult crossings. The main route passed to the east of Djado and Siggadim, the latter being the northern outpost of the communities along the Wadi Kawar, and still a principal staging post on today's cross-Saharan routes. The long wadi's towns—Gazabi, its ancient capital, Dirki, its current political capital and residence of the local sultan, and Ashinuma—owe their existence to the water that lies shallowly underneath, left over from "the long ago." Salt mined in Dirki is a pretty pink in color.[15]

The largest settlement between the Wadi Kawar and Chad is Agadim, a notorious haunt of freebooters and slave raiders in the old days and still a rendezvous point for the smugglers of human contraband.

෴

LIBYA THE RIVERLESS is mostly stony plain and craggy rock, volcanic peaks and boulders, some of them square cut and hundreds of feet high, more resembling the work of prodigious artificers than that of any natural agency. Alexander Gordon Laing, the British explorer who met a treacherous end near Timbuktu in 1825, wrote of Libya's "forlorn, black-looking plains; the eye of the traveler roams in vain over the wide, unvarying superficies, in search of some object to rest on, till at length, wearied by the bleak and tedious sameness, he is willing to pull the folds of his turban over his eyes and to shroud his head in a burnoosa."[16] The landscape is made up of sandstone escarpments, volcanic moonscapes, *regs,* and shifting seas of dusty gray sand. An arm of the Tibesti Mountains stretches northward from the main massif in Chad; Picco Bette rises to 7,500 feet on the border. While there are no perennial rivers, the numerous wadis are filled by flash floods during the rains but quickly dry up or are reduced to an intermittent trickle. Elsewhere in Libya matters are less grim: The Al-Kufrah oasis was famous the desert over for its fruits and its dates, and the province called Fezzan contains many somnolent towns and was a desirable prize for a sequence of conquerors over the centuries.

Somewhere in Libya is an imaginary north-south line. The Sahara on each side is indistinguishable from the other, but all ancient travelers knew where it was: When they crossed it, they moved from the East, called the *Mashriq* (Egypt, Mesopotamia, Arabia, and the Prophet's birthplace, that is, civilization), to the West (the *Maghreb*),

frontier country. In modern terminology, the word *Maghreb* is colonialist shorthand for the coastal states that stretch from Morocco
(sometimes included, sometimes not) eastward to Libya; it is used
in the same way that the term *Levant* scooped up Lebanon, Palestine, and a vague area of the eastern Mediterranean, and was often
in French writing given a slightly derogatory cast.

The modern country of Chad, south of Libya, is essentially a
huge basin surrounded by massifs, lined with clay and sediment left
behind by the ever-shrinking Lake Chad. Only three rivers are left
in the country: the Chari, which flows into Lake Chad from the
south; the Logone River, which joins the Chari; and the Ko-
madougou, which runs only intermittently and flows from the west
before petering out in the north. Otherwise, the country is a land of
stony, eroded landscapes. The sandstone peaks of the Ennedi
Mountains, and the crystalline mountains of Qaddaï to the southeast of Tibesti, are more open, softer, broader than Tibesti itself or
the Aïr. North of Ennedi is the Mourdi Depression and the Erdis
Plateau, both hyperarid and lifeless, but on the escarpment nearby
rain sometimes falls, and the nomads pasture their cattle in its lee. A
lion was killed there not long ago, a long way from its normal habi-
tat, following a nomad's herds; its skin is now in the Museum of
Natural History in Paris.

☙

MOST OF WHAT is now Sudan and Egypt remained unvisited
by Leo; he dismissed it (and its inhabitants) with a single sneering
paragraph as "inhabited by certain Arabians and Africans commonly called Leuata; and this is the extreme easterly part of the
deserts of Libya." The people who lived there, in Leo's view, were
"black, vile and covetous, yet exceeding rich."[17]

"Sudan," in classical usage, is elusive of definition. The word *Sudan* (as in *Bilad-as-Sudan*) is used at different times and by different
classical writers to mean different things. Until this century the
word was used to describe either the southwestern Sahara or all of
the southern Sahara, and even now in common usage "eastern Su-

dan" is a loose term that includes a number of rather far-flung independent countries.

Sudan, the country, is Africa's largest, almost 8 percent of the continent's landmass, and one of its poorest. It straddles black Africa and the Arab north, and has ancient links with Egypt and Ethiopia. Geographically, Sudan is about a third rock desert, a third flowing dunes, and a third clay-pan basin known as the Sudd Marshes, where the Nile pauses on its way to the sea.

These marshes, home to more than one hundred thousand people, are perhaps the most extraordinary feature of the Sudanese landscape. What is now marsh was once a great lake, but even these remnant marshes hold a great deal of water, which is greatly coveted by the Egyptians, who are rapidly running out of water of their own. The Sudd Marshes represent Egypt's only possible source of extra supplies—draining them, by some measure, would each year add almost a billion cubic meters of water to the Nile. Sudan, not surprisingly, is vigorously resisting this notion.

The northern part of the country is rock desert, the central portion undulating dunes, eight hundred miles of unrelieved rolling billows, each about ten feet high and perhaps a hundred yards long, a corduroy of sand from horizon to horizon, monotonous and disorienting. Curiously, craters and even small hills are found in various places that consist entirely of small round stone balls the size of peaches, "as nearly globular as anything in nature—a bubble, a drop, a planet. They must be cemented with some tough ingredients, as they were excessively hard to break."[18]

✧

EGYPT IS, crudely drawn, the Eastern Desert and the Western Desert, with the Nile, of course, as the country's lifeline. Without the Nile, Egypt as we know it would not have been possible. There are no other rivers in Egypt, and it scarcely rains.

The Eastern Desert, almost a quarter of the country, extends from the Suez Canal, the Gulf of Suez, and the Red Sea to the Nile. A limestone plateau lines the Mediterranean shore, which breaks up around

Qina into cliffs about 1,600 feet high and is deeply scored by wadis, which make it very difficult to traverse. Wonders exist there too. Pliny had reported "emerald mountains" somewhere in the desert; James Bruce, the Scot who explored Ethiopia in the eighteenth century, came across them when he traversed the desert from the Nile at Karnak to Cosseir (now Quseir). Not emerald, exactly, but "eight miles of dead green supposed serpentine marble, by far the most beautiful kind I have ever seen." Nearby, too, were mountains of red marble, "in prodigious abundance."[19] The Western Desert, some 262,000 square miles between the Nile and the oases of Farafra and Bahariya, is one of the driest parts of the Sahara, though even here, in ancient days, there was apparently some water, for satellite photos show a skein of erosional channels, as faint and elusive as Martian canals. The region slopes gradually westward from the Nile to the first of the depressions that are its most characteristic feature. Here too is the oasis variously known as al-Dakhilah, Dakhla, Dakhleh, or El-Dakhla, already famous when Herodotus was writing his histories, two and a half millennia ago. In this everlasting oasis are the oldest ruined buildings in all of Africa, Neolithic huts dating back perhaps twelve thousand years, as well as Egyptian temples, tombs, and an entire buried Roman city, a Pompeii of the desert, smothered not by volcanic ash but by the relentless drifting sand. Northwest from Bahariya the plateau, now a landscape of ridges of blown sand interspersed with stony tracts, continues to fall toward Siwa and the Qattara Depression. Qattara itself was once the home of one of the ancient world's preeminent oracles, the Oracle of Ammon, to which Alexander the Great came, demanding and imperious.

This is desert that belies the monotony of Saharan reputation. Between the oases there are giant white chalk formations, like tombstones in a futuristic cemetery. Elsewhere the palette of the dunes and striated rocks is rich in reds, from pomegranate to rose; mica glitters in the sun; there are ridges of charcoal and gray and a startling purple. The lake in the oasis at Fayoum is that same brilliant purple.

Some of these oasis lakes have turned saline. Some are large enough

Ancient mosque at the Dakhla oasis. (State Information Service, Egypt)

to have a fishing industry. A few years ago, to the astonishment of or-
nithologists, cormorants showed up in the Western Desert oases,
somehow attracted by the fish that had been introduced to the lakes,
and they stayed, a very long and dusty flight from the ocean.

ᢏᢌᢎ

I F Y O U F L Y over the Sahara in daylight—say from Cairo to
Bamako, Mali's capital, or Marrakech to N'Djamena in Chad,
crossing as you do so the desert's invisible frontiers—you can spend
six hours staring out the window at the ground and not see a living
thing. Even at relatively low altitudes, the game trails and wandering human tracks that mark the most arid landscapes of sub-
Saharan Africa are almost entirely absent. What you see is a color
palette peculiar to the place. The immense sand seas (those massive
stretches of caramel and beige) blend into the grays and duns of the
hamadas and the dusty silvers of the salt pans; here and there are
sharp spikes of black basalt and patches of iron where the central
mountains have punctured the planet's skin, leaving monstrous
scars. If you pass over a few isolated oases, you may not see the

towns that infiltrate them—they are dun against dun, and unless you see the flash of the sun on metal or glass you won't know they're there—but you will, if the sun is in the right quadrant, spot the dusty green of a date grove. No matter how large, those groves look pathetically small and brave against the awful immensity on every side. They look as though they are clinging to life, being overtaken by the desert, as indeed many of them are. The massive, inexorable, inescapable desert itself, fearful and deadly, looks for its part as though it has been there forever—which is not, by any means or any definition, true.

CHAPTER TWO

❦

From the Distant Past

IN THE DUSTY little hamlet of Tin Téhoun, forty miles or so into the desert north of Timbuktu in Mali, earthworms tunnel in the moist soil around the town's only well. Dig a shovel down into the soil, a yard, two yards, maybe more, and there they are, looking no different from earthworms in Asia, Europe, America, or elsewhere in Africa, six or eight inches long, dirty red in color, slimy to the look and the touch, unprepossessing and unlovely. To farmers and gardeners, and to ecologists and the ecologically correct, they're the preeminent symbol of an ecosystem's health. Indeed, the date growers of the Sahara frequently judge the fertility of local soil by the number of earthworm casts to be found in it. Earthworms aerate the soil, bring it nutrients, prepare it for planting, though in this unlikely place only the odd date palm grows.

Desirable as they are, earthworms are also vulnerable creatures. They are extremely sensitive to the loss of body water, and will die within hours if exposed to the air, particularly aquatic species. Yet earthworms exist in all the damp places of the Sahara, and aquatic worms in oases a very long way from places where rain commonly falls or rivers commonly run—in Tin Téhoun, for example. Tin Téhoun is a small hamlet, not much more than a few ramshackle houses and the well, shabby and down-at-the-heels. Even the palms look dispirited, poor cousins to the robust groves of the northern oases. The nearest occasional water, the Niger River floodplain, is at least fifty miles away to the south. To the north, sixty or seventy miles away, is another hamlet not much different. Maybe two hundred miles to the northeast is the drainage basin around the Timétrine Mountain, a flattened adjunct of the Adrar des Iforhas, but the drainage basin hasn't actually drained anything for millennia, and is as arid as the surrounding desert. Yet here are earthworms, as slimy and glossy as ever.

How did they get here? Where from? Why here? How long ago? Did they migrate here, in different times, or are they retreating? Were they always here, and are now cut off from their "cousins" elsewhere? And if they did arrive in the deep desert in earlier epochs, when? In any case, their "migration routes" shed some light on geological events and on the history of human interaction with the Sahara, as an Egyptian team thought when they began an esoteric and unlikely study of deep-desert earthworms.

The Egyptian study, by S. I. Ghabbour of Cairo University's Institute of African Research and Studies, had become interested in genus, and then in species. Earthworms may look alike, but different parts of the Sahara are inhabited by different species, with some curious connections. The worms of the northwest—Western Sahara, Morocco, parts of Algeria, even the offshore Canary Islands— are identical to those in Spain and Portugal. Species found in eastern Algeria, the Tripoli area of Libya, and as far east as Siwa in Egypt are similar to those found in Sardinia and Sicily.

The worms of the eastern Nile region can also be found in the Levant and as far north as Rumania. The earthworms of the southern Sahara live along four distinct tracks. The first follows the Blue Nile north from the Ethiopian Plateau; the second starts in Kenya and ends at the Siwa oasis in northern Egypt; the third starts near

Africa's Great Lakes, especially around Lake Victoria, passes through Sudan, and finishes in Tunisia; the fourth, most curious of all, is a long and sinuous trail that starts in West Africa, in Liberia, and follows the southern Sahara all the way to the Nile and thence north to Lake Dahshour, near Cairo, a distance of more than three thousand miles.

The migration patterns, if that's what they are, of the Saharan earthworms in some ways confuse as much as enlighten. But their widespread dispersal in the desert is clear and unambiguous evidence that the Sahara was once a great deal more humid than it is now, at some or many times in the distant past. The earthworms aren't by any means the only evidence, but they are conclusive. The earthworms didn't hitch a ride on a camel; they came on their own, through soil that was moist and nutritious, and were trapped in the few places where moisture remains.

☙

GEOLOGICALLY, the entire desert sits on the African Shield, bare and intricately folded pre-Cambrian crystalline rock. This shield, like those in North America and elsewhere, has remained stable through many geological epochs. About 580 million years ago, this stability was rudely (if briefly, in geological time) interrupted by the so-called Pan-African Episode, a violent twisting of the continent's surface, caused by tectonic plates colliding. Its effects were startling, long north-south folds in the continental structure, including two in the Sahara: The Dahomey-Ahaggar belt between Ghana and Algeria, and the Mauritanide belt from Senegal to Morocco. Subsequent depositions of rock during the Paleozoic epoch, somewhere between 570 and 250 million years ago, have remained relatively unchanged, but nevertheless the shield structure is scarred with numerous basins and depressions in the north, and in the south, where it slopes away, it enfolds the huge basin sometimes referred to as Mega-Chad, which is where Lake Chad itself is now to be found.

The Paleozoic rocks were in turn covered by Mesozoic deposits (250 to 66 million years ago), among them the limestones of Algeria, Tunisia, and Libya, including the Nubian limestone of the Libyan desert, in which "relic" deposits important to humans are now to be found, such as petroleum and, more curiously, water. Pools of petroleum, remnants of forests-that-were, are found in a massive band across the northern fringes of the Sahara. Oil was first found in significant quantities at In'Salah in Algeria in the 1950s, but reserves exist in Morocco, Tunisia, Chad, and Niger; major fields of natural gas are found in Algeria, Libya, Tunisia, and Egypt. As for water, caverns in the deep rock contain massive aquifers of fossil water, some of it very old. Flat and forbidding northern Mali may be, but a vast water-bearing stratum is known to lie several thousand feet below the surface, just as others do in Algeria, Libya, and Egypt, and Malian engineers are looking enviously at what Colonel Qaddafi is doing in Libya, diligently mining water for new agricultural zones along the coast.

Underneath, far below the earthworms of Tin Téhoun, the Sahara is not at all the austere place it seems on the surface. The sifting-sieve of geologic time has given the desert its normal share of planetary rocks and minerals. Along the Moroccan-Algerian border are deposits of manganese and zinc and cobalt; there is iron in Mauritania and all the way across to Libya. Copper is found in Algeria, phosphates in Morocco and Western Sahara. There is mercury at Azzaba in Algeria.

It is said that the gold of Old Ghana once stuck up out of the ground in large rods or spikes, there for the taking. These golden rods have gone now, if they ever existed outside the campfire stories of avaricious traders, but alluvial fields are still worked in the southern Sahel, and prospectors keep looking for more.

And there is salt, of course. The trade in Saharan salt kept the caravans moving long after the gold and then the slaves had diminished; and although the towns of the Sahel and the north now have to compete with cheap imported salt in hundred-kilo bags, caravans still travel the increasingly obscure roads to Taghaza or Bilma.

৵৲

IF YOU THINK of yourself as the leader of a caravan threading its way, not as the modern ones do from oasis to oasis through the stony *regs* where nothing lives, but rather backward through the long tunnels of geological time, through fossil and ossuary and shell and forest-turned-to-stone, the landscape would morph into something magically different: humid, fecund, full of molds and moisture, dense with jostling wildlife.

There were dinosaurs in the Sahara, as there seem to have been pretty well everywhere, proof enough that the desert was once humid and fertile. About 100 million years ago the whole Sahara was forested, moist; home to dinosaurs, crocodiles, massive turtles, pterosaurs, and fish of all sorts. To the south of Tazolé, which is about sixty miles east of Agadez in Niger, is a dinosaur cemetery, one of the world's most extensive and important. The fossils are spread over a belt ninety miles long, some of the bones peeping coyly from the sand at the top of the dunes, buried and reburied a thousand times. Now they are picked over by the odd tourist or hacked up by the Tuareg to make anklets and bangles.

In the same Ténéré Desert, a team from the University of Chicago in 1997 uncovered an enormous predatory dinosaur, with a skull like a crocodile's and foot-long thumb claws. The sickle-shaped claw was protruding from the desert, exposed by the wind; one of the Chicago team, David Varrichio, almost literally stumbled on it. Excavation led to four hundred more pieces of the skeleton, buried just inches under the desert floor. The creature, a "spinosaur" called *Suchominus tenerensis*, would have been thirty-six feet long and twelve feet high at the hip. "This," said team leader Paul Sereno with some understatement, "would not have been a friendly place. If you weren't grabbed by a spinosaur, you'd likely run into a 50-foot crocodile." Farther to the east, the Cairo

Fossilized skull from the Sahara. (Middle Tennessee State University)

Geological Museum has uncovered what it calls "giant prehistoric amphibians" in the Bahariya oasis in the Egyptian desert; these strange creatures, up to sixteen feet long, lived as recently as 94 million years ago.[1]

Signs of ancient forests, too, are everywhere in the desert. In Algeria, Niger, and Chad are forlorn stands of fallen forest giants turned to stone, petrified after they fell, now impervious to decay, if not to erosion. Near the deep Saharan village of Uigh es Serir in northern Chad, "the last well before Tibesti," are the remnants of petrified tree trunks, as thick as boulders in places, some several feet across but mostly splintered into smaller fragments of light brown stone on which the growth rings of the trees can be clearly seen.[2] In the Tiguidit cliffs of Niger, fallen forest giants turned to stone have been dragged away by the nomads to mark their wells. All over the desert, indeed, these melancholy relics are stood on their ends by the Tuareg as trail or water markers, and generally treated with casual contempt; pieces are chipped away to give as souvenirs, careless of their possible historical significance.

Reeds and grasses petrified too: Around many of the salt pans that were once lakes, particularly in the southern Sahara, are curious calcified reeds, looking oddly glasslike and resembling nothing more than tiny ventilation shafts, marking out the former extent of now vanished lakes.

&

IN CHAD'S BAHR-EL-GHAZAL (not the same as Sudan's Bahr-el-Ghazal, which is a tributary of the Nile), shells as large as dinner plates litter the former riverbed, as do the fossilized bones of fish six feet or more in length. Paleolithic fishing settlements dating back fifty thousand years or more have been found in the region, with stone harpoon-heads, large heaps of mollusk shells, shells of turtles and fish bones. One theory is that the Ténéré desert represents the ancient bottom of a much-expanded Lake Chad.[3] Indeed, every large depression in the desert has its store of shells, frequently stirred to the surface by the shifting winds. The bones of crocodiles, hippopotamuses, elephants, zebras, Cape buffalo, elephants, and gazelles have been found, as well as windblown ridges of lake-bed chalk[4]—more evidence, were it still needed, that the region has been dotted with bodies of freshwater. Far to the west, along the boundless plains of Western Sahara and Mauritania, there are flattened mesas, crumbling vestiges of a larger plateau, made not of sand but of tiny shells. Antoine de St. Exupéry's airplane was once forced down on just such a mesa in the Rio de Oro region in the far western Sahara, and he slouched about, disconsolate, kicking up the "sand" when his boot hit a "a hard, black stone, the size of a man's fist, a sort of molded rock of lava incredibly present on the surface of a bed of shells a thousand feet deep."[5]

The evidence is there for the tutored eye. Geologists "see" the Sahara by looking at remnants of vast drainage systems: the presence of large numbers of dry lakes, deposits of travertine, the presence of soils that form under tropical conditions, rock weathering requiring standing pools of water, vast dune areas that were once fixed in place by vegetation, alluvial deposits interpreted in terms of climatic change—all evidence that the desert had a much more verdant past.[6] In the rare wet winters, ancient landscapes magically reappear, the water like some invisible ink made visible through trickery, and the wadis flow once more, the depressions fill to become pools, and the salt pans momentarily become still waters.

❦

THE FETID SAHARAN SWAMP (or verdant paradise, depending on your ecological perspective) existed in all its profusion in the late Tertiary period, not much more than 5 million years ago, when the monsoon line was almost a thousand miles north of where it is now. There were dry patches even then—Algeria's Great Western Erg has no prehistoric remains, indicating it was arid throughout the period[7]—but most of the desert was dense with humidity.

After the Tertiary period, the almost tropical wetland dried up. Once, twice, three times, possibly more—the Sahara has been a desert more than once. It was humid, according to the geological evidence, several times during the long Pleistocene period (from 1.6 million to twelve thousand years ago). The "fossil aquifers" that underlie much of Libya and Algeria have been dated to between ten thousand and thirty-five thousand years old, which means that the water seeped into the soil from Pleistocene and Holocene (the past twelve thousand years) rainfall. Desertification followed humidity once more, and once more, and again, in roughly ten-thousand-year cycles—the desert came forty thousand years ago, thirty thousand years ago, twenty thousand years ago.

The end of the last glacial period, about fifteen thousand years ago, was everywhere marked by a tremendous increase in rainfall. The Sahara had been a desert throughout the Ice Age, but during this early Holocene period, as the ice melted and the rainfall increased, lake levels in America, Europe, and everywhere else, including Africa, peaked approximately twelve thousand years ago (the so-called Allerod Warm Stage) and then again about nine thousand years ago (the Boreal Warm Stage). The record of the Nile sediments is similar. The Nile, and probably the Niger River too, became completely blocked with drifting sand during the latter arid years of the Pleistocene, when glaciers gripped the continents north of the tropics. When solar radiation increased and the glaciers began

their retreat, the rains came back; the tremendous increases in the
Nile flows, and therefore its sediments, also occurred twelve thousand and again nine thousand years ago.

These fecund Holocene years showed increased monsoonal rains.
Once again, the Sahel, the southern desert boundary, was four to five
degrees of latitude farther north than it is now, and contained a series
of lakes that flooded annually with water draining from the Saharan
highlands. Savanna grasses spread across the desert; the lakes and
wadis filled up, and rivers teemed with fish. Lake Chad was fifteen
times its present size. Forests appeared: Atlas cedar, sycamore, ash,
linden, and willow grew throughout the modern Sahara; oaks and
cedars grew in the highland areas of the Ahaggar and Tibesti.

In the mid-Holocene period, mean average temperatures were
two or three degrees hotter than today (four degrees in Arctic and
sub-Arctic regions). These were ideal conditions for the flowering of
human cultures. The summers were balmy and the growing seasons
extended a month each way, and a number of civilizations flowered,
in Mesopotamia and elsewhere. Some twelve thousand to ten thousand years ago, the first signs of a more sophisticated human occupation came into sight in the Sahara.

Then, six, seven, eight thousand years ago the Sahara began to
dry up again, transforming itself in the process into the greatest
desert on earth. For the last three thousand years or so, the climate
has remained what it is today, as hot and arid as any place on earth.

∽

IF THE SAHARAN CLIMATE has remained stable for the
last three thousand years, has the desert itself? The evidence is ambiguous. In fact, whether the desert's boundaries have remained stable, and remain stable, is a debate of furious intensity and acrimony
in academic journals.

The Sahara might be growing, it might be shrinking, it might
simply be shifting its boundaries. If it is changing, it might be due
to human carelessness, ill-understood climate cycles, planetary mo-
tions, axial tilt, or all or none of the above. For every theory there is

a countervailing theory, and for every piece of evidence another that contradicts it.

The arid conditions of today have prevailed at least since Roman times, if not before. For many years the Romans succeeded in keeping the desert at bay: The greatest engineering culture of the ancient world was never deterred by anything as mundane as a lack of essential resources, and they built aqueducts to bring in water from very long distances; in numberless northern oases the sinuous curves of the old Roman carriers still stand, or lie half buried like giant sandworms. Farther to the east the Greeks, using a system of stone cisterns in still more difficult circumstances, maintained fields and vineyards extending all the way from Cyrenaica in Libya to Alexandria in Egypt. Like the Roman aqueducts the Greek works, too, are in ruins, but the damage was human-caused, not a consequence of climate change, or the further failure of what little rain did fall. They were pulled down in a fit of destruction by invading Arabs in the eleventh century.[8]

Some of the changes in desert ecosystems are relatively new. A French military man, Lt. Gralt, writing in 1945, pointed out that "not long ago it was possible to travel from the Aïr to Termit [to the southeast], finding water every day where now there are no wells for 150 miles."[9] In Roman times in certain eastern oases the wells were no more than fifteen feet deep; now, some of them go down more than four thousand feet, and the water tables are still dropping.

On the other hand, in Sudan and around Lake Chad there are dune patches that were set in place a few thousand years ago when the rainfall belt was almost three hundred miles south of where it is now; within the last millennium they have been colonized by vegetation—do these shifting boundaries mean the desert is actually shrinking?

☙

WHAT IS NOT at all in dispute is the rapidity with which the Sahara, in its current form, became a desert last time around. It changed, in fact, from verdant savanna to desert with worrying speed.

The most plausible explanation for this transformation combines a theory of axial tilt with new notions of positive feedback loops in an intricate interplay of ocean, land, vegetation, and atmosphere. In this hypothesis, slight and gradual changes in the earth's orbit and axis accumulated until they caused abrupt changes in vegetation and climate, so abrupt that in a mere three hundred years or so the Sahara changed from grasslands to the desert that exists today.

That the earth's axis tilts and that the tilt angle changes have long been a commonplace of astronomy. The tug of gravity from Jupiter, the solar system's giant, and from Venus, smaller but closer, affects the earth, causing it to tilt, and it is this tilt that gives us the seasons: Summer happens when one hemisphere or the other is tilted toward the sun. Over the course of a forty-one-thousand-year cycle, the tilt ranges from 24.5 degrees to 22.1 degrees. At the same time, the gravity tug from the sun and the smaller countervailing one from the moon cause the earth to wobble slightly, which changes the time of perihelion, the point on the earth's orbit where it comes closer to the sun. These two cycles, and a theoretical third cycle affecting the shape of the orbit itself, determine the intensity of sunlight falling on the earth. These cycles were first proposed by the mathematician Milutin Milankovich in the 1930s as part of a theory of ice ages; they are now called the Milankovich cycles.

Around nine thousand years ago the tilt of the earth's axis was 24.14 degrees. Today it is 23.45 degrees. Before the change, perihelion occurred in July. Now it takes place in January. Before the change, the Northern Hemisphere was bathed in brighter and longer sunlight, enough to amplify the African and Indian summer monsoons. At the time, pollen studies show, the Sahara was covered with savanna grasslands and low shrubs, with pockets of forests.

For a few thousand years, the changing axial tilt had no measurable consequences. Yet, very small changes were going on, too small by themselves to have an effect on life in the Sahara, but nonetheless building up momentum. A study by the Potsdam Institute for Climate Impact, reported in the journal *Geophysical Research Letters*,[10] suggests that the transition from savanna to desert took place in two discrete "episodes," the first between 6,700 and 5,500 years ago, and the second in a 300-year burst sometime between 4,000 and 3,600 years ago. The first episode was dangerous, but not disastrous. The second, appallingly short in geological time, tipped the climate system completely, and life in the Sahara changed abruptly. Summer temperatures climbed dramatically, rainfall almost ceased (down to less than two inches a year), rivers and lakes dried up, and water tables began dropping.

The theory suggests that very little of this cataclysmic change was caused by ocean temperature changes, and even less by human action on the environment. Martin Claussen and his team concluded that atmosphere and vegetation feedback loops were substantially to blame. Feedback loops are complicated and interlinked, the study suggests. "We've shown that this can be described as a natural phenomenon . . . just a vast weird clockwork . . . that connected Jupiter to the acacia trees [of the Sahara], with Earth's tilted axis, the summer monsoon, and the brightness of the desert sand all acting as intermediate cogs . . . and it all happened very fast . . . well within the limits of cultural memory." Claussen, not one to shy away from controversy, added that "global warming . . . could, a century or two from now, provide the nudge to the monsoon that the tilt and wobble of Earth's axis did in the middle Holocene."[11]

Another study, by the U.S. National Center for Atmospheric Research,[12] suggests that the moisture retention of the soil and its vegetation was part of what kept the Sahara lush in earlier times: The soil itself gave off more moisture, helping to create rain clouds. A third study, by John Kutzbach and his colleagues at the University of Wisconsin,[13] agreed with this conclusion. Using a university supercomputer to model the Saharan climate, the Kutzbach team sought a solution that would explain the archaeological evidence such as fossilized pollen grains and relics from ancient fishing villages. When the team factored Claussen's changed axial tilt into their model, they found, to their surprise, that nothing very much happened. The previous tilt would cause only about 12 percent more rain, not nearly enough to fill up lakes. "We had more rain on the edges of the Sahara this way," Kutzbach explained, "but it didn't make it far enough in." His initial model assumed that the soil itself held no more moisture than it does now. When he refined the model to assume that six thousand years ago the Saharan soil would retain more moisture, mainly because more vegetation was growing there—something known from the fossil record—new simulations showed that water trapped in plants and in the soil itself would have increased humidity levels and boosted rainfall a further 16 percent, quite enough to shift the desert's southern boundary hundreds of miles north.

How it works is simple enough. The ground covered by plants is darker than a desert. The Sahara would not be that "brilliant band of caramel and beige" so visible from space were the desert covered with vegetation; and darker plants absorb more solar energy than lighter sand, which reflects most of it back into space as infrared radiation. Also, plant-rich soil is by definition wetter than bare sand; when the moist soil absorbs sunlight, some of the water evaporates. It rises, condenses, and forms clouds, the prerequisite for rain. As Claussen puts it, "It is a self-reinforcing feedback loop: The vegetation gets thicker, the ground moister and darker, which leads to more rain, which thickens the vegetation."

෴

THE DESERT as a whole may or may not be expanding, but no one doubts that localized areas of desertification do exist, almost all human-induced, especially along the Sahara's southern fringes. In fact, the United Nations has recently encouraged changing the definition of desertification from "spreading of a desert" to "arid land degradation," to take account of new thinking.[14] As vegetation is stripped from the land, the surface dries out and reflects more of the sun's heat. This condition in turn alters the thermal dynamics of the atmosphere in ways that suppress rainfall. Increased dust (itself a product of desertification) or other atmospheric pollutants are causing changes in the climate. Desertification results in declining water tables, and the salination of topsoil and the remaining water. Increased erosion and the extinction of vegetation, however caused, make the climate drier.

Population growth, the engine of all increased resource demands, is at the heart of the desertification problem. More people means more animals, and more vegetation cut for fuel and construction. The additional herds needed by greater numbers of humans trample and compact the soil, reducing the infiltration of the little water that exists, causing erosion and damaged soil. In the Sahel, humans have come to use cattle dung as a source of fuel, but even so what sparse vegetation remains is being hacked back for kindling, a violation that leads to increased erosion and wind damage.

Even within natural deserts, human activities can magnify the effects. In southern Tunisia, for example, the native plant cover, such as it was, was replaced by olive groves, cultivated in a dry farming system. This meant repeated "cultivation," which in practice was the opening and destruction of the soil surface, which in turn provoked deflation and soil erosion. The paleontological record shows that this degradation happened in several steps, dating back to the sixteenth and seventeenth centuries, when newfound political stability encouraged nomads to stay put on the Jeffara plain.

The Tuareg rebellions in the Aïr mountain region of Niger in the 1980s and early 1990s are another example of soil degradation caused by politics. Because of the warfare, the Tuareg nomads could no longer easily wander off to find new forage for their camels, and since they were unwelcome in the cities, they were forced to rely on cultivation, based on irrigation from shallow wells. Some of the wells, inevitably, went dry. In other cases, the soil began to erode, and stone walls built to impede the erosion only made things worse by preventing the water from infiltrating the ground. Small dams accelerated evaporation instead of hoarding the water, increasing the salinity of the soil.

Other economic and social factors have also taken their toll. Diesel deep-water pumps at oases throughout the desert have enabled the tapping of ever-deeper aquifers, which have, in turn, encouraged herdsmen to give up their nomadic but sustainable way of life and remain near the wells, and made it possible for them to raise even more livestock. Overgrazing resulted, the animals tearing up plants by their roots, destroying their ability to reproduce. The insistence of Western donor countries on "modern" methods and commercial models meant that the most fertile lands were reserved for cash crops alien to the region, cotton and peanuts, for instance, for sale in Western markets. This led to the increasing cultivation of ever more marginal land. At the same time, in imitation of Western agricultural models (based on more temperate climates and better rainfall), farmers began working their lands with only one or two years' fallow time, whereas before they had left the land for fifteen or even twenty years to recover on its own. It is the classic vicious circle: The desert causes ever more desperate measures by humans to survive, and those human activities make the desert worse.

However, skeptics about desertification do exist. A 1998 study reported in the journal *Science* disputed what it called "the popular belief" that the Sahara was growing southward. The study did acknowledge that "land degradation proves to be a problem in this area, reflecting the more localized effects of grazing and foraging for fuel," but it claimed to have established that, overall, the shifting desert boundaries were not, in fact, human-induced but were caused by the natural ups and downs of rainfall. The study also maintained that while the natural climate has shifted the desert's edge, there was no change in the total amount of vegetation. Desertification, in this view, was a small, and altogether localized, phenomenon.[15] A Ph.D. dissertation by Ahmed Mokhtar Brere on the application of Landsat imagery to monitor dune movements in the Sahara found plenty of movement but little sign of spread.[16]

Even the best evidence sometimes seems ambiguous—petrified wood, for example. Petrifaction is a curious thing. The botanists call it a "pseudomorph," where the natural wood fibers are replaced by silicon dioxide or by what is called "cryptocrystalline quartz," or chalcedony. The process involves the trees imbibing solutions containing silica, presumably from alkaline-saturated water; the mimicry is so accurate that the original cell structure can still be determined after the

Petrified trees. (Marq de Villiers)

transformation is complete. Fossil wood is found everywhere in what the specialists call the "Inter-Calary Continental," a layer of sedimentary rocks that underlies the greater part of the Sahara, together with fossils of fish and reptiles, and has popularly been used to date the changed Saharan climate.[17] Vintage geological texts assumed millions of years for the process, but more recent theories have reduced this to thousands of years, and the fossilized wood now found in Niger and Algeria is assumed to come from trees that were living ten thousand years ago. But tantalizing anecdotal evidence indicates that the process can, indeed, be much faster. The British writer Nigel Heseltine recounted how he had seen, "among the darkened ration tins at Uigh-es-Serir, a half orange petrified in exactly the same manner, which could not have been thrown there much earlier than fourteen years before."[18]

❧

AXIAL TILT CONTINUES its inexorable progression, and climate continues to change, whether through human agency or not. The consequences for the Sahara of short- or medium-term global warming are not readily calculable—they might be a hotter desert, or a cooler one, or a drier one, or a wetter one. The two forces combined will no doubt, in five millennia or so, bring grasslands back to the Sahara, if overpopulation or other degrading factors don't intervene. But even a slight change in temperature or aridity would alter the desert profoundly. If it became hotter, this would dry up the wells, make the residual caravan traffic impossible, and drive the nomads from the desert. If it became cooler or wetter, pastureland and oases would multiply, making rivers flow and bringing new agricultural zones to the interior. The Sahara would, in effect, be either uninhabitable, or desert no longer.

But the nomads of the deep desert don't monitor the climate or track the arcane academic debates in the specialist journals. The rain doesn't fall, as it didn't for their fathers' fathers and as they fully expect it won't for the sons of their sons. They learn to make their way in the desert-that-is, and not even in the legends, the collective unconscious of folk memory, do verdant grasslands play their part. Sand is their ever-present reality.

CHAPTER THREE

⟡

The Sand Seas

IT WAS EASY to imagine, in the steely sun of midmorning, that the sand had advanced, had crept farther into town. It crunched underfoot on the packed-earth walkway; there were little eddies in the el made by the house and the public bake oven to the left, already smoldering with a small fire of camel dung this early in the day. A probing finger of sand crept under the curtain serving as the house's front door, pushing for the center of the room, and there was more sand on the sills. In the road, if the sand was deeper by an inch or two, it wasn't immediately obvious as the roads are made of sand in any case.

Down the street to the east, toward the edge of town and the desert beyond, the stubby square that served as the minaret of the mosque, or what had been the last of the town's three mosques, still peeped from the sand, an incongruous sight, a massive building drowned in sand. At the far end of town, the houses were buried, only their roof parapets still showing. The houses a little nearer were only half covered, as though the street were slowly sinking into the sand, burrowing into the desert. Outside a nearby building, on a crude bench made of breeze-blocks, men sat in the lee of a wall, in the sun, smoking and gossiping. One sucked on a plastic bottle of imported mineral water. A crowd of children had already assembled, yelling for *un cadeau, un cadeau*, a gift, a gift, the universal child's yell that greets outsiders in these parts. The women were already working, as diligent as locusts in a cornfield, stooped in a ragged row, near a house that was buried to its lower windowsills. Working away, as though it meant something. The women with their buckets and their brooms and their stubbornness. Sweeping, sweeping. The sand women of Arawan.

℘

A R A W A N   I S in the Malian desert six days' weary slogging north of Timbuktu, the last real town before the salt mines of Taoudeni and Taghaza. Modern salt gatherers still use the town as a way station, much as René Caillié, the French explorer, did in 1824. Caillié was in a caravan that paused for a week at Arawan on its way north. Just outside the town, it came to the last wells to be found for more than 180 miles. All stopped to fill their waterskins and, an ominous sign to a pseudo-Muslim and a not-very-devout Christian, to pray for God's mercy. Then they set forth into the void, a land-

Arawan. (Penn State University)

scape, as Caillié described it, as "nothing but an immense plain of shining sand, and over it a burning sky."[1]

The town was founded, according to local tradition, before Timbuktu, which makes it more than nine hundred years old. Local legend says the name means "water hauled up on a rope" in Tamashek; it was in the middle of the *Majabat al-Khoubr*, the Empty Quarter, but the Arawan oasis had sweet water in wells that were deep enough but not too deep, and vegetation for the camels. The caravans almost always paused there for a few days, or a week, gathering their strength, girding themselves for the forty or so grim days they were still to face on their trek north. They wouldn't see another oasis like this one until they got to the Drâa Valley in Morocco, some eight hundred miles to the north.

Three thousand people lived in Arawan in its heyday, in the days when caravans meant something. Caravans of ten thousand camels were far from unknown. Now only a handful of people are left, perhaps thirty families, perhaps fewer, most of them Mauritanian Moors.

In the middle of the twentieth century, for reasons no one has fully understood, the dunes came to Arawan, and began to roll inexorably through the town.

The process was slow at first, insidious. There was no tsunami of sand; terrified residents were not forced to flee the enveloping dunes. And it wasn't as though Arawan hadn't become accustomed to sand—there was sand, after all, for hundreds of miles in every direction, sand underfoot, grit under the houses, sand in the wells, sand in the gardens. The roads were made entirely of sand. But over the course of a few years there was more of it than ever. The winds had always blown little eddies of sand through the town; now those eddies became larger, stayed longer. Little rivulets of sand built up around the buildings and in the streets. It took a decade or more for the first buildings to become engulfed, which was more or less when the villagers realized that something different was happening.

They didn't know why, of course. No one knows why to this day.

Were the wind patterns different? They didn't think so. Did the climate change? Not appreciably, or at least not locally. Did the driest place on earth become even drier? The wells still yielded water, as they always had. The date palms didn't die, not at first, but their fruit was meager and they were scrawny to the eye.

But sand attracts sand. It's how dunes are made—a little patch makes a bigger patch, the patch makes a mound and the mound a hill. In a short while, after a few years in which the townsfolk struggled to keep the growing things alive, most of the trees in the oasis were engulfed, and the wells had to be deepened, the shifting sand making for perilous digging. The first mosque was buried, houses smothered. People had been leaving Arawan for years, but now the desertions increased. The town was being suffocated, and by the early 1980s had been reduced to barely a quarter its former size.

In 1988 an unlikely savior arrived, in the person of Ernst Aebi, a Swiss-born surrealist painter from Manhattan and a member of the Explorer's Club, who stumbled on Arawan in his Sahara wandering, and stayed. Whatever his reason, he simply said he was unable to resist the challenge because "it is easy to visit remote places but [much harder] to change them for the better."[2] By dint of persistence and eloquence he persuaded the remaining people to plant more trees in the path of the shifting sand, irrigated by water drawn by a solar pump, trees that he himself had hauled across desert from Algiers, nearly a thousand miles away. A communal garden was also planted, and vegetables. Aebi built a school and even an eight-room hotel, which he called—in pure Manhattan irony—the Arawan Hilton. And beautiful it was, too, a Malian whimsy in mud, with ornate decorations and (an even greater whimsy) trees in its courtyard.

He enlisted the locals in his quixotic project, and it became a daily chore and a lifetime's work for the sand women of Arawan to keep the garden going and clear away the desert one bucket at a time.

It was no use. You cannot stop the Sahara by an act of will, no matter how obsessive or how admirable the goal. No one came to the

The Arawan Hilton. (Ernst Aebi)

hotel except a few functionaries bent on tax-collecting and leathery French tourists intent on their own strange spiritual quests. The major trans-Saharan caravans had ended many years before, but even the small convoys heading for the salt mines stopped coming, for in the early 1990s the nomadic Tuareg rebelled, stirred to bitter complaint, convinced that the Malian government favored the Bambara people of the settled south with what meager aid was available during the long drought. The village was too poor, and too small, to become in any way self-sufficient, no matter what the dream. The Arawan project was doomed and Aebi left.[3]

You can reach Arawan these days, if you care to, grinding north along the old caravan routes in a truck. The Tuareg are quiescent, or so the authorities say, and a few *caravanniers* are once again making their plodding way to Taghaza to buy salt. There's nothing to see along the way and not very much to see when you get there, unless you are interested in sand, and in hopeless human quests. Against the largest desert on earth, Arawan is just a small human outpost, and it is not much of a contest. Most of the gardens have long gone, withered for lack of water. The sand women, though, are still there, sweeping and brushing and scooping.[4]

&

THE FATE of the town of Arawan is grim, but hardly unique. On whatever side of the Sahara you now look, the same process is taking place. On the desert fringes and in the *ergs* the dunes ebb and flow, a viscous tide, rolling up against beleaguered desert towns and drifting through the streets of Taghit and Tellit and Tamanrasset. Sometimes the towns must move, sometimes merely endure for a while. At In'Salah, an epicenter of the Algerian oil industry, the houses get buried but a few years later emerge from under the sand wave, and if their original inhabitants are still in town, they reoccupy the buildings. The same thing happens to the palm groves; the dunes shift slowly but irresistibly toward the west, and the palms emerge dead and must be replanted to their east as the wave passes. The gateway to the desert from the northwest is Ain'Sefra, also in Algeria, a beleaguered outpost where enormous dunes are blowing up against the foot of the mountains and the town is doomed by the scouring wind and entombing sand. In Chad, north of the Ennedi Mountains, oases that had sustained commerce for a millennium have vanished completely. El-Gedida in western Egypt, despite a stubborn resistance, is being overwhelmed by sand, its easternmost houses facing a looming pile of sand a dozen feet high, and still growing. Along the Sahelian southern fringes of the Sahara, the ancient towns of Timbuktu and Gao and Agadez are all under siege.

Nor is Arawan's doom, or the uncertain fate of so many other Saharan towns, fairly attributable to man-induced global warming or latter-day desertification. Along the Mediterranean shores, the ancient seaports of Leptis Magna and Sabratha, recently found, had been buried for centuries under deep layers of drifted sand. Indeed, the wayward flowing sands of the Sahara caused the ancients along the Mediterranean littoral to think of the land beyond the Atlas Mountains not as a sea but as an immense river of sand, across which no bridges led, a treacherous thing whose turbid currents could sweep away the unwary to lands unknown.

Numerous stories exist about armies lost in the sands. Most of them are so tangled in myth and legend that their factual veracity is doubtful, even if they speak psychological truth. One such is the story of Dhu'l-Adhar, "a king of Yemen at about the time of Solomon"—the reference to Solomon is a clue that mythmaking has been going on—who raided the Maghreb and forced it into submission. His son and successor, Yasir, is said to have reached the Saharan Sand River beyond the Moroccan Rif and to have halted, dismayed, unable to find passage through the "seething currents of sand." Adhar fled back to the coast, and his lineage vanished from the stories.[5] Another story has Al-Sa'b Dhu l-Qarnayn, said on no historical evidence to be "one of the earliest Arab invaders of the Maghreb," reaching the Wadi l-Raml with his army, and stopping, as dismayed as Yasir had been. He found it to be flowing with sand like towering mountains. "He ordered [one of his commanders] to cross the Wadi with 20,000 men. The commander advanced until he vanished from his sight and not one of his men returned. Next Qarnayn sent [a second commander who] crossed over with 10,000 men but he and his companions did not return . . . and they vanished from his sight. When he saw that he knew that knowledge of its [cause] was hidden from him."[6] Both the above tales were among the "Alexandrian cycle" of stories that spread through the North African littoral well after the Arab conquest.

More factual, because more is known of the protagonists, was a tale recounted by Herodotus, as an aside in his *Histories*, an account of the Persian Wars, written about 450 B.C. This was the story of Cambyses, the Persian conqueror of Egypt in 525 B.C., who dispatched an army to quell the stubbornly oppositionist Ammonites, keepers of the oracle at Jupiter Ammon, at Siwa in the Qattara Depression in the Egyptian Western Desert (the same oracle that confirmed Alexander's ballooning opinion of his own abilities). But Cambyses's assault was not to be. "The men sent to attack the Ammonians, started from Thebes, having guides with them, and may

be clearly traced as far as the [Kharga Oasis], seven days journey
across the sand. Thenceforth nothing is to be heard of them, except
what the Ammonians report, that the Persians set forth from the
Oasis across the sand, and had reached about half way when, as they
were in camp breaking their fast, a strong and violent south wind
arose, bringing with it vast columns of swirling sand, which covered
up the troops and caused them to disappear. Thus, according to the
Ammonians, was the fate of this army."[7] Forty thousand men, with
their panoply and pay chests, with their animals and their food
stores, with their armor and weaponry, with their commissary and
their water skins, perished in the sand, their skeletons polished and
preserved, perhaps, but never found.

∽

THE·OVERWHELMING IMAGE of the Sahara, especially
in the minds of outsiders, is that of sand—sand, and sculpted dunes,
and perhaps, for those of a more optimistic state of mind, waving
palmeries in verdant oases. But in fact only about 15 percent of the
Sahara is sand. More than four-fifths of the desert consists of mountains, jagged and forbidding, stony gashes graven across the landscape, and massive plains of gravel and rock—rock and gravel,
indeed, is the characteristic Saharan landscape, more common by far
than dunes. Caravans will try to avoid dunes if they can, the camel-
masters threading their camels between and around them, searching
for "desert pavement," level plains of lag gravel cemented by gypsum
deposits, plains called *reg* or *areg* in the western Sahara and *serir* in the
east, rather like the *hamada* of Morocco and Algeria, bare rock with
just isolated boulders, as though to emphasize the emptiness.
    Each sort of desert has its own characteristics and its own name.
The Tuareg, so intimately attuned to the landscape, have many fine
subdivisions and definitions of desert-ness. The Arabic word *Sahra*,
which simply means desert, has given a name to the whole, but the
Arabic word is derived in turn from the Tamashek *Sahar*, which
properly means "sand alone, without stones, rocks, or water, with a
smooth horizon and no permanent paths." Other Tuareg gradations

include *ghrud,* dunes and sand hills of whatever height; *serir,* plains of gravel, whether rounded, sharp, or polished; *warr,* a rough plain with some boulders, very difficult to thread one's way through (the word is sometimes a synonym for fatigue); *hatiä,* implying places of potential fertility, with a few scrub bushes and grasses, on which a camel may survive; *wishek,* sand hills or plains, usually used for new desert, a productive area now made infertile; *ghraba,* date groves with no town attached; *subkhar,* salt plains, sometimes marshy in winter but usually as hard as stone; *wadi,* a valley in which shrubs grow and in which, when the rains do come, torrents may rush; and *jebel,* which defines a stone mountain or mountain range.

Most of the *regs* are plain beyond belief, without color, without any memorable feature whatever. It is quite possible to wake up in the morning, travel all day, camp, wake up the next morning, repeat the previous day, and all the while to have seen neither a tree, nor a shrub, nor a blade of grass, nor a boulder of any size, nor a hill or mountain or mesa, nor a wadi, nor a well—to have seen, in point of fact, precisely nothing but a flat gravel plain. It is not surprising that newcomers to the Sahara are prone to taking refuge inside their own minds, fevered by the heat; and that the nomads have peopled the emptiness with djinns, the spirits who embody nothingness, whose only sound is a moan and whose dominant characteristic is malice.

In parts of the Sahara, though, the landscape is more surprising. On some of the *regs,* the rocks are glossy and quite beautiful, polished to a patina in a palette of reds and ochers, a varnish two thousand years in the making, minerals extracted from the earth by dew and polished to a high gloss by the endless susurrating winds. Turn over a pebble and it will be brilliant orange, rich in iron, a flower of the desert. South of Murzuq, in southern Libya, rocky crags are banked with smothering dunes. Camels' feet pick their way through coconut-sized stones, a startling black and orange, their ferruginous dark shells easily broken, the thickness of orange peel. The kernel is sandstone, very soft, "of invariably the liveliest hues, from light yellow, through all colors of the rainbow, to deep purple." The Tuareg, who waste nothing, "heat these nuts and throw them into milk to preserve it by the iron thus absorbed."[8]

In a number of places in Libya's Fezzan province and in many other places in the eastern Sahara, the sandstone, which contains threads of iron, looks on the outside like basalt, but when broken is a startling red. Where layers have hived off, usually on the west sides of massifs, the mountains are carved into fantastic shapes, gothic cathedrals, castles, obelisks, and monuments, carved as though by human art, and splashed with red and ocher. The early European travelers, seeing the appalling sprawl of jagged rocks and cracked cliffs of the Saharan landscape, assumed they had been produced by millennia of alternative bouts of cooling and heating, but the reality is more curious than that. Moisture is the cause of the mayhem: Dew is the agent, chemical reactions the instrument. The wind is at work too, endlessly eroding, leaving huge sheets of lag gravel, where the finer particles have sifted away. Wind also causes blowouts, sometimes called "deflation basins," which are circular or oval lowlands scoured out by constant blowing. Elsewhere it has made ridges and flutes in the bedrock, the result of sandblasting.

All over the Sahara are "ventifacts," rock polished by the sand, or carved into complicated shapes. Glass bottles left exposed are soon pocked and pitted, and after a few years will disintegrate altogether.

క్ర

NEVERTHELESS, despite the desert's being only 15 percent sand, every Saharan country does have massive dunes and seas of sand that can reach for tens, sometimes hundreds, of miles. In the Mauritanian desert north of Mali's capital, Bamako, for example, the golden dunes are streaked with reds and browns of a startling intensity. The Moroccan desert south of the Drâa contains classic dunes the color of caramel, while the old Songhai town of Gao in southeastern Mali is famous for the dunes that border the Niger River, massive sand hills three hundred feet high and miles long, the color of a delicate pink rose. In the Erg de Ténéré in eastern

Niger, the Sands of Nothingness stretch toward the ancient salt mines at Bilma; some have called them the most beautiful dunes in the desert, golden and gorgeous, deep and deadly. Farther north, in the Great Ergs of Algeria, drifting tides of sand are the size of Belgium; south of there, the Grand Dune near Amguid, on the western edge of the Tassili n'Ajjer range, is really a sand mountain, maybe thirty miles long and more than four hundred feet high, so big that you can camp warmly on its slopes on chilly winter nights, for it still radiates the heat accumulated during the day. Dunes of dark chocolate shot through with veins of red in northern Chad surround eroded sandstone pillars, jagged and forbidding, the size of skyscrapers. In all these places, the desert is shifting, a ponderous ebbing and flowing.

Where did so much sand come from? Is it just degraded fertile soil, desiccated and turned to powder by the aridity and the winds? Or the remnant of stone mountains worn down to dust? Almost all windblown sand is quartz, which accumulates when rocks are weathered away because it resists chemical breakdown better than most minerals. But the current thinking is that, ironically, the desert sands may also be a by-product or aftereffect of water, the same force that sculpted the rocks and weathered the massifs. The sand is most probably a relic, left over from the shallow sea that lapped the Sahara in the long Tertiary period (65,000,000 to somewhere around 1,600,000 years ago) followed by some still-mysterious uplifting of the seabed to its present elevation. Sand accumulation may also have occurred in ancient lakes.[9] In some places in northern Algeria gypsum crystals of sand size are still deposited each year on the beds of ephemeral lakes as the water dries out; they are then blown like sand to form dunes.[10]

Typically, the "mix" of sand in dunes differs from that of the flatter portions known as sand sheets. The sand in dunes doesn't vary much, the grains ranging from 0.008 to 0.016 inches. The sand on sand sheets is much more varied, with very fine sand mixed in with other particles as large as fine gravel. Examined under a microscope, the coarser grains are rounded and pitted by the sandblasting effect of tinier particles, giving the sand a somewhat frosted look.

☙

HOW QUICKLY the dunes move! One day there's nothing much, the plain bare and scrubbed, barren soil, thorns, broken stone, gravel, ocher and dun, shimmering in the incandescent desert heat. Then, just a few weeks later, there it is—a full-fledged dune the color of honey, sculpted by the wind into ruffles and flutes, a knife edge to leeward, fifty, eighty, a hundred feet high.

Dunes form in a bewildering variety of shapes—tied dunes, which form in the lee of hills; echo dunes, which appear to windward of other dunes; barchans, which are shaped like crescents; and seifs, which are sharp-edged, but sinuous in shape, meandering, and often isolated on larger sand sheets. There are many others, too: parabolic blowout dunes; transverse dunes, and the shifting shapes associated with the sand seas; S-shaped or sigmoidal dunes; pyramidal dunes; domes; and star-shaped dunes. They range in size from a small pile of sand about a meter in height to giant sand mountains of sixteen hundred feet or more, mountains with hills of their own on their slippery backs, the shifting and chaotic topology of the desert. The desert seems a strangely living thing, a shifting, capricious, willful entity, obliterating all in its path. The nomads' tents, like barques on a heaving sea, move to take account of these miraculous appearances, and tuck up against the rising waves.

If you put your ear to the ground when the dunes are coming, you will hear nothing but the susurration of the wind in the membrane of the inner ear, because the sound of their movement is below the threshold of human perception. Only later, when the dune is more massive, do the shifting sands create an eerily evocative hissing, especially at night when the desert air is sweet and still. In the full glare of the sun, when the thermometer climbs past 120 degrees and the hot winds blow, the earth is made sky and the horizon disappears; the whole landscape seems to migrate, inexorable and inescapable. The sand accumulates, but first it chokes and stifles, and makes men feverish, as claustrophobic as miners at a deep seam. In a high wind, the dunes smoke and a low-pitched drumming is heard, the spirit of Raoul, the Drummer of Death, and the Tuareg, the Blue Men of the desert, draw their veils across their faces, and cast their eyes downward. The Tuareg often seem to live in a curtain of sand, and make their lives accordingly.

Less romantically, the drumming is the avalanching of billions of tiny grains slowing as they reach the bottom of the slip face, the sounds also caused by the piezoelectric property of crystalline quartz, in the same way that, under controlled circumstances, the needle on a phonograph translates vibrations into sound.

∾

COUNTERINTUITIVELY, the Saharan dunes move not by drifting but by jumping. When the tiny sand grains, quartz ground fine as flour, skitter across the sere landscape they do so not in fluid motion, in straight lines, but in little hops. They don't roll, or slide. They skip, cause ricochets, knocking other tiny grains into movement, into jumping. This phenomenon is called "saltation."

The dance of the grains is, in its way, oddly beautiful, a seeming chaos that devolves into pattern, random movement shifting into ponderous purpose. At the first breath the grains do roll, not hop, but as the wind picks up the momentum increases, and little collisions occur, or the grains hit a tiny gash or bump in the earth, and become airborne. In the air, the wind gets a better grip, and the particles pick up speed. Sometimes, when they come down, they rebound even higher, whereupon the wind accelerates them even more, and the hopping process is magnified. If the wind reaches thirty miles an hour and the surface is resilient, saltating grains can spring several feet into the air and travel a distance of two yards, or even more; rebounds can take them even farther, maybe fifteen or even twenty feet. When they fall, they drop in the wind at angles of between ten and sixteen degrees. This means that a grain that merely reaches a yard in height can actually hop ten or fifteen feet across the desert. And the grains multiply, each saltating grain pro-

ducing others, for unless the incoming grain lands directly on another, it splashes down among other grains, creating a small crater
and blasting half a dozen new particles into the air. So whenever the
wind picks up and attains an effective velocity, a curtain of saltating
grains rises into the air. Over dunes or other soft surfaces, this curtain is quite small, no more than half a yard high, and even on the
windward side of a dune the saltating grains seldom rise above knee
height. But over less yielding surfaces such as stony plains the curtain can easily reach seven feet or more, the height of a tall man or a
small camel.

It doesn't take a gale to shift the sand. A wind of eight miles an
hour, measured at a height of thirty feet, can move fine grains (0.008
of an inch in diameter), and a thirteen-mile-an-hour wind is enough
to move larger grains (up to 0.024 of an inch in diameter). Once the
sand gets started, less intense winds can keep it moving, but the initial impulse needs at least that much energy. The mass of sand moved
is an exponential factor of the wind speed. An eight-mile-an-hour
wind can carry half an ounce an hour, a sixteen-mile-an-hour wind
will carry 9.6 ounces an hour, and a thirty-mile-an-hour wind forty-
one ounces an hour.

Maybe three-quarters of the sand in a dune-in-making shifts in
the little bopbopbops of saltation. The remaining quarter, the larger
pieces, moves slowly along the surface in a process known as "impact creep," kept in motion by the bombardment of the saltating
grains. A saltating grain can move by impact particles six times its
diameter and two hundred times its weight, and thus small pebbles,
up to two-thirds of an inch in diameter, too big to be moved by the
wind, can be driven steadily along the ground. Wind can't match
water for shifting gross weight, but it can take material a lot farther.
Sand shifted by saltation and impact creep can travel tens to hundreds of miles.

Obviously, dunes are formed because jumping sand bounces
more easily off hard surfaces than off soft ones, so that more sand
can be moved over a pebbly desert surface than over a smooth or
soft one. Even a slight hollow, though, or a rock, will reduce the

Star dune. (Sheila Hirtle)

amount of sand that the wind can carry, and a small sand patch begins. Very quickly, this patch will trap more sand. When the patch
is big enough, it begins to change the wind velocity about it. The
winds decrease near the surface and deposit more sand on the patch.
Quickly, the dune is built up.

If the conditions are right, the dune will grow very rapidly: In
days it will be taller than a man, and in just a few weeks it can reach
sixty-five or one hundred feet, and keep growing. Over time, the
windward slope eventually adjusts itself, and the wind velocity close
to the sand increases to compensate for the drag imposed by the
sandy surface. The smooth leeward slope steepens until the wind
can't be deflected down sharply enough to follow it, leaving a "dead
zone" into which the sand falls. When this so-called dispositional
slope reaches the natural slope angle of dry sand (about thirty-two
degrees), the added sand cascades down the slope, now called the
"slip face." The dune has stopped growing—there is no net gain or
loss of sand—though it continues to move forward as a whole,
slowly, ponderously, relentlessly.

Dunes also form around hills or rock formations that the geogra-

phers call "topographic obstructions." The nomads know that shel-
tered zones, wind shadows, are found on the lee of small hills into
which the sand migrates to form one or two long, narrow trailing
dunes called *seifs*, depending on the width and height and shape of
the hill. If the wind meets a high scarp or massif, an echo dune is deposited on the upwind side, separated from the scarp by a rolling
eddy of air that keeps a corridor free of sand. Many oases are found
in this kind of corridor. Echo dunes are the largest dunes in the
desert, sometimes reaching a height of more than sixteen hundred
feet. The crescent-shaped *barchan* dunes are seldom greater than
750 feet.[11]

The Sahara always moves, changing daily, hourly. Sometimes
dunes seem to take on a grotesque life of their own. A massive dune
will sometimes roll over a smaller one and they will mate and then
roll on, leaving behind a new small dune. Tuareg women have been
known to make coarse remarks about the mechanics involved.

Dunes don't always move in the same direction; they shift as the
winds do and, when they grow big enough, create their own wind
patterns. They advance, but they also retreat. They grow, but they
also diminish—dunes can vanish as quickly as they came into existence, and even a massive dune can turn into a flat sand sheet a
month later. Beneath the sands lie many relics of the past, stone-age
artifacts, forgotten armies, hunters who lost their way, murdered
and plundered caravans, vanished explorers, dead camels, and, increasingly, the detritus of "civilized" life: plastics and wrought metal,
derelict trucks and shredded tires. All these are buried and exposed
and reburied in endless cycles.

∾

∧´ Y Ó B ∧ , a *caravannier* who lives mostly in the Tiguidit area
southeast of Agadez, in Niger, knelt to the desert floor and beck-
oned. "Come and look!" he said. The surface on which he was
kneeling was rippled, and in the wind it seemed almost to smoke. It
looked hazy, as the ripples, in parallel rows about six inches apart,
shifted through traction and creep and saltation. These little ripples

were no more than an inch or so high, but they were moving swiftly, maybe a foot every two minutes.

He pointed to the hazy ridges of the ripples.

"See those?" he said, gesturing. "What do you think we can learn from those?"

A nagging question for some days had been how they, the *cara-vanniers* heading out to the salt mines at Bilma, in eastern Niger, navigated across featureless wastelands, with each horizon of dunes apparently identical to the hundreds that went before and the many hundreds to follow. Perhaps an answer lay in these ripples?

A'Yóba grinned, delighting in the lesson. "It means nothing," he said. "You can learn nothing from it. The movement is random. When the wind gets up, and a storm is coming, the ripples disappear, the surface becomes smooth, and visibility diminishes. But we don't need tiny signals to tell us a storm is on the way. It is already obvious."

Entire dunes migrate downwind, he pointed out, but winds are necessarily variable. There are generally prevailing winds, of course, but in the course of a year, the dunes may shift in several directions. They will move, but they might also grow, or diminish, be absorbed into others, disappear entirely. Dunes will move but dune patches will tend, he said, to stay in more or less the same place, within a few dozens of miles. The *ergs,* the sand seas, don't move. Only the dunes.

What he was describing was a movement rather like swells on the ocean. The swells seem to roll onward, but they don't really—the water remains in place. But A'Yóba had never seen a sea, or any other natural water except at the bottom of a well, and the comparison was meaningless.

❧

THERE CAN BE few more dispiriting, and exhausting, activities than traveling across unstable sand in the middle of the Sahara, lurching forward in small increments, sometimes only a few feet at a time, knowing that there are dozens, perhaps hundreds, of miles to go.

It requires considerable experience to drive safely across a sand sea whose "waves" crest at four hundred or five hundred feet and are sometimes intimidatingly steep. To travel at all across the desert, you need to know, first, the direction of the prevailing winds (not the zephyrs, but the larger winds) and, second, how dunes are made, and to pay attention to their structure. Dune surfaces can be firm enough for traveling, or very soft. Most sand in a dune is laid down on the "slip face"—as the dune moves forward, the sand is constantly being reexposed on the windward slope, which makes for very soft sand, in contrast to the sands on top of or between dunes, which will support a considerable weight.

Long ridges like the swell of a rolling sea can be soft and treacherous, and even camels will sink to the knees or deeper. In places, the Tuareg say, you can encounter light and soft sands that neither man nor beast can traverse. "If they try it they will sink and be lost forever," said a Libyan camel man called Ali, who had, he said, been on the edge of some such sand, in which one leg sank to the thigh while the other was still on firm ground.

If the whole desert were dune, travel would be difficult, maybe impossible. By contrast, the sand sheets, which are scoured by the wind and relatively flat, make travel possible, though all drivers bog down in the desert at some point, no matter how carefully they watch for sheets with sharp ripples (safe) or rounder ripples (soft, with sand often more than axle-deep). Dead grass will generally hold the sand together enough to support a vehicle, but often what looks like an area of flat rock is really desiccated clay, nasty pools of gray, powdery sand called *fech-fech,* which smokes when you walk across it, and in which a vehicle will sink to its axles or beyond.[12] They're almost impossible to see until, alas, it is far too late.

℘

GHIB'AN, a man of mixed Hausa-Tuareg ancestry of which he was inordinately proud in a prickly sort of way, especially among the ethnically conscious nomads, tried to beat the soft sections by sheer bravado. His Landcruiser had been headed to Tamanrasset, in southern Algeria, but had turned back and was once again aiming for Agadez. The map acquired in Agadez called the road an "indicated route," which supposedly meant there were signs, if one knew where to look and what to look for. In reality, though, there were no indicators, no markings, no signage, not even any tracks. Ghib'an seemed able to spot the soft sand, yet his preferred method was not to skirt it—this apparently took too long, was too uncertain, held no cachet—but to shift up rapidly through the gears and take it by storm, trusting that his momentum would carry him on through. In an astonishing number of cases, he made it to the other side, the vehicle lurching and pitching, the motor screaming, but making it to hard ground, his passengers strapped in tight and clinging to stanchions that were custom-installed for the purpose. Just as often, though, he didn't, the vehicle slamming to a halt with a bone-jarring thud. A'Yóba would look gloomy. "Camel much better," he would say in deliberately pidgin French, which Ghib'an would interpret as a slight on his driving and a slur on his competence, his knowledge, and his manhood in general.

"Camel dead by now," he snarled after one of these unscheduled halts.

"Camel in oasis by now, drinking water," A'Yóba said, needling.

Like every other desert vehicle, they were carrying *tôles*, nonskid boards for placing under the tires. Usually these are just planks, although sometimes they are made of metal mesh. Ghib'an's were wood, with bottle caps nailed in neat rows every six inches or so; he had them strapped to the roof with whatever other baggage didn't need protection from the sand. The passengers unstrapped the two *tôles* and shoved them forward of the front wheels, from which most of the air had been let out to give them better traction. Ghib'an gunned the motor and slipped the clutch, and the vehicle leaped forward, grinding through the patch onto harder sand. The process repeated itself, once, twice, sometimes more than a dozen times in a row. In bad sand, it can take eight hours to travel five miles. The prudent, of course, carry two sets of four *tôles*, thereby giving the vehicle a continuous nonskid surface,

but most Saharan travelers can't afford them. Ghib'an carried only
two, or one half set.

This went on for an hour, two hours, but eventually the sand
ended and a gravel plain appeared ahead: *hamada,* by far the best
terrain for desert travel. This one was a dreary gray in color, and
quite featureless, but with the consistency of a good unpaved road.
Sometimes, though, *hamadas* themselves hold unexpected perils;
where in one place the gravel will be rounded, and therefore afford
easy passage to camel or sandal or tire, sometimes for no apparent
reason it can turn to sharply pointed stones that will damage a
camel's soft pads, destroy sandal leather, and ruin car tires. A Roman
army was said once to have torn its sandals to shreds on a *hamada,*
and perished miserably on the plains, with nowhere to go and no
refuge in sight. And indeed, west of In'gal, which is itself on a
branch of this same Tamanrasset route, near a well known as Targa,
is just such a plain. In the middle, derelict, is the hulk of a truck, left
over from the early days of motoring. The wheels have no tires; apparently they were shredded before the vehicle had crossed more
than a quarter of the plain. The driver tried to continue on the rims,
but they sank, eventually, into deep sand and the vehicle moved no
more. The vehicle has been stripped, but the bones of the driver are
still there, toppled over now from where he had propped himself up
against the door. The remains of the other passengers, if there were
any, are nowhere to be seen. Perhaps they attempted to walk out to
find water and died somewhere in the sand. Perhaps a dune covered
them, and only the archaeologists of the future will be able to read
in the runes of the skeletons their terrified and lonely deaths.

The *hamada* Ghib'an reached, however, remained benign as he
knew it would, having crossed it on the way out of Agadez a few
days earlier, and his party reached the artesian wells northwest of the
city without further need for work, or for remarks on the benefi-
cence of camels.

Late in the afternoon, close to the city, they passed through an
area of smooth golden dunes. As they were traversing a ridge, they
looked down the valley and saw, as far as could be seen, dunes as

smooth as silk, the color of honey caramel, golden billows to the far horizon. Heaving out of the valley floor, in the middle of the gold, were two sinuous black ridges, curved "dunes" of iron and gravel. From on high they looked like the vertebrae of some long-dead giant. The gravel and half-buried mica glittered in the sinking sun. Then dusk came and the color faded like a dream that was hard to hold in memory. The exhilaration that this image induced, though, persisted through the next day's travel, and the one after that, and it became easier to see how the nomads could refer to the desert as Allah's garden without being ironic. Austerity and serenity intersected, and the emptiness was not empty at all, but pregnant with meaning.

A'Yóba understood the feeling, he said, and approved. Familiarity was not breeding contempt. It showed a desert heart. He meant this as a high compliment.

CHAPTER FOUR

જી

The Winds

THE BORDER CROSSING from the arid north of Cameroon to the arid south of Chad and its capital, N'Djamena, is a dusty and desultory affair. This is not among the more tension-filled borders of Africa, and the soldiers who guard both sides of the pole barrier are rather more prone to sitting with their feet up and drinking copious drafts of orange Fanta or fermented palm juice than they are worrying about contraband or insurgents. For the first fifteen minutes or so, they didn't even deign to notice the idling Toyota whose occupants were waiting, more or less patiently, to be let through. A wind had picked up and was rattling the corrugated iron shed where the soldiers were sitting with relatives and girlfriends and hangers-on, a clamoring and gossipy crowd, ever friendly. By the time the car had been processed and all the papers inspected and they had asked (on the Cameroon side) for a little *dash* to make things go more smoothly and (on the Chad side) why on earth the travelers were traveling in this be-nighted weather, a gale was already blowing. Half the Sahara seemed to be passing overhead, visibility was down to less than one hundred yards, and the air was thick with grit. The *harmattan*, or what the Tuareg call the Hot Breath of the Desert, was strengthening. The wind's name is supposed to be derived from the Arabic word for "evil thing"; if it is, most people in the desert would agree it is well named.

ભ

SAND — AND WIND, its master.

Planetary rotation and solar radiation cause climate, and climate causes winds and is caused by them in return, the most common of meteorological commonplaces. The Sahara has two major contending wind systems, those of the subtropical north and the tropical south. In summer they meet across a vast west-east swath of the central Sahara, from Taoudeni in western Mali, flirting with the southern edges of the Ahaggar and the northern fringe of the Aïr Mountains, petering out somewhere east of Bilma, near the Chad border. In winter the whole front shifts southward. These massive wind fronts are described by meteorologists as mid-latitude low-pressure systems, or "extratropical cyclones," part of the continuing march of air masses and fronts driven by the sun and the earth's spin, and wrenched in turn by the massive furnace of the Sahara itself. The desert nomads for their own protection have learned a good deal about the winds and their patterns. They may not know the climatological factors involved—that winds generally circulate in a clockwise direction in the northern hemisphere, or that high-pressure systems tend to dip down to the east so that winds are stronger there—but they do know that the wind patterns, overall, are mirrored by the patterns etched into the sand. They understand the wind, and respect it, and fear it when they should.

"When the wind blows the desert trembles," the Tuareg say; the dunes literally shiver and shift and horizons disappear. A chronicler in France's Foreign Legion wrote: "And across all the *harmattan* was blowing hard, that terrible wind that carries the Saharan dust a hundred miles to sea, not so much as a sand storm, but as a mist or fog of dust as fine as flour, filling the eyes, the lungs, the pores of

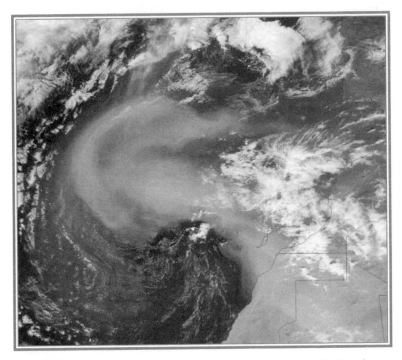

Sandstorm driven by the harmattan. (NASA/Goddard Space Flight Center)

the skin, the nose and throat, getting into the locks of rifles, the works of watches and cameras, defiling water, food and everything else, rendering life a burden and a curse."[1] He didn't know the half of it: The *harmattan* brings out Raoul, the Drummer of Death, and his reach is greater by far than the Great Nothingness of the Sahara. Three hundred, four hundred, five hundred miles to the north the Hot Breath of the Desert layers fine dust on Marseilles, on St. Tropez and Nice, and the swimming pools of the rich in the hills above the Côte d'Azur turn to gritty milk. Dust from North Africa is commonly found in England and northern Germany as well as in France.

In 1989 the winds were so strong that fully grown grasshoppers were carried across the Atlantic from the Sahel, to be dropped on the canefields and beaches of Antigua five days later. In the last year of the millennium a reddish-brown river of dust, picked up from the deserts and the eroding grazing lands of the Sahel, a plume hundreds of miles wide and thousands long, was whipped across the Atlantic by the trade winds. Planetary ecologists say somewhere between 60 million and a billion tons of the Sahara's iron-rich sand blows across the Atlantic each year, an estimate, obviously, with a fair degree of elasticity.[2] Even the lower number sounds like a massive amount of sand, but it is quite small in planetary terms, and in any case most of it falls into the sea. Nevertheless, the number has been going up steadily over the past twenty-five years, and at the same time, the mortality rate of creatures like Caribbean coral has risen sharply. Eugene Shinn, a researcher with the U.S. Geological Survey in St. Petersburg, Florida, has tracked the coral's declining health to fungal spores and bacterial cysts hitching a ride on African sand; in 1998, scientists identified an African soil fungus as the cause of the decimation of sea fans across the entire Caribbean, an object lesson in the interconnectedness of life.

The dust also is now known to be bringing traces of pesticides banned in the United States but still used in Africa, such as chlordane and DDT, back to American shores. This African dust is not universally harmful—orchids growing in the upper canopy of the Amazon rain forest actually depend on it for a proportion of their nutrients—but it is generally worrisome.

Another U.S. Geological Survey report in 2001 said that what the researchers called "opportunistic pathogens" were hitching rides from Africa on the wind—the sand is heavy enough that the dust clouds block enough solar radiation to protect bacteria on their journey to the New World. Large dust arrivals from Africa have now been found over 30 percent of the continental United States; although no one has yet estimated its mass, it would be a small fraction of the amount that leaves the Sahara. About half the volume that reaches the United States settles on Florida. On any given day, a third to a half of the dust drifting through Miami comes not from local beaches but from Africa. "It may," the study suggested, "pose a significant public health threat."[3]

This might seem something of an exaggeration, but in the sum-

mer of 2001 a NASA-funded study tracked a cloud of Saharan dust
to the Gulf of Mexico, where it settled with unnerving consequences—causing a huge bloom of toxic "red tide." The Saharan
dust reached the West Florida shelf around July 1, increasing iron
concentrations in the surface waters by 300 percent. Through a
complex process involving enzymes and plantlike bacteria called tri-
chodesmium, the iron enriched the nitrogen content of the ocean,
and in October an 8,100-square-mile bloom of red algae (*Karenia
brevis*) had formed between Tampa Bay and Fort Myers, Florida.
Red tides give off toxins that can cause respiratory problems in humans, and also poison local shellfish. Anyone eating the contaminated shellfish would suffer paralysis and severe memory problems.
This red tide also killed millions of fish and hundreds of manatees.[4]

☙

NOT EVERY SAHARAN WIND is fierce, or unwelcomed.
In summer lows, moist winds are pulled in from the Guinea highlands southwest of the desert, and rain falls on the central mountains.
In winter, highs over the Ahaggar pull in the eastbound polar fronts
from the Atlantic, bringing snow to the Atlas and rain to the northern oases.

However, many of the winds are hated and feared, and every one
of those has a name. The dry northeast wind is called the *alizés,* and
blows hot toward the equator. The dry, desiccating south winds that
carry the glowering towers of dust are known variously as the *ghibli,
chili, samun, jefhya,* and *irifi.* The *ghibli* is bad, and can seem never
ending. In the Fezzan of southwestern Libya, the camel-masters say
that if the *ghibli* blows forty days, God preserve us from the evil!
The camel becomes pregnant without the intervention of the male.
"Nothing can be more overpowering than the south wind, *El-ghibli,*
or the east wind, *El-shirghi,* each of which is equally to be dreaded,"
the British explorer George Lyon wrote in his journals in 1818. "In
addition to the excessive heat and dryness, they are so impregnated
with sand that the air is darkened by it, the sky appears of a dusky
yellow and the sun is barely perceptible. The eyes become red,
swelled and inflamed, the lips and skin parched and chapped, while

severe pain in the chest is invariably felt in consequence of the quantities of sand unavoidably inhaled."[5]

Yet the *harmattan,* which blows north and west, is the worst, the
driest, hottest, most enervating of all. It is known as the *khamsin* in
Libya and Egypt, and as the *sirocco* in Algeria, but among the Tuareg
and Tubu clans of the Ahaggar and Tibesti, it is called the *shahali* or
shai-halad, the mother of storms. In the North African Campaign
of World War II, several major battles were interrupted by the
khamsin. Gales of ninety miles an hour and electrical disturbances
so profound that compasses became useless forced the troops of
both sides to hunker down, waiting for a lull.

The coming of the *harmattan* strips the air of what little moisture
remains. Humidity has been tracked to fall from 80 percent to 10 percent within hours. When the gale is in full cry, visibility is reduced to
a few yards. Sand penetrates everything. There is grit in the food, grit
in the water, grit on the sheets in the hotels. If you close the windows
against the sand, as you must, the temperature can climb steadily, and
reach 120 degrees, 125 degrees, and the air sears the lungs.

Sandstorms can be black as night or a lurid yellow or a bleak
gray the color of old ash; they may hiss or roar, or rumble like
thunder; the air is oven hot and crackles with static and a hand
run over a canvas tent pops and sparks like methane breath on a
smoldering coal tip; nerve-ends tingle with electricity and firefly
sparks jump and snap. Even camels' tails spark and crackle. The
camels squat in the sand, their backs to the wind, and close their
long-lashed and double-lidded eyes; the Tuareg hunker down, still
as an empty tomb, and seem hardly to breathe. A car's headlights
can't be seen at ten paces. Abrasive sand beats on metal with a
sound like heavy rain. It can rattle against legs and arms and
face like hail.

Owen Watkins, a literary-minded surgeon traveling with Kitchener's army toward Khartoum, described the effect: "Such was the
hot dryness [that] whole blankets, as they were being drawn one over
another, or even slightly shifted, blazed up like sheet-lightning in the
dark tents. These fits of diamond-like virtue occurred stronger in the
hot nights of May."[6]

Northern Algeria, 1927. Train to Touggart derailed during a sandstorm. (Marcel Zoltowski)

Gustav Nachtigal, the German explorer who spent years in the Sahara and was the first European to penetrate the Tibesti Mountains, used to sit on the terrace of a friend's house, watching the storms. "Fraulëin Tinné's large dog could not be stroked without producing crackling sparks," he wrote.[7]

Not everyone survives these "fits of diamond-like virtue." Alongside the road from Agadez to Bilma is the burned-out hulk of a bus. It has been there for twenty years, the *caravanniers* say, since the day it exploded and burned to a crisp when they were filling its tank before a windstorm. Someone hefting the can had drawn a spark from the heavy static charge that had built up on the surface of the vehicle, and there was an instant conflagration. Luckily the passengers had piled out to watch, but all their belongings were lost. Looters picked through what little remained after the fire.

Watkins once saw a train engulfed by an awful sandstorm. At first, he thought it just a thunderstorm like any other, but "men who had been in the country for years had never seen the like." Then it dawned on him that it was a sandstorm, and he fled for shelter. "It was quite the most grandly awful sight, a great bank of dust about 100 feet high, stretching for miles and miles in front of us and rushing upon us with a dull roar. In camp not a breath stirred, everything waited in expectation. As it came nearer, the edges of the cloud were tinged with purple and gold by the sunlight, whilst here and there in the mass were black yawning chasms, like the mouth of an inferno, swallowing up mile after mile of fair country. Then it struck us! Swallowed us up! The sun went out, and in an instant we were plunged from bright sunlight into pitchy night. We barricaded doors and windows, but the fine sand silted through every crevice, and laid over us all a white coat of dust; the heat was so intense that it seemed too close to breathe; perspiration started from every pore, and running down our faces cut channels through the thick coating of dust. When at last the storm ceased, the sun had set, the moon was high in the sky, and the cool evening air was like a breath from heaven to our dust-choked lungs. The [invalid convoy] train we had seen start had to pull back into the station, and another train a few miles out into the desert had to stop, being nearly swept off the line by the force of the wind. After that experience I find it easy to believe the stories, often read before in skeptical spirit, of whole caravans being lost and buried in the desert."[8]

Even on still days there can be dust devils, the *ebliss*, miniature tornadoes that can carry small plants and animals high into the air. True desert tornadoes, which are common along the southern fringes of the Sahara, are worse. In a curious little memoir called *Desert Life: Recollections of an Expedition in the Soudan*, the author, who titled himself "B. Solymos (B. E. Falkonberg), Civil Engineer," recalled that these "radiate to great distances heat and pungent smells; snatching up and throwing about bedsteads, saddles, quadrupeds, men; and piercing camels through and pinning them to the ground with a blunt tent-pole or a stake; and stealing soldiers' metallic weapons and sending them down from the heavens in other latitudes."[9]

A tornado passed through an oasis in Mali in 1999, missing the settlement but tearing out by the roots all the date palms, the reason for the community's existence. Less than a week after it happened, the entire oasis was deserted. No repair crews, no builders, no gardeners or planters, no herdsmen or householders, no *haratin* were working away. It was empty, abandoned. The houses had been stripped, the camels moved off. Everyone had left.

෪

MOST OF THE WORLD'S GREAT DESERTS, like the Sahara, are found either side of the humid and steamy equator. Why they are where they are is pretty straightforward, a consequence of what the climatologists call a "Hadley Cell," a closed circle driven by the energy of the sun. It works like this: The solar energy reaching the earth is at its greatest at the equator, and the air near the ground is therefore heated more quickly than air elsewhere. As it rises, it expands. When it reaches higher altitudes, it cools, and when it cools it condenses, causing rain to fall in tropical storms, great drenching sheets of water. The now drier and less dense air continues to rise, and at high levels moves away from the equator, pushed outward by the wall of continually rising hot air. Over the subtropics it cools further and starts to descend. It has already lost most of its moisture near the equator, and as it descends it is compressed and becomes warmer, its relative humidity declining even further. By the time it gets to the ground it is very hot and very dry, and it rushes back toward the equator to complete the cycle as hot, arid wind, deflected slightly westward by the earth's rotation in the "Coriolis effect." The area between where it descends and the humidity of the equator is where the deserts are found.

The Sahara, north of the equator by between nine hundred and twelve hundred miles, is massive enough to contain two climatic regimes of its own. To the north is a dry subtropical climate; to the south, a dry tropical climate. They are in many ways quite similar, but have somewhat different patterns of moisture, temperature ranges, and wind.

The great swath of the Sahara from northern Mauritania in the west, across southern Algeria and Libya, northern Mali and

Niger, across the top of the Tibesti Mountains and so into parts of Egypt's Western Desert, has cool winters, very hot summers, and extreme temperature swings. In the Libyan winter it is quite possible to have frost at night and temperatures of eighty degrees or more during the day. Average monthly temperatures in winter are only 55°F, but the summers are a different story. The highest temperature so far recorded in the Sahara is at Al-'Aziziyah, in Libya, on the northern margins of the desert, where the thermometer once reached 136°F. When it does rain—a total of less than three inches a year falls between December and March, with another small peak in August—it rains torrentially, in thunderstorms that cause flash floods. The massifs of central Sahara still occasionally get a sprinkling of snow in winter.

The southern Sahara, the dry tropical zone, doesn't have the same wild daily swings of temperature. Its cycle is more an annual one, following the sun: a relatively milder winter whose days and nights differ by little more than 20 degrees, with a hot dry season preceding sporadic seasonal summer rains yielding about 5 inches a year. Daily temperature swings rarely exceed 30°F, and the average is much less. Winter temperatures are moderate, usually in the fifties, although in the Tibesti Mountains lows of around 5°F are not uncommon. Summer highs of 120 or 130°F, on the other hand, are far from uncommon. A test done at Bouroukou, in Chad, measured an evaporation rate of more that 304 inches per year, the highest yet recorded; and in the summer on the mountains the relative humidity is so low it can be life threatening—2.5 percent, compared to a "norm" of 30 percent. Sebhah, Libya, has the dubious distinction of being the most arid place on earth.[10] As in the north, what rain does fall comes in dramatic thunderstorms, accompanied by flash floods. Winter is the time of the *harmattan*.

✧

THE SAHARA'S CLIMATE, like that of most deserts, is a complex and shifting amalgam of factors, both internal and external. Among the most obvious are the presence of the Canary current, the configuration of the mountains to the north, the existence of the supersaturated equatorial forests to the south, and the self-reinforcing nature of desert ecologies. All these are important. But large as it is, the Sahara is neither isolated nor, climatically speaking, self-sufficient. The oceans are larger still, and climatologists are now only dimly beginning to understand the effects of shifts in ocean temperature on planetary landmasses. It is not yet a meteorologist's truism that climate anomalies in any one region can be linked to ocean surface temperatures on a global scale, but there are many tantalizing hints that ocean temperatures a very long way away can have direct consequences on what happens in the deep Sahara. The oceans, those heat capacitors for the planet, may not have caused the desert, and may not be keeping it arid on their own, but they have a hand in its climate and, more particularly, its weather.

The Sahel, the southern Saharan fringe, was unusually damp in the 1950s, and suffered unusually devastating droughts in the 1970s and 1980s. These rainfall data correlate neatly with temperature shifts in the oceans, whether higher than normal temperatures in the southern Atlantic or Indian Oceans, or lower than normal temperatures in the north Atlantic. A one-on-one causality is far from proven, but the coincidences are startling.

This even works in the short term, a matter of years or even months. If the temperature of the ocean goes up, evaporation goes up, too, and massive changes are precipitated. A relatively small change of one degree can, in the tropical oceans, cause a massive increase in oceanic evaporation; the increased water vapor in the lower atmosphere is condensed where the air rises (called convergence zones), which process unleashes the latent heat of condensation, which in turn provides a substantial portion of the energy needed to drive tropical circulation. El Niño is the best known of these cycles.

☙

I T W O R K S the other way, too. The oceans affect the Sahara, but the great furnace of the Saharan summer "twists" the prevailing winds; the rising vortex over northern Africa sets off a chain of dis-

A hurricane's path, from Africa to the United States. (NASA/Goddard DAAC)

turbances in the cold moist air of the eastern Atlantic, a series of highs and lows that increase in number as the summer progresses. As early as June or July a few of these lows intensify into tropical depressions that begin to coil their way across the ocean, heading for the Caribbean islands. Some of them dissipate their energy in midocean; others pick up velocity and energy and mutate from storm to hurricane. In the "hurricane season" of late summer and early autumn a procession of a dozen or more of these massive, deadly lows threads its way through the islands and toward the coast of North America. Most of the destructive storms that pound the Gulf of Mexico and the Carolinas and all the way up the coast to Canada's eastern seaboard start in the open ocean, but many do owe their provenance to the arid landscapes of the greatest desert of all.

The pop science saying that "a butterfly fluttering somewhere in Manchuria can help set off a tornado in Kansas" considerably overstates the complexity of weather making, but its spirit is right, and the one-man weather office in Timbuktu and the slightly more sophisticated operation in Niamey, Niger's capital, are indeed taking observations of phenomena that directly affect America's weather.

Timbuktu's sole meteorologist observes the old-fashioned way—by going onto the roof in a thunderstorm, eyeballing its extent, and hoisting aloft a handheld wind velocity meter. He is there mostly to warn the pilots of Air Mali's venerable Fokker aircraft on their thrice-weekly runs into the city from Bamako, Mali's capital, if it is safe to proceed or more prudent to turn back. But his handwritten notes, forwarded later to the capital, are assembled into broader databanks and used by others to track storm patterns.

The systems that he and his colleagues in Niamey record are the same lurid thunderstorms so vividly described by Owen Watkins more than a century ago. The hot air rising rapidly from the furnace of the desert collides with cooler ripples descending from the Tibesti Mountains of Chad and to a lesser extent the Aïr Massif of Niger, deep in the heart of the Sahara, forming thunderclouds that some-times—the exact mechanisms are not known—coalesce into violent weather systems, big enough to alert American meteorologists who are monitoring satellite images across the Atlantic. The behavior of these storms, known to meteorologists as low-pressure systems, is erratic and unpredictable; some of them lose their coherence over land; others drift westward; a few even make it all the way out into the Atlantic, where they are energized as they are buffeted between the cooler air over the Atlantic—the Canary current is a cold-water current—and the furnace behind them. This increased energy is ex-pressed in a number of ways; one of them is that the low-pressure systems begin slowly to spin.

More than a hundred such low-pressure systems drift out of the Sahara into the ocean each year, rotating slowly counterclockwise. Most of these, once again, dissipate their moisture before they get very far. In others, the spin increases as the storm moves south and west, and if it is still spinning as it reaches the tropical oceans where water temperatures can reach eighty degrees, the effect is like taking the lid off a pot of steaming water—moist air ascends ever more rapidly, moisture and energy are dumped, surface winds rush into the vacuum thus created and in turn force the winds to rotate ever faster. After a few days, the tropical depression escalates into a tropical storm. If the sustained winds reach seventy-five miles per hour, the meteorologists reach for their naming dictionaries and give the new hurricane a moniker.

There is now considerable evidence that when the Sahel's rains come early or more copiously than the norm, Atlantic hurricanes intensify; the correlation between the number and intensity of hurricanes and the weather of the Sahel is too close to be merely coincidence. Saharan droughts, it seems, can be good for the Florida insurance industry. Does this imply that if the Saharan climate changes for the better—that is, if the desert becomes verdant again—the western Atlantic will be battered by more violent and more frequent storms? The climate models hazard no guesses, there being too many unknowns. On all the evidence, though, the Sahara is less distant than one might think.

CHAPTER FIVE

❦

The Surprising
Matter of Water

IN A WADI in the Ténéré, a shallow well had been dug. Nearby was a young woman in a black robe, black *aba* hood over her head. She herself was small and black with a toothless smile, bold eyes, legs stringy with muscle, bare feet. She had two small children with her, but they kept their distance, wary of strangers. A small flock of goats, not at all wary, butted their heads into anyone who would let them. The young woman carried a small metal basin, and a tin can on a string, which she threw into the well to haul the water to the surface. She poured the first few cans into the basin and the goats sucked greedily. Only then did she offer the children a few sips from the can, and lastly she herself drank, but sparingly. To drink too much or more than you need is anathema.

Like most wadis, this one was broad, flat, sandy, with occasional acacias rooted in the sand, their leaves torn and tattered from rasping goat and camel tongues. The river that had once run here would have been placid, slow-moving, and the well was almost in the center of what would have been its course. It was only four or five feet deep, but there was better than six inches of water at the bottom. It was kept from collapsing in on itself with a crude bracing of acacia branches, but in a week or so it would fill in anyway, and need to be reopened. The young woman offered her visitors a can. The water was clear, a change from normal Saharan standards, and had a slight metallic taste, perhaps the fault of the tin can used to draw it to the surface.

The young woman belonged to a family of nomads camping a

Young woman and one of her children at a well. (Marq de Villiers)

mile or so away, in the lee of an escarpment. The men were absent on some errand, she didn't know what, and had taken with them the family's camels. The women had been left behind with the children to tend the goats. When asked why they hadn't camped closer to the well, she shrugged. To walk a mile or two to the well with the goats helped fill up the day.

The well wasn't the only one of its kind in the wadi. Within sight were half a dozen other mounds of excavated sand. Several of the other wells had already filled in; some were dry. They were all, not surprisingly, more or less in the center of the dry watercourse. If water existed in the region, this is where it would most likely be found. Desert life is full of probabilities and guesswork, and most of it is based on long experience.

❧

IF IT HARDLY RAINS in the Sahara, and there are virtually no perennial rivers, where does this water come from? How did it get here, and how long has it been lying under the surface, waiting to be tapped? And the water that makes oasis life possible—how much exists, and where did it originate? In all, how much water is there in the desert, and how long will it last? Is it being renewed, and if so, how fast? These questions underlie all desert life and though they are seldom stated they are always there, a threnody of anxiety that permeates decisions every family must make, and by extension every state.

❧

IF ONE WERE SOMEHOW able to see through the desert sand and its underlying rock, and if somehow in this magical lens water was to appear in brilliant color against the underlying dun, one would see a complicated, slender, three-dimensional lattice of blue, in some places shifting and changing with the seasons, in others remaining stable for geological epochs. At times there would be splashes of blue underneath ancient river courses and wadis, shal-

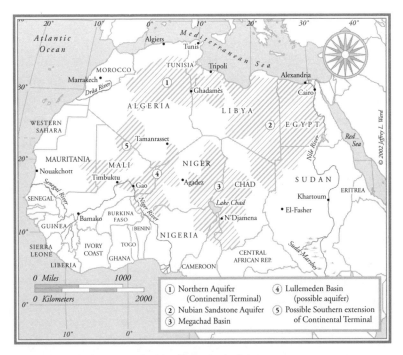

Sources of water in the Sahara.

low, erratic, spiky with endless branches and tributaries, with neither beginning nor end, dependent on ancient drainage systems but
no longer containing enough moisture to reach the oceans or any
other outlet. Some of these would be permanent water, shallow but
not transitory, left over from earlier epochs. Others would come and
go, apparent briefly after the "rainy" season, thin and tenuous or absent entirely at other times. Sometimes there would be vertical
"pipes" of emerald, dropping through fractures in the crust to pools
of water lying on the impermeable layers below; some would go
down a hundred feet, some many thousands; some would be a sliver
wide, others dozens of yards. And in places, very deep down, in
the permeable sandstone laid down on the oldest rocks, would be
virtual seas of blue, the size of the American Great Lakes. These are
the Nubian Sandstone Aquifer and the other great reservoirs that
underlie so much of north and central Sahara. They are "fossil

aquifers," so called because they were filled with water in earlier geological epochs.

The first answer to the question of how much water exists and how it got there must thus be sought by going back into geological time. Even though the Sahara has been a desert in prior epochs, and more than once, it is now well established that in the later Pleistocene and Holocene epochs—and more especially in the period from thirty thousand to ten thousand years ago—the present territory of the Sahara was akin perhaps to the Ukrainian steppe: grasslands, dotted with hundreds and perhaps thousands of lakes, with rivers flowing from the mountains and making their way to the sea—to the Atlantic, as the Moroccan rivers like the Drâa would do today if they didn't seep into the sand and disappear first, or to the Niger River to the south or the Nile to the east. The patient sifting by archaeologists has provided ample evidence of the copiousness of prehistoric water, ranging from fish and shell fossils to ossuaries of hippos and other aquatic creatures. Newer technology adds to what archaeology has shown and what history has suggested: Using radar, scientists[1] have peered through the sands of the Egyptian Western Desert and found evidence of dense riverbeds, dried up and buried, wending their way through the desert like vipers. And it is clear that Nabta Playa, a depression, was a great lake that once would fill with the summer monsoons. The study suggests that what was true for the Western Desert would also be true for the Sahara as a whole. And indeed, a NASA earth-observing "synthetic aperture radar" in the early 1980s was able to penetrate the dunes and see that the whole desert was underlain with a network of ancient riverbeds.

The water cycle of this prehistoric time would have been identical to that of the modern period, differing only in intensity. Water circulates through the earth's systems, from a height of fifteen kilometers above the ground to a depth of some five kilometers, transferring from one "reservoir" to another in complex, self-regulating cycles, governed by gravity or solar energy, over periods that range from hours to thousands of years. These reservoirs include atmospheric moisture (cloud and rain); the oceans, rivers, and lakes; groundwater (usually known as "the water table"); subterranean aquifers; the polar icecaps; and saturated soil (tundra or wetlands). The system makes human life possible because more water evaporates from the oceans than returns to it directly, the balance falling on land as freshwater. The period water stays put in any one place is called its "residence time." Residence times vary tremendously, from ten days for the atmosphere to many millennia for the sea. The residence times of the underground aquifers beneath the Sahara would be measured in tens of thousands of years, perhaps very much longer. Water in the Sahara's Nubian Aquifer has been dated to somewhere between ten thousand and thirty thousand years old.[2]

These massive aquifers were "charged," in the jargon of hydrologists, in the way all the world's aquifers are, by infiltration of surface water from above. The process is well understood, though its measurement is still haphazard. Rainfall, at least that part of it that doesn't directly join free-flowing surface water or become absorbed by plants, seeps into the soil zone, the upper few feet or so of earth. At first, it makes a "zone of aeration," in which the small interstices between soil particles are filled with a mixture of water and air; if the precipitation continues, complete saturation of the soil zone occurs and the water continues to descend until, at some point, it merges into a zone of dense rock. Rocks too dense to allow penetration by water are called "aquicludes." Others are more porous and can store considerable amounts of water. These supersaturated rocks, together with the interstices between them and their own natural fissures, are called "aquifers." The geology can get quite complicated. Aquifers can sometimes lie underneath layers of aquicludes, and are then called "confined aquifers." In other cases, called "unconfined aquifers," there is nothing around the aquifer but unsaturated and permeable material, such as gravel, shale, or sand. The boundary between the unsaturated and the water-bearing material is called the water table. In water-rich regions like Canada, northern Europe, and parts of the United States, the water table is relatively close to the surface, sometimes only fifteen or twenty feet below it, or even less. In the Sahara, where the aquifers are not being replenished, or are being replenished very slowly, the water table is often thousands of feet down. In most of the Sahara, where no permeable rocks exist, there is no water table at all. In other places, such as in the oases that make desert life possible, there are artesian "springs," which are really just water being pushed up through natural fissures in the rock from confined aquifers that are under hydraulic pressure.[3] These aquifers, then, are not pools or lakes of water in the conventional sense—even if you could somehow reach them you could not swim in them—but merely supersaturated porous rock and gravel, charged in earlier geological epochs, and recharged only erratically after that. Wells drilled into the aquifer work by creating open spaces into which the water from the surrounding rock can flow, and from which it can then be pumped—you could, in fact, "swim" in the wells, were you of a mind to.

Possibly these aquifers were filled once again in Europe's "little ice age" of the sixteenth to eighteenth centuries, when copious rain was thought to have fallen in the deep desert. If they were left alone, they'd lie there, virtually forever, immune to evaporation, with no further place to seep.

Even much of the shallow groundwater of the Fezzan in Libya and other districts is derived from rain that fell in earlier epochs. It is generally found either as springs or as *sebkhats*, terminals of desert wadis. When these *sebkhats* are penetrated by digging, the hydraulic pressure may cause a localized near-surface water table, and water will be available in shallow wells over a considerable area. Most of this "paleowater" remains very clean. It could have been paleowater the young woman in the wadi was giving her goats. If so, it might have been topped up, every now and then, by the rare rains and resultant floods, but it had essentially waited there for her for several thousands of years.

☙

WATER IN SERIOUS QUANTITIES was first discovered deep under the desert in the 1970s, in the Al-Kufrah region of Libya, far away in the southeast quadrant of the country, where it converges with Egypt, Sudan, and Chad. It was an accident—the prospectors were looking for oil, not water. The massive oil fields in the Sirte Desert to the northwest were good for generations to come, it was believed, though it never did any harm to find some more. They found something all right, but it was clear, clean water instead of black gold. A few more wells were test-drilled in the region and they all told the same story: Underlying the desert, in the saturated sandstone and in the interstices of the underlying shield, was an immense reservoir of water, which came to be called the Nubian Sandstone Aquifer. A few years later more water was found, this time to the west of the country in the Murzuq basin. It was, the geologists reported, another massive aquifer, probably unrelated to the first and separated from it by a thick layer of marine deposits. This one, which they called the Continental Terminal, spills across the border into Algeria, and possibly even beyond that to the Niger Taoudeni basin and even part of Mali, which would make it the largest known arid-country aquifer on the planet, bigger even than the Ogallala, which underlies the proto-deserts of the American High Plains states. It could, however, be two or even more discrete aquifers; the water under Mali might be unrelated, a separate pool. It will be years, if ever, before the answer is known, since no one outside Libya has the money for exploration, and what money they do have is spent on more urgent matters.

The geology is nevertheless fairly well understood. Massive depressions in the so-called basement rock, generally pre-Cambrian and very old, were later filled with more porous sedimentary deposits, which now form reservoirs deep underground; these reservoirs reach thicknesses of more than three thousand feet. Yields from wells in these areas can be astonishingly high, up to twenty-five thousand cubic feet of water per hour. But the water is all "fossil water," deposited in the soils in the long-ago verdant phases. Geologists have assumed until recently, from the lack of surface water and the paucity of rain, that these aquifers are not being recharged at all, and that the water, once used, would be gone forever.

Libya's mercurial Qaddafi, however, whatever his politics and his quirks and his erratic ambitions, is not a man to think small. When his engineers told him of these surviving "fossil aquifers," he conceived the grand notion of taking this remnant water from the deep desert and piping it to the coast, there creating new agricultural zones, a new source of nourishment for growing things in his riverless country. He called this the Great Man-Made River, and for once this is not just hyperbole: a gigantic network of massive pipes, each thirteen feet in diameter, hundreds of miles long, taking water to Libya's coastal plains from wells thousands of feet deep. Under Qaddafi's insistent prodding, the Sahara gave up one of its greatest secrets, something it had kept hidden for ten thousand years.

To non-Libyans (and no doubt to many Libyans as well), the Great Man-Made River seemed mad, a product of senseless ambition combined with endless flows of money. To build the largest civil engineering project on the planet, to spend $32 billion to take water from the desert to the coast, to allow the population to increase and industry to establish itself as a result of ready access to water—to build all this, to see irrigation sprinklers in the desert, knowing that in thirty years, or forty, or perhaps fifty the water would inevitably run out, seemed insane.

Qaddafi's defense was simplicity itself: Water was of no use deep under the desert floor, and if it was exhausted in time, at least it would have done some good in the interim.

More recently, however, geologists have been revising their estimates. It has begun to seem possible that the ancient aquifers are being recharged at a faster rate and in greater volume than suspected. Perhaps the rivers that flow into the desert and disappear and the flash floods that ravage parts of the southern desert in what passes for a rainy season—perhaps these are adding greater volumes of water to the groundwater reservoirs than had been anticipated. If so, Qaddafi's "river" will last longer than the forty or fifty years that pessimistic predictions had at first indicated.

cↄ

IF THE SAHARA had been dry forever, these aquifers would
not exist—nor would any of the other water still to be found in the
great desert. Relative to the immensity of the whole Sahara, of
course, these signs of water are thinly spread and perilously few, but
they do exist. There are even fish, deep beneath the desert sands. In
the middle years of the last century the French academician Jacques
Couëlle dug a well in the desert near El-Goléa, south of the Western
Great Erg, and at 130 feet his men struck water, brackish and churn-
ing, but water nevertheless. The next day the crew returned with bas-
kets, and found themselves pulling out fish, "completely blind, with
only a membrane where there used to be eyes; they have reproduced,
surviving more than 10,000 years. There were hundreds of thousands of them. We cooked some of them and they were delicious."[4]
An explorer in the deep Algerian Sahara near Tamanrasset came
across an artesian spring, hydrologic offspring of a deep-level aquifer,
which flowed into a sluggish creek no more than a few hundred yards
long, in which wriggling tadpoles and small fish could be seen.[5] Paul-
Xavier Flatters, who led a doomed French expedition into the Sahara
in 1880 (his whole party was massacred by Tuareg), stumbled
through the Tassili escarpment, which he found generally "sinister,"
his views no doubt colored by his suspicion of his fate. "We are at
this moment at the foot of a mountain of enormous rocks," he wrote
in one of his last letters to his wife, "cut by a gorge at the bottom of
which runs a stream: The first running water we have seen in the Sahara! There are fish in the water."[6] This was at Amguid, to the west
of the massif. The survivors of the expedition, twenty-seven in all including guides, made their way into the gorge after the massacre.
There they paused a few days. "Beautiful acacias grow at the entry [to
the gorge] of which the interior is carpeted in oleander," one of them
was reported as saying afterward. "The cold, clear waters nourish numerous fishes. We caught one as big as a human leg (crocodiles also
live there). So full of fish was it that Messaoud [one of their guides]
threw in his shirt and recovered six little ones."[7]

In Chad's Archeï region, near the town of Fada, is a canyon whose water, fertilized by camel droppings, produces algae that are eaten by fish that are preyed upon by an isolated group of crocodiles, an entire ecosystem in miniature, a closed cycle, each component trapped and dependent.[8] Slightly to the west, a traveler passing an evening in an outpost of the Foreign Legion noticed "in the fireplace a small stuffed crocodile, about three feet long, one of the dwarf Saharan race from the lake of Archeï." Said the lieutenant, "There is no shortage of water here. Anywhere you dig in Fada you find water at six or eight feet."[9]

In the great massifs of the central Sahara—the Ahaggar, the Tassili, the Aïr, the Tibesti—there are deep canyons where the sun seldom penetrates; sometimes water collects there, forming rock pools that are almost, though not quite, perennial. Wadis in some of these mountain folds can contain considerable amounts of subsurface water—not enough to turn the Tuareg into farmers, exactly, but enough for gardens and to grow forage for the livestock.

Most curiously of all, perhaps, water can even be found on occasion in the largest dunes. Oddly, if any rain at all falls, sand makes a better base for cultivation than other soils, because it absorbs water easily, the high air content in the upper levels insulates the water from evaporation, and it readily gives up water to plants. Dunes "fixed" with vegetation can support dense agricultural populations, as in northern Nigeria and Senegal. In the very largest dunes, rare "seeps" can be found, the sand weeping water, though the surrounding desert floor is dry to a depth of many feet. If you know what you're doing, even in the deep desert you can dig down a yard or so in the dunes and press moisture from the sand.

However, it is never enough to live on. Many a traveler has sucked damp sand, but died of thirst nonetheless.

❧

IN CERTAIN PARTS of the desert, there is even standing water, open to the sun and its fierce evaporative powers. There are not very many lakes, of course, in the vast scale of the desert, but the occasional one does exist. In Libya, east of the Ubari Sand Sea and north of the Murzuq *hamada* is a series of eleven extraordinary saline lakes whose origins and qualities continue to puzzle hydrologists. They are known—like the other lakes in the desert—to be spring-fed from subterranean aquifers, but the mechanisms remain obscure. Mavo Lake changes color—sometimes the water is blue, sometimes green, and sometimes a striking red. When the water is pink, it is usually because it is tinged with billions of tiny shrimplike creatures known locally as "doud," Arabic for worm. The people who live around its shores, accordingly, are known as Dauada, which seems to mean "wormers," or possibly worm eaters. Another of the eleven lakes, Lake Gabraoun, is as salty as the Dead Sea, but if you dig a shallow pit, even a few feet from the lake's edge, it fills with freshwater. Date palms and reeds thrive on its shores.[10]

The lake near Ashinuma in the Wadi Kawar, in eastern Niger, is about half a mile long by about two hundred yards broad, but only about two feet deep, a reddish brown color, like a still-fermenting dark beer. Springs on the east side boil up in several places; the water is salty and very bitter.[11] On the north side below the bank a black substance like mineral tar oozes into the water, and a crust of salt forms on the top like half-thawed ice. Natron, hydrous sodium carbonate produced by the weathering of granitic rocks or sandstones, forms in cakes at the bottom; the local people use it for tanning, for baking unleavened bread, as an animal feed, and to mix with pipe tobacco, among other things. The Egyptians used it as part of the recipe that mummified the pharaohs. Water from the nearby wells is brackish and stinks, and can cause severe intestinal disorders.

In northern Chad, a massive lake once stretched from Gouro in the southern Tibesti to the Ennedi Mountains, some 150 miles; only fragments remain in the half-dozen small lakes of the Ounianga Kebir and Serir. One is called Red Lake, another Blue Lake,

Lake Yoan (Klaus Daerr)

and they are, indeed, painted in startling primary colors. Lake Yoan is the most dramatic of these; you can stand on a cliff two hundred feet above the water and hear the whisper of the waves, a magic moment there in the bitter heat.[12] On every shore there are springs, freshwater but very hot, more than eighty degrees, heated by molten lava somewhere deep below. The lake itself has a greasy feeling and is strongly salty, but waterfowl thrive, and flocks of ducks can be seen. So, alas, can billions of tiny black flies, a constant irritant to travelers. Legends say these flies were released by the goddess of the lake, a giantess with golden hair, who mated with a shepherd to become the ancestress of the Ounia people.[13]

Lake Chad is the greatest body of freshwater in the Sahara or on its fringes. The lake was known to Ptolemy, and was the subject of legend in the European Middle Ages. But to the African traders it was no legend: One of the oldest trans-Sahara routes, that from Tripoli to the Hausa trading cities, teases the lake at its northwest corner, and the ancient Egyptians passed by on the way to the gold mines of Old Ghana. Fragments exist from the Denham-

Clapperton-Oudney expedition of 1823: "The great Lake Tchad, glowing with the golden rays of the sun in its strength, within a mile of the spot on which we stood. On the shores there were prosperous little villages, most of the houses having a cow or two, some goats, and chickens in the yard and the lake itself was thronged with birds and animals."[14] All was not, however, as peaceful as it seemed, for the villages were subject to constant raids, not only by the Tubu in the north, but by the piratical Buduma, a warlike people who inhabited the islands of Lake Chad and controlled the waters from their battle canoes.

Some believe Lake Chad is the remnant of a much larger ancient sea, sometimes referred to as the Paleochadian Sea or, less formally, as "Mega-Chad." This immense body of water covered some 154,000 square miles and would have been more than 600 feet deep. When it flooded in those ancient times it flowed northeastward. You can still see the channel, winding for 400 miles along the Bahr-el-Ghazal, the "River of the Gazelles," and so into the vanished lakes of the Djourab and Bodélé regions of Chad, now deserts to the northeast. The disparity in altitudes makes it seem unlikely that those vanished lakes ever emptied into the Nile, but it wouldn't have taken a great tectonic shift to make impossible something that had been entirely normal.

Much more recently, within the last two hundred years, the lake was more massive than it is now; on some maps it is still shown twice its actual size, for it is shrinking fast, almost a hundred yards a year. These days, it is less a lake than a large bathing pool for hippos, and if you're a reasonable size and don't fall into a hole, you can wade across it. In the drought of the eighties it once dried up altogether, except for a few pools where desperate wildlife gathered (the fishermen starved). What water is left is divided into two lobes separated by a sandy ridge penetrated by only one channel. To its north, in the Kanem region, the once-notorious but now peaceful Buduma inhabit the huge dunes that barricade the shores. In the south the shores are flat and swampy.

The lake has elicited many a colorful and unlikely legend, some of them more recently cobbled together than others.

"Dawn," wrote Olive MacLeod in 1912, "found us at the edge of the lake, gazing out across a little bay at Hajer-el-Hamis [on the southern shore of Lake Chad], which, though actually but a few hundred feet in height, seems a veritable mountain in that sandy plain, where for several days journey these rocks are the only eminence. Till comparatively recently Lake Chad surrounded the hills and there are traces of water action as high as 50 feet upon them. The rocks are magnificently rugged. The effect is of irregular fluted columns, intersected by many caves inhabited by strange fluffy owls and millions of blue pigeons, the descendants perhaps of that messenger dove who brought the olive branch to the Ark."[15]

Here, on the southern shore of Lake Chad, on the hills of Hajer-el-Hamis, is where Noah's Ark came to rest, at least according to one medieval folktale. Maybe they thought so because the place was so wretchedly distant, and had water in such benightedly unexpected a place. "And it was here that the Ark rested when the Flood subsided, evidence of birds and beasts, for these could hardly have found their way here in such variety and number had it not been for their historic origin. The name of the surrounding country, too, bears its testimony to the past: Bornu, Bur-Noah = the land of Noah. As the name Hajer-el-Hamis denotes, it is a place of pilgrimage, and for centuries men have traveled thither to make sacrifice, sacrifices that were once of human beings, though humbler offerings are made now. Once certain pilgrims, who lived not far from Chad, journeyed to Mecca, and when they had come there they made plaint before the Mallam, saying, 'See how far we have come, and what we have suffered on the way.' The Mallam made answer, 'You had no need to come thus far. In your own country there is a holy mountain where you may worship,' and they retired discomfited."[16]

Rich Neolithic sites have been reported in the Bodélé area northeast of the lake and, even more remarkable, enormous slag-heaps, providing evidence of iron working. This can hardly have been carried on much earlier than the beginning of the Christian era, so Bodélé must have been inhabited by a sedentary population long after Neolithic times. Like much of Africa, the region seems to have skipped the Bronze Age and proceeded directly from stone to iron, in defiance of what was once thought to be man's orderly technological progression.

Though called *Bahr,* or river, no river any longer flows there. Immense bones of animals and fish, some of unknown species, have been found, petrified. The nomads say "they went to take them up as bones, but by a trick of *Iblis* [the devil] they proved to be stones." As we have already seen, some of these fish must have been ten to twelve feet long; and shells are still found embedded in the earth, some of them finely polished, "some so large that the Negroes make trumpets of them."[17]

Now Koro Toro, on the Bahr-el-Ghazal, is a southern gateway to the Sahara.[18]

❧

TO SEE LAKE CHAD proper is to see what the Sahara must have been like in its last verdant incarnation. However, it is no longer easy to find. Twenty miles or so past where it was supposed to begin, a dugout canoe paddled gently among the reeds and papyrus beds, the muddy marsh that marked the edge of the lake, and a little to the side lolled a hippo, with its enormous mouth wide open and a bird pecking away at its teeth. The paddler was probably one of the Buduma, reduced to scratching a living from the meager fishing of the lake. He agreed to a day without fishing in return for a fistful of Central African francs, though there was nothing more to see than mud and swamp and islands of reeds, ten to fourteen feet tall, bulrushes and papyrus and choking hyacinths. If there was a lake somewhere, it was hidden in the grass and the haze. And if its water was fresh, it nonetheless smelled strongly of rotting vegetation. None of the lake's famous flying fish were visible—only crocodiles, which are very dangerous in these parlous times because there are far too many of them and they are hungrier and angrier than usual.

❧

IT DOES RAIN, albeit erratically and infrequently, even in the desert's furnace heart.

In the north, the rain falls in winter, and the rivers that begin in the gravel valleys of the Atlas and Anti Atlas Mountains run continuously until they vanish beneath the surface in the *ergs*. In the central massifs, rain can occasionally fall in torrents. After such a rainfall, the valleys are covered by a green carpet of plants. Permanent or semipermanent streams flow in the higher altitudes, while, lower down, water collects in small lakes or pools in the crystalline rocks of the valleys and hillsides.

In the Sahel, on the desert fringes, savage summer thunderstorms last for several hours. They have oddly precise boundaries—it can be bone dry on one side of a dune, and pouring rain on the other. These electric storms cause shock waves and flash floods that rush into areas the rain never reaches, causing widespread damage and drownings. Entire herds of goats have vanished in these floods, which appear out of nowhere with frightening rapidity, scouring the wadis with a deafening roar, the water disappearing almost instantly. Nothing is eerier than a flash flood where no rain has fallen and no water otherwise exists. The torrent appears under a cloudless sky, in the full light of day, with no warning other than a distant and barely audible rumble, as boulders are shifted and stone banks collapse; then the water is there, acacia branches tumbling in a flood the color of coffee, and just as soon it is gone, and all that is left is a hissing as the water is sucked into the already drying sand. By the next morning, there will be no sign the flood ever happened.

Heinrich Barth was actually saved by a flood from an attack by Aïr Tuareg, who had been harassing his caravan. "An immense quantity of rain fell in our locality which changed our valley into the broad bed of a massive river, placing all our property in the utmost danger, a stream violent enough to carry away the heaviest things, not even excepting a strong, tall animal like the camel, a grand and awful picture of destruction. Our little island attacked on all sides by the impetuous mountain torrent, swollen to the dimensions of a considerable river, was fast crumbling to pieces."[19]

The town of Ghat, in Libya near the Acacus Mountains, was built of mud in an area where it hardly ever rained. It suffered a freak downpour in the 1960s, and mostly melted into the ground, a misfortune from which it never really recovered, and it is now only used as an occasional camp by itinerant Tuareg. Tamanrasset in Algeria, the Tuareg capital to the west of the Ahaggar, was largely destroyed by such a flood in 1922. Many travelers have recounted similar stories, from many epochs. Teminhint, an oasis on the way to Murzuq in Libya, was "a beautiful spot of about 800 inhabitants,"[20] Gustav Nachtigal reported, but more than a third of the houses had been destroyed the summer before he got there in a torrential downpour, much to the bewilderment of the inhabitants. Six men and fifty animals died, drowned in the Sahara, a bitterly ironic end. The sheikh of Kharifa, in the Fezzan, Ali Tibbo, told a visitor that in 1822, a year of cursed memory, the rain had fallen in such torrents from the hills that it filled the wadi below until it resembled a sea, and that the town of Tiwiwa was entirely washed down from its hills. The dunes on the north side of the wadi were then covered with fine grass, and for two years following crops thrived where none had grown before. Or since.

So accustomed are the desert dwellers to water's absence (and occasional ferocious appearance) that some have come to look on flowing water with suspicion. In the Fezzan area south of Tripoli, the inhabitants sometimes pray to be spared rain—partly, of course, this is because their houses are made of clay, and deteriorate rapidly when it rains, but also, as Nachtigal noted, "because for the date palms and gardens the inhabitants prefer well water." A date palm, the desert saying goes, should keep its "feet in the water and its head in the fire."[21] Similarly, rainwater was described as *meyi*, dead, while the water in the wells was *hai*, life-giving.

In parts of the desert, especially in the uplands, it may rain "regularly," maybe two inches a year, maybe as much as six. In the highlands of the Mauritanian Adrar, at Guelta Zemmour in the Western

Sahara and at the Adrar des Iforhas in Mali, it is damp enough that pastures and even date groves grow 180 to 450 miles north of the Sahelian frontier, deep into the desert.[22] Near the massifs, heavy dews are common, and dew collectors, large dishes made of fine mesh, can collect enough water to keep a family alive.

Elsewhere in the Great Thirstland the "rain" can be a grim mirage. The air is like dry fire, and water sizzles and just disappears. In the desert's heart there may even be atmospheric rain that lasts several days, but no water reaches the ground: The raindrops evaporate in the ovenlike air mere inches above it.

೧

A FEW RIVERS do flow in the Sahara, though seldom all the time. The only perennial river in the central Sahara is the Iherir, in the Tassili region of Algeria, whose modest flow seeps out of the cracks in the massif and runs through several twisting gorges before disappearing into the sand. Several major rivers originate outside the boundaries of the Sahara, and then flow through or disappear into the desert itself, impacting in various ways on its surface and groundwater. The Drâa and the Saoura flow from the Atlas Mountains along the northern periphery. The Drâa winds its way as far as Agdz, where it turns into a spectacular 150-mile oasis before drifting south into the desert, past Tamenougalt (from which the Sa'adis overran Morocco six hundred years ago) and Tamegroute (which preserves magnificent illuminated Korans in its seventeenth-century library, a legacy of its rich political past and of being the locus for many of the counting-houses of Saharan trade). Once at M'Hamid, what used to be the longest river in Morocco is finally swallowed up by the sands, though it is possible to track its underground passage all the way to the Atlantic, where the part of it that has not seeped into the deep aquifers pumps sluggishly into the sea at Tan Tan Plage. The Saoura heads directly southward into the desert, the so-called palm road, past Beni Abbés, and finally peters out 120 miles later in the deep desert west of In'Salah in Algeria, where it gradually spreads out and disappears into the sand.

Some of the greatest Saharan rivers rise in the tropical highlands to the southwest. The Niger rises in the sodden hills of Guinea but traverses the southern end of the Endless Desert. On Mauritania's southern border is the Senegal River, at 1,015 miles one of west Africa's longest, often confused with the ocean outlet for the east-flowing Niger, which rises in the same moist highlands. The Nile, the longest river on the planet, is of course a Saharan river for much of its course, though it rises in the humid hills of Burundi and rests awhile in Lake Victoria. This, the so-called White Nile, then wanders through the Sudd Marshes of Sudan before flowing between the Nubian and Libyan deserts, and the ancient strongholds of Meroë and Kush, the far reaches of Pharaonic Egypt and then Egypt's own Western and Eastern deserts. Still, most of the Nile water, the so-called Blue Nile, comes from Lake Tana in Ethiopia.

In planetary time, the Nile's present course is not old. Somewhere around 30 million years ago, the early Nile had its source in the present Atbara River, which also flows from the Lake Tana region; this would have been, more or less, the course of the present Blue Nile. The Sudd Lake, now the Sudd Marshes, was to the south, and self-contained—this early Nile was still cut off from central Africa. However, at some point the East African lake country—Lake Victoria—developed a new outlet, which sent its water northward into Lake Sudd. With the accumulation of sediments over a long period, the water level of this lake rose gradually; as a result of the overflow, the Sudd was drained, spilling over to the north. These overflowing waters formed a riverbed, and so linked the White to the Blue Nile, thus unifying the drainage from Lake Victoria to the Mediterranean Sea.[23]

For more than 750 miles the Nile cuts through bare desert, a ribbon of green, a glimmer of hope in the desolation. Did not Mohammed, the Prophet of God himself, say that the "Nile comes out of the Garden of Paradise, and if you were to examine it when it

The Nile. (State Information Service, Egypt)

comes out, you would find in it leaves of Paradise"?[24] It is a very
narrow ribbon, and a slender hope, for the floodplain is seldom
more than ten miles wide, even at high water, and that perilously
narrow channel forms Egypt's only agricultural zone. No wonder
the annual inundation of the Nile was so eagerly anticipated. In
midsummer, the *fellahin*, the peasant husbandmen of the Nile
floodplains, used to wait anxiously for the Night of the Drop, when
a drop of dew of marvelous power, made in the heavens, fell into the
Nile and impregnated it, bringing forth the life-giving floods. Many
used to stay up late to wait for the Drop, "and are often persuaded
that they see it shooting like a star towards the river, now shrunk
within its narrowest limits."[25] Less romantically, it was the annual
drenching from the heavy rains in the Ethiopian highlands that
caused the annual deposits of silt in the Nile Valley and especially in
the delta; it was this nutrient-rich silt that enabled a sustainable
agriculture along the lower Nile and, at least arguably, contributed
to the flowering and fecundity of ancient Egyptian civilization.

The Pharaohs apparently learned very early to manipulate and control the water: An Arab manuscript of fairly recent vintage (1686) quotes an earlier book, now lost:

> Achmed, son of Ti Farshi, in his book of the description of the Nile, says historians relate that Adam bequeathed the Nile unto Seth, his son, and it remained in the possession of these children of prophecy and of religion, and they came down to Egypt. Idrisi the prophet [of this line] began to reduce the land to law and order. He is the first man who regulated the flow of the Nile to Egypt. Idrisi gathered the people of Egypt and went with them to the first stream of the Nile, and there adjusted the leveling of the land and the water by lowering the high land and raising the low land and other things according to the science of astronomy and surveying. Idrisi was the first person who spoke and wrote books on those sciences. It is said that in the days of Am Kaam, one of the Kings of Egypt, Idrisi was taken up to Heaven, and he prophesied the coming of the flood, so he remained on the other side of the equator and there built a palace on the slopes of Mount Gumr. He built it of copper, and made eighty-five statues of copper, the waters of the Nile flowing out through the mouths of these statues and then flowing into a great lake and thence to Egypt.[26]

Idrisi was, it seems, the world's first hydrological engineer.

His modern equivalents, at the urging of the pan-Arabist Gamal Abdel Nasser, finally put a stop to the Nile Delta's infusions of silt in the 1950s by building the Aswan High Dam, an act of engineering hubris that has set off endless controversy among hydrologists and agricultural engineers. Before the dam was built, the river at Aswan, at low water, was not very formidable, but in the annual floods "it would become a mighty irresistible torrent, boiling and roaring over the granite rocks."[27] These floods often took the hapless fellahin by surprise, and villages and fields were torn away. The dam put a stop to the destruction. On the other hand, that nutrient-rich silt no longer reached the farmers' fields, but instead built up in useless tons behind the dam's retaining wall. Without it, Egyptian farmers were obliged to resort to chemical fertilizers and intricate networks of irrigation canals, now, alas, infested with bilharzia, that lethal water-vector disease of Africa.

Perhaps fortunately, a major part of the Nile is actually hidden from sight. Egyptian hydroengineers have calculated that despite its equatorial origins, much of the river would disappear in the Sudanese Sahara were it not for the fact that a considerable part of its flow is groundwater, recharged aquifers under the sand, that are relatively impervious to evaporation. Nevertheless, Egypt, which is famously thrifty with water use, is rapidly running out of usable water—it is using almost all of its supply and there are a million new Egyptians every nine months. In recent years Egypt has pondered draining the Sudd Marshes, for to its jaundiced and water-scarce eye the marshes "waste" huge amounts of the Nile water by holding it for evaporation. Water wars have several times been threatened by Egyptian planners should the Sudanese ever think of using that water for themselves.

෴

THE NIGER, which derives its name from the phrase *gher n-gheren*, meaning "river among rivers," in Tamashek, skirts the Sahel and keeps the desert cities of Segou, Timbuktu, Gao, and Niamey alive. For 1,010 miles (a third its length), it flows through Mali. Before Timbuktu it spreads out in a wide valley, almost an inland delta; the countryside is flat, the river's descent almost nonexistent, and it spreads into a complex network of branches and lakes, allowing rice to be cultivated on the fringes of the desert itself. The river's curious and unexpected course—it first flows northeast, then east, then takes a bend to the south to the Niger border, after which it plunges southward and enters the Atlantic in a festering, malarial delta in the Gulf of Guinea, a further 1,600 miles or so—baffled early explorers. Herodotus, for example, confused it with the Nile, as did so many later writers. He asserted in his *Histories* that the Nile

flowed eastward "out of the Libyan desert" before it swerved to flow
north. He quoted Etearchus, king of the Ammonians at Siwa in
Egypt, as recounting the tale of certain of his young men who had
daringly crossed the desert "to see what they might see beyond the
utmost range of travelers." They were, the king admitted, wild and
violent men, but they made it safely and came across a city near a
great river that flowed eastward. This was no doubt the Niger and
the city some precursor of Gao, but they took it for the Nile, and
thus "proved" Herodotus's earlier assumptions.[28]

Idrisi, the twelfth-century Arab geographer, believed the Niger
flowed westward, and thought it had a common source with the
Nile. Ibn Battuta passed through Timbuktu early in the fourteenth
century, when it was already a trading depot of note, and a university town with extensive libraries. But on the Niger he was unhelp-
ful: He left no word of its course. Leo Africanus, alas, spoke of
traveling "downstream" from Timbuktu to Djenne to the west,
thereby indicating that he didn't know nearly as much as he let on.
Mungo Park, who reached the Niger in 1796 on an expedition fi-
nanced by London's Africa Society, saw for himself that the river
flowed eastward. A Moor in Timbuktu had told a friend that "below
Ghinea, is the sea, into which the river of Tombuctoo disembogues
itself."[29] But Park was unable to believe it—flowing eastward, it
seemed impossible for the river to end in the Atlantic. Ghinea, or
Guinea, he incorrectly placed somewhere east of Timbuktu, along
with Ghana, then a name of ancient renown but uncertain location.
He excused the Moor by saying he had confused the word for "sea"
with the word for "lake"; Park then repeated rumors he had heard of
a great lake to the east, which he called Wangara, and which must,
he thought, surely be the terminus of the river. Whether this imagined lake was really Lake Chad is not known.

ॐ

FOR MILLENNIA caravans have crossed the desert, but never
in straight lines; the tracks zigzag to where the water is. Such maps
of the desert as do exist mark the known wells and oases, generally

with stark annotations: good water, water lightly salted, bad water. Many Saharan wells are no more than holes in the ground, sometimes covered over by sand or even camouflaged by their diggers, and so finding one requires both skill and a fair measure of luck. Even when not camouflaged, wells can be almost invisible from just a few paces, a few small sticks laid in a square on the ground their only markers.

The camouflage was often malicious in intent. Nomads tell many stories of roving bands preying on caravans that had missed the concealed wells, or found them empty, or got there after the predators had deliberately collapsed their sides, making the water impossible to find. Such devices have a long history. Pliny had noted wells choked with sand. "It has been impossible," he wrote, "to open the road to the Garamantian country because brigands of that race fill up the wells with sand."[30] It is still a favorite trick of Tuareg bandits to fill in an old well, and then plunder a caravan when its members are reduced to delirium from thirst. At remote wells in the first year of the twenty-first century freelance and unauthorized tax collectors have set themselves up in many places in Niger and Algeria, demanding payments they call "maintenance fees" for the wells. Travelers must pay or risk a perilous ride to the next well, which itself may be similarly occupied.

Even now, a common task of a caravan that arrives in an oasis or at a water-bearing wadi is to dig a well, not just draw from an existing one. The larger the caravan, the more necessary the wells, and opening new ones is quicker than waiting in a long line for a slow well to refill.[31]

Sometimes wells dry up altogether, their underlying aquifers exhausted. This occasionally happens in clusters of oases, or even in regions if the sparse rainfall that feeds the springs is absent for too long. The results are almost always disastrous. If a source dries up, its former users must find water elsewhere, but most desert water is already spoken for. Threats follow, and mini–water wars are common. These have a long history: The Egyptians of the Twelfth Dynasty built a wall from Heliopolis and Pelusium to stop raids from desert dwellers intent on stealing water, and such incursions still happen. In 2000 a Mauritanian mob desperate for water stormed across the border into Mali and attacked an oasis there; they were beaten back and dozens were killed.

In the oases, water supplies are usually meticulously allocated. Gardens and date palms are watered by an intricate system of carefully measured sluices and furrows, each plot owner jealously watching that his water rights not be preempted by others, or somehow "stolen" by the unscrupulous. Despite all the care, oasis gardens are often poisoned by salination of the soil caused by the intense evaporation. And of course they are sometimes just overwhelmed by the dunes, and the wells are abandoned.

The oasis town of Ghadamès in western Libya, in medieval times, had taken this business of measuring water seriously indeed. Water from the springs and wells was conducted by underground conduits to a tiled and vaulted chamber, where it was carefully measured by the watermaster, called the *gaddas*, before being released into narrow channels and sluices that took it to the town's gardens. The gauge was a bucket with a hole in the bottom, which emptied at a known rate. For each bucket emptied, the *gaddas* tied a knot in a string. The knotted strings were filed with the town's *khadi*, ruler, for later adjudication should it prove necessary. Three *gaddas* were on duty on a twenty-four-hour rotation. They were, it goes without saying, men of the utmost probity, and were not paid for their work.

∽

THE EARLY EUROPEANS tried to help assure a steady supply of desert water, but in a neat metaphor for colonialism, usually ended up making things worse. "Blinded by their nationalist idealism, competitive spirit and desire for promotion and decoration [France's Saharan officers] refused publicly to admit [that] the French conquest and occupation had upset the fragile economy of the oases, and all of southern Algeria." To increase the water supply, the French military sank deep wells, appalling the desert dwellers at the amount of water they consumed. When François Lamy took over as commander at El-Goléa in 1891, he found that he had to dig extra wells for his garrison of 230 men. Once the bedrock was pierced, the water came rushing out, 50 gallons a minute, from the first attempt. But the artesian wells were a mixed blessing. "As [most] oases occupied depressions in the desert, the water had no place to run, so it collected in stagnant, fetid pools [in which] malarial mosquitoes bred, as did other diseases, like typhoid. Ouargla, El-Goléa and other settlements, which had once been havens for nomads in the summer months, were, within a few years of the French occupation, deserted by people fleeing disease. At the same time, the artesian wells lowered the water table and dried out the oases while flooding them. The military engineers, or *génie militaire*, charged with digging the wells, became known as the *génie malfaisant* or evil genie."[32]

Modern deep-water diesel pumps have changed oasis life, again not always for the better. The water is sweeter and more controlled, pressure valves doing what Lamy's soldiers didn't know how to do— shut down the flow of an artesian well. But reliable water has merely caused the oasis population to swell and the nomads to settle in shanties instead of living in movable tents, thus joining the new urban poor who have become a fact of life in so many parts of Africa, dependent now on state welfare and the rudimentary money economy to keep alive.

To help reduce the incidence of malaria, *gambusia* fish, which have a voracious appetite for mosquitoes, have been introduced to oasis ponds, though the nomads don't like them, considering them unclean. The ponds can be foul with decaying vegetation and infusions of camel dung, but the Tuareg think the fish dirty the water, and kill them when they can.

ও

WHERE THERE ARE NO MAPS and the routes are uncertain, desert travelers judge where water is, the *caravannier* A'Yóba said, from the lie of the land. Indeed, the Tuareg nomads generally find water not by prior knowledge but by looking at the topography; where there was once water, there probably still is. It is obvious, for instance, that most of the shallow wells lie in or close to the wadis, the ancient watercourses, and close to the so-called alluvial fans that are found all over the desert, debris at the base of mountain drainage systems where once water flowed. If there's a dried-up saline lake nearby there will be efflorescences of "thermonatrite," which looks like salt incrustation but is really natron reduced by dehydration. This is also a reliable sign that water lies somewhere beneath.

Even outsiders can learn the trick of finding water. Heinrich Barth reported a conversation with a Tuareg chief in Agadez. "After exchanging compliments with me, he asked me, abruptly, if I knew where water was to be found, and when I told him that, though I could not exactly say in every case at what depth water was to be found, yet that, from the configuration of the ground, I should be able to tell the spot where it was most likely to be met with, he asked whether I had seen rock inscriptions on the road from Ghat; and I answered him that I had, and generally near watering places. He then told me that I was quite right, but that in Tafilalt there were

A Tuareg getting water from a well. (Fuoristrada)

many inscriptions at a place distant from water. I told him that perhaps at an earlier period water had been found there."[33]

❧

WITHOUT WATER, a man will last little longer than a day in the desert, two at the most. It doesn't matter if he's from the water-fat Outside or is a wiry nomad whose metabolism is tuned to desert ways. Without water, he dies. And he loses perhaps ten liters of water a day through sweating, double that if he's forced to keep on the move. Outsiders sometimes don't even know they are sweating, because, in truth, there is never any sign of moisture—the "sweat" dries instantly—and so they often don't realize how much water they need. Water loss must be replaced, and very soon. If it isn't, the thirst rises up, a ravaging need much more urgent than hunger, an *adab* as the Berbers say, a demand-that-must-be-met. True thirst is all-consuming, exhausting, an imperative that floods the brain as the moisture leaves it, impossible to control. In less than a day the body becomes weak and lethargic; the brain is disoriented, incoherent; visions flood into the mind, but they are disconnected, random, useless. The next day the fever comes, quickly followed by merciful death.

Musa, a Tuareg from the Aïr, was once caught in the open desert without enough water, and he almost died. His mistake was to trust technology. He had abandoned his camel for a truck left over from the French, and he headed out for Bilma with thirty liters of fuel but only five of water, reasoning that since a truck covers the distance five times faster than a camel, he would need five times less water. Alas, the truck died and after a day the water was gone.

"I sat in the sand and pulled my turban over my nose," he said, "and my head filled with pictures. It was not unpleasant, not after a while. I was regretful, but not unhappy."

"Were there pictures of water?" he was asked. "An oasis, perhaps, a well?"

But there had been none of that. No grasping at a shimmering mirage, palm trees and cool water in the burning sand. "I saw my son," he said, "my son and his woman. I saw the moon, I saw the camel's nose, nostrils closed against the sand. I saw things I've always seen, only they were not there." He hadn't expected, he confessed, to see a vision of Paradise, a foretaste of things to come. He didn't consider himself devout enough to see the ineffable. He saw only humdrum things.

What happened, in the end?

"A small caravan from Zinder came by," he said, "and they gave me water and a camel to ride."

The water, from *guerbas* slung under the camels' bellies, had been shared ungrudgingly. It was the desert way. However, when a man is found dying of thirst, the common practice is to not let him drink right away. Wash his brow, and his neck, and if you have food let him eat a date, or chew on a biscuit, and only then do you moisten his mouth before letting him sip slowly. Gulping a draft too soon can cause severe retching, enough to draw blood from a damaged throat.

One of the most difficult tasks for any Saharan caravan is to maintain water discipline after a crossing in which one or more wells have been found dry, or during which the men and beasts have endured long stretches without water. The Tuareg pride themselves on their restraint, even when a well is sighted after a hazardous crossing, but other travelers are not so self-possessed or so strong-willed. There are many desert tales of traders from the southern salt mines or goldfields, or from the northern oases or urban centers, who seemed to lose all civilized restraints when driven by urgent need: "Beasts and men ran toward [the well] and I was presented with a hallucinatory vision," wrote Lieutenant Léon Lehuraux, a French soldier in Algeria in 1916, who watched one parched caravan rush toward a water hole. "Children crushed, camels, donkeys, zebus rushed with their heads lowered into the mob to get closer to the precious liquid."[34]

Custom often trumps common sense, even among the immensely practical men of the desert. Wells are often surrounded by mounds of camel excrement. In the desert sun, it dries quickly, but when water is spilled onto the pile, as frequently happens, it softens and often runs back into the well, to be drawn up by the next bucket. The water is frequently brown or dirty green, and slimy to the feel. An oasis between Agadez and Tamanrasset was contaminated in the late 1990s by the bloated corpse of a camel, just as Lehuraux's was. No one removed the camel because no one knew whose it was, and it is a serious matter to tamper with another man's camel, dead or alive. Cautious travelers dug shallow wells nearby, others simply dipped their containers in the pool as far from the corpse as they could.

"Didn't it make people sick?" a caravan leader was asked.

"Oh, yes, many became sick. Many camels died."

And in the end?

"After about a month, the army came, and burned the camel, and pumped out the pool."

Contamination of the meager water supply is a constant problem. But even if water is contaminated, you must drink. If you don't, you die anyway. Which is also why it is an ancient Saharan tradition, still rigorously maintained, alive despite the desert's long history of banditry and well-tampering, that if you see a man in the desert, or a woman, a goatherd, a rider on a camel, someone afoot, alone or in a group, you stop. There may be "water need," in the simple phrase of the desert. Similarly, if someone shows up at your tent or encampment needing water, it is your obligation to provide it.

༄

SOMEWHERE in the Erg de Ténéré, not too far into the dunes, a pair of nomads, afoot, suddenly appeared over a ridge. The Toyota Landcruiser that had been rumbling through the sand ground to a halt. Everyone got out and hunkered down in the lee to exchange civilities and news.

All the men, from the desert and the Landcruiser alike, were veiled, only their eyes showing. The two groups squatted down about six feet apart.

Are you well?

Thanks to God, I am well. And you?

God bless you, I am well. Is it peace?

Peace has come. It is peace with you?

It is peace. How is your family?

They are well, thanks to God. And yours?

They are well.

May your sons remain in the hands of God.

And your sons too.

How did you spend the heat of the day?

There was shade, aaaiiii, but we traveled far.

Did you pass a good night?

It was restful, yes. And you?

All was well.

And so on and so on. No hands were shaken with strangers, and all parties to the conversation were careful to keep their staffs upright, planted firmly in the sand, as unthreatening as possible. Among the Tuareg, these ritualized greetings can last five minutes or longer before the time for real news arrives. None of the questions and answers are "real," in the sense that they require an accurate answer. If your father has just died, and you are asked in these preliminaries how he is, the proper answer is "He is well, and yours?" Only later, and only if you know the person, would you provide the real news. Among the Tubu these formalities appear to be quite without end, but to neglect them is a grave offense; the insulted party is thereby given the right to an indemnity, and violence in retaliation is approved. In the old days, the systematic refusal of salutation between two families nearly always ended in murder.[35]

It is considered polite among the Tuareg to occasionally interrupt a conversation by bowing and asking "How are you?" without in any way expecting an answer.

Eventually, the news is given.

From where do you come?

From Wad' el-Raml. And you?

From Agadez.

Where do you go?

What have you seen?

Is there water near? What is its condition?

Do you need water?

Aiyah, yes. Both the nomads nodded. One carried a *guerba,* tattered and evil-looking, that was two-thirds empty. The other had a battered aluminum kettle, empty.

They filled them up from the plastic literjohns in the back of the Toyota.

When the last salutations had been satisfactorily made, the nomads trotted off with their water into the desert. Where were they going?

"To their people," Wantam said, pointing vaguely northeastward. "Maybe one journey away."

One journey meant one *journée,* a full day's march, perhaps thirty miles. Why had they come?

"They came to fetch the goats that had been left in a wadi. And then, when water grew short, they came to the road."

"To wait here for water? In case someone came? What if no one had come?"

"Oh." Wantam shrugged. "They would wait. There's always someone. Almost every day."

ↄ

BUT THERE IS NOT "always someone" in the desert; it is why so much lore is focused on water, and why so much effort goes into its discovery and conservation. And it is also why water that flows freely on the surface is regarded as so extraordinary.

The oasis of Timia in the Aïr Mountains is reached along a dusty wadi from the old provincial town of Assode, which is now abandoned. The track is alternately stony and sandy, with treacherous patches of *fech-fech* to trap the unwary. Sometimes it runs along the middle of the wadi itself, which is dry even in the rainy season but is pierced with numerous wells, and for many miles there are Tuareg gardens—not just date palms, but onions, peppers, garlic, and even tomatoes. This unnamed wadi has been a refuge for the nomads since not long after the Arab conquest, its subterranean water, not much more than four or five feet down, among the most reliable in the desert, having yielded up enough for gardens even in the bad drought years of the 1980s.

Timia is itself picturesque enough—a smartly restored fort from the French colonial period perches on an outcropping over-looking the village and the wadi itself, and the beige-colored mud houses are neatly made—and as backdrop, there is the looming presence of the peak called Adrar Egalah, at 1,974 meters. On all sides are the dramatic upthrusts of the Aïr, black basalt infused with red streaks. Nevertheless, the best-known feature of Timia is

The waterfall at Timia. (H. Kochenderfer)

none of these things, attractive as they are. Travelers who take the track that climbs the three thousand feet from Timia up toward the remote village of Kripkrip, the passage from these hidden valleys toward Agadez, 150 miles away to the southwest, will pass a gully of boulders and head-sized rocks. On a level stretch about a third of the way up is a small pool, too small to be called a lake. And tumbling into it, no more than a few yards wide and a few feet high, is a waterfall.

No more incongruous sight can be imagined, here among the bony rocks where not even grasses grow. Nor is this the only falling water in the Sahara, or on the Saharan fringes. There are one or two waterfalls in the Ahaggar, at Tamekrest and at Imeleoulaouene, overgrown with reeds and even trees, an astonishment there in the bleak rock. The Iherir River that flows from cracks in the Tassili has little tumbles that could charitably be defined as waterfalls. There is a waterfall of some substance in Tunisia, and also one or two in the High Atlas, at least after the rains.

There are stories in the Aïr villages of a party of Italians, men and women, who had passed through Timia a decade before. They were said to have stripped down and bathed in the little lake, deliriously washing off the dust of the desert in the chilly mountain water. They were shot to death for the privilege, their bodies tossed into a ravine and their vehicles stolen and stripped into their component parts. It seems almost certain that the story is just a legend—the Italian consulate has no record of missing tourists. Besides, many travelers have paddled decorously in the little pool and come to no harm and met no apparent rancor, and the local people, children and adults alike, will splash in the tumbling water after the rains come and the torrent broadens—but the story is widely told in the region and has a definite subtext. The little cataract has for centuries been a special place to nomads, to whom tumbling water is a miracle, easily soiled.

There is another level of meaning. The Tuareg have long memories, and the massifs like the Aïr and the Ahaggar are places with a history much more pregnant than having served as a source of forage for goats and as places to grow dates. The mountains were where the nomads went when the invaders came, some fifteen hundred years ago; and it was to the mountains that the unruly clans of the desert retreated whenever they needed a refuge. Given the weight of history, it is no wonder the Tuareg are so protective.

CHAPTER SIX

ᕙᕗ

The Massifs

IT IS NOT very far from the Algerian oasis town of Tamanrasset to Assekrem, which in the language of the Tuareg means the End of the World, maybe thirty miles or so. But this is a landscape as violent, fractured, and torturous as any on earth, a prodigious place in a land of prodigies, and it is not difficult to feel intimidated as well as awestruck, as though one is creeping slowly through an immense graveyard, desecrated not by man but by the long centuries of warfare the planet has been waging on itself.

The four-wheel-drive, a hybrid vehicle cobbled together whose skeleton, at least, was an ancient Landrover, ground steadily north-eastward from the town into the mountains, turning off from the main north-south highway—to In'Salah and thence to Algiers, more than twelve hundred miles away—through a deep gully. It crept up what seemed at first sight to be a sheer cliff. The road up to the End of the World was narrow and boulder strewn, the drop steep, the cliffs excessively unstable. The short journey takes most of a day.

The road rises steadily, twisting and turning, and as it ascends brief glimpses can be seen of the country of the Ahaggar interior, the mountains of the region called Atakor. The geology texts say volcanic eruptions some two million years ago covered the underlying granite with nearly six hundred feet of basalt, and no doubt it is so. To the untutored eye, it seems more that the granite has fractured into gigantic splinters, and out of the enormous heap of slag that was the underlying Ahaggar Plateau thrust massive needles of rock, some of them thousands of feet high, split by weathering and cooling into prisms and jagged pyramids. The French called them organ pipes, but that is altogether too benign a description. They look more like thousand-foot stone daggers thrust into the bedrock, more than three hundred of them in a few hundred miles, giving the horizon a fantastic air of unreality.

The ancient Landrover reached Assekrem just before sundown. The view from the top, toward Mount Tahat, Algeria's tallest mountain, was an apparently endless vista of jagged and eroded sandstone peaks in a palette of rich reds and ochers. With not a blade of grass nor a shrub in all that immensity, the jagged peaks glowed as though an immense furnace were lighting them from

Needles of rock in the Ahaggar. (Fuoristrada)

below. The next morning the view was no less startling, but in the sunrise 'the dark reds and maroons changed to burnished gold, shading every minute into a bewildering array of secondary hues, as far as could be seen, fifty, sixty miles or more.

At 6,500 feet there is a primitive inn, a shelter, and a rough stone building with a small sign identifying it as the hermitage of Charles-Eugène Foucauld, the French explorer and military man who came to the End of the World to study the Tuareg language and to contemplate the manifold sins of his own people. Foucauld had participated in putting down a nomad insurrection in 1881, but he soon left the army, dispirited with its harshness and code of violence, and became a Trappist monk. He spent some years as a solitary ascetic in Palestine, but in 1901 he returned to the Sahara and built himself the crude stone shelter that still exists in Assekrem. The Tuareg admired the austerity of his ways, and helped him compile a dictionary and grammar of Tamashek, their spoken language. He was unfortunately killed there in 1916, almost certainly by mistake—his own guards shot him in a vain attempt to drive off a raiding party of local rebels against France.

℘

ALL OF THE central Sahara's mountain ranges—the Ahaggar, the Tassili n'Ajjer, the Aïr, the Tibesti, and the Ennedi—were part of the tectonic upheavals that rent much of Africa some 300 million years ago, scoring the continent with a network of gigantic faults. This fracturing was accompanied by volcanic eruptions and basaltic upwellings, just as it was in other parts of Africa, especially in Ethiopia. The Great Rift that runs through East Africa almost down to Malawi was part of the same geological reordering.

The Saharan massifs are substantial enough to exert considerable influence on climate and weather—it is the cooler air coming down off the Tibesti that precipitates the thunderstorms of the southern Sahara, and is the birthing chamber for many of the Atlantic hurricanes. In the days when the Sahara was still verdant,

Assekrem, "The End of the World." (Tourism Algerie)

the massifs were the source for the rivers and lakes that dotted the landscape, many of which, dried up and barren, turned into the sand seas of the desert. Nothing, however, grows up high on the plateaus—from the End of the World not a plant is to be seen—because rainfall is sporadic and brief, even at higher elevations. Nevertheless, in all the mountainous regions of the Sahara, in steep-walled canyons that delay evaporation, water collects in rock pools, and tenacious shrubs grow. Aerial photographs of ravines in the Ennedi Massif show ribbons of green deep down in many ravines. There are oases hidden in the canyons of the Ahaggar and the Aïr, and seasonal rock-ribbed pools in the Tibesti. The water that collects in these places occasionally seeps out of the massifs, through cracks and fissures in the escarpments. Such is the Iherir, the central Sahara's only perennial river, which cascades prettily north from the Tassili in Algeria and ends its brief life somewhere in the Erg of Issawan; it still contains four species of fish and the occasional crocodile. Another is the wadi that feeds the oasis of

Tamanrasset: On the outskirts of the town small springs can occasionally be seen, some of them frequent and persistent enough that tadpoles have been found swimming in them.

ের

PERHAPS THE BEST WAY to get a feeling for the massive size of the Ahaggar Plateau and its violent mountains is to drive in from the north, from the date-growing and industrial town of In-'Salah, a main stopping place on the road from Algiers.

For the first hundred miles or so there is nothing to see but sand and gravel, the horizonless *hamada* that covers so much of the desert. The road traverses the arid plateau of Tademaït, so flat and featureless that a golf ball would be a noticeable obstruction. Not far to the north are the two greatest sand seas of all, the Great Ergs of Algeria, whose fine sand often drifts overhead, giving the air a curious opacity, the land and the sky blurring, without definition, a vagueness of outline in which it is impossible to gauge distance. Fifty miles or so farther, near the well the locals call Tirhatimine, the distant view begins to change, to darken, gradually taking shape in the otherwise milky air. Once past In'Ecker, an undistinguished village that became briefly notorious in the 1960s when the French used it as the locus for testing a series of thirteen nuclear devices, massive cliffs appear, great towering walls of rock, the outermost bastions of the Ahaggar themselves. To the left and the right stretch endless walls of rock; perhaps sixty miles are visible from the road. Yet this is a tiny part of the whole, and doesn't even hint at the geological turmoil within.

To the geologists the Ahaggar are not really mountains at all, but part of an eroded and twisted high granite plateau sometimes called the Mid Sahara Rise, sprawling over a vast stretch of the middle desert, some 965 miles north to south and 1,300 miles east to west. But there is also a smaller and even more tumultuous region also called Ahaggar, and it is this smaller area that is generally meant when people speak of the "Hoggar Mountains," or the mountains of the Ahaggar. At its heart are the peaks called Atakor, which is where the Tuareg located Assekrem, the End of the World—true mountains that squat on the plateau itself, whose lava flows have splintered and sloughed off into enormous cliffs and fissures, adding even greater depth to the crevasses in the granite beneath. These mountains, reaching their greatest elevation at Mount Tahat's 9,573 feet, themselves cover an enormous area, more than 210,000 square miles, some 400 miles on a side, about the size of France. Within it are some of the Sahara's most dramatic landscapes. A submassif called Tahaggart, southeast of Tamanrasset, is described on an Algerian government Web site as "an enchanted castle of spires and towers," towering rocks carved into intricate shapes, rising abruptly from golden dunes as fine as flour. To the northeast are the peaks of Ahnet, looming over beautiful dune fields that were once ancient lakes—the Tuareg have for centuries mined salt at Amadror, the bed of one such lake.

To the north, east, and south, the Ahaggar Plateau confronts the surrounding desert with massive cliffs. Only to the west does it diminish somewhat, sloping downward to end in that most desolate of places, the Tanezrouft. In some ways the Ahaggar resembles a medieval European fortress writ massively larger: The brooding cliffs that surround it are the ramparts; the Atakor peaks the fortress where the feudal lord held sway. It is not surprising that the Tuareg, who believe in the djinn of the desert, have invested many of the peaks with names and personalities, and have attributed to them the legendary exploits of ancient heroes.

ᘯ

NORTHEAST of the Ahaggar is Tassili n'Ajjer, which is, even by Saharan standards, a wild landscape. UNESCO, when it declared the area a World Heritage Site (mostly for the more than fifteen thousand rock paintings found deep in its interior, making it "the world's largest open-air museum"), pointed out in its tidy bureaucratese that the area was "of outstanding scenic interest with eroded sandstones forming forests of rock." And indeed, the eroded sandstone pillars thrusting out of hidden ravines and unclimbable gullies reach hundreds and sometimes thousands of feet into the air. The landscape is a mind-boggling palette of black through dull red to

Massive formation in the Ahaggar. (Fuoristrada)

umber with occasional veins as bright as fresh blood, iron and manganese in the sandstone oxidized and hardened to form a patina, land-
scaping by chemical action. Between the gullies and the rocks, eroded
into infinite and disorienting labyrinths, are smaller sand seas—Tiho-
daïne, Admer, Merzouga, and many others. The triangular Tifernine
dune field to the northwest is one of the more famous in the desert,
lapping up against isolated sandstone towers, stained umber and orange from erosion. Yellow-blond sand with a topping of red stain—
from the air it looks like nothing more than a one-hundred-mile-long
slice of cherry cheesecake. What is now Tassili National Park, also created with UNESCO's help to protect the rock paintings, is to the
southeast of the massif, near the border with Libya and Niger.

The Tassili Plateau originated in the same geological upheavals
as the Ahaggar. The massif is really a series of narrower northwest-
southeast plateaus separated by a massive sandstone trench, yielding a
network of steep-sided valleys; narrow, deep gorges; and dry riverbeds.

Only in the deepest ravines is there water, but it is from the Tassili
that the Iherir River makes its way into the desert. The canyon of the
Iherir is one of the great curiosities of the Sahara: Mosses that grow

in the river have over the centuries conjured into being little cascades and pools made of travertine, the purest honey-colored marble, calcite and aragonite precipitated out of the springwaters by the vegetation, giving certain stretches of the river an unreal air of being relicts of some vanished empire of master builders; in the slanting sun of evening, the marble glows like liquid gold.[1] The Iherir, though, is not typical of the landscape. Not surprisingly, in view of the aridity and extraordinary topography, the population of the Tassili is sparse. Probably no more than one thousand to three thousand people live there at any one time, most of them nomadic herdsmen.

It was between the Tassili and the Ahaggar proper that poor doomed Flatters met his end. On the start of what was to be his last week, the Flatters party broke camp, and passed through an ominous black gorge lined on both sides with sheer sixteen-hundred-foot cliffs. The foothills of the Ahaggar were just visible to the south and west, and to the northeast the jagged and tortured shapes of the Tassili. For several days they passed through a haunting landscape of stark cliffs and ravines, and across a broken plain strewn with gigantic boulders (some of them an unnerving six hundred feet high, remnants of some great catastrophe). It was somewhere on that ghastly plain that their Tuareg guides fell on them and hacked them to pieces.

Not far from the town of Ghat is another surreal piece of Saharan landscape, what the Tuareg call Tantanah, the magic mountain, a curious formation in which the cliffs are crosshatched with natural crack lines, so that the entire mountain looks to be built of gigantic stone blocks, set in place and mortared. Gigantic indeed: The "blocks" are steep and precipitous, more than a thousand feet high. There are Tuareg all over the desert now, but in ancient days Tantanah marked the start of "Tuareg country proper," beyond the reach of the sultans of Algiers or Tripoli, a place where the nomads were the acknowledged masters.

&

TO THE SOUTHEAST of the Ahaggar, and in some ways an extension of them, is the Aïr Massif of Niger, hundreds of miles of striated rocks reaching 6,500 feet, pierced with valleys called *koris*. Individual mountain masses make more or less separate islands within the Aïr. From north to south these are Tazerzaït (which includes the highest peak in Niger, Mont Gréboun, at 6,562 feet), and others, their Tamashek names tongue-twistingly tangled to Western ears—Tamgak, Takolokouzet, Angornakouer, Bagzan, Tarouadji.

The Aïr is home to the Kel-Oui Tuareg confederacy, as it has been for many centuries. Early in his wanderings in the Sahara in the nineteenth century, Heinrich Barth was given a curious small insight into its significance for the nomads. He was traveling with a small caravan of Tuareg on the northern fringes of the Aïr, and as they passed by what he called "a remarkable ridge," four men suddenly appeared in front of them. A troop of men lightly armed with bows was dispatched from Barth's caravan, presumably—or so he thought—to reconnoiter. Barth followed, and there saw a peculiar sight. The archers were sitting quietly on the ground, while the four strangers were dancing wildly around. Before Barth could react, one of the strangers dashed up, grabbing his camel's rope, and demanded tribute. Barth cocked his pistol and was about to shoot when one of his own party yelled to him to stop. That remarkable ridge, it turned out, was significant in local legend and history, "for here it was that the Kel-Oui (at that time an unmixed and pure Berber tribe, as it seems) took possession of the country, a compromise or covenant was entered into between the red conquerors and the black natives that the latter should not be destroyed, and that the principal chief of the Kel-Oui should only be allowed to marry a black woman. And, as a memorial of this transaction, the custom has been preserved, that when caravans pass the spot where the covenant was entered into, near the little rock Maket n'Ikelan, slaves shall be merry and be authorized to levy on their masters a small tribute. The black man who stopped me was the *serki-n-baï*, or chief of the slaves."[2]

The Aïr is as much a moonscape as the Ahaggar, one of the most spectacular sights in the desert, as large as Switzerland, hundreds of miles of black rocks with peaks like needles. Five millennia or so ago, farmers, fishermen, and pastoralists shared the

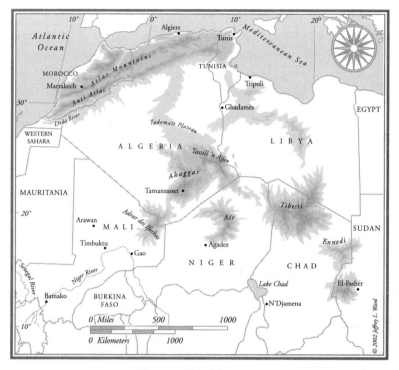

The mountains of the Sahara.

valleys, leaving behind them hundreds of cave paintings of extraordinary detail, depicting hunting scenes, rituals, gods of unknown provenance, and, in one fresco near Assode, what looks
very like a massive banquet. Water still runs in the mountains, and
even hot springs at Tafadek, water sweating from a landscape in
high fever. The oases of Timia (where the Aïr's waterfall is found)
and Iferouâne are green islands in the desolation. Even where water runs, the soil is now thin and sour, overlain with salt. Nevertheless some vegetation grows, and the Tuareg pasture goats there
and grow small gardens. *Ergs* stretch out on either side. To the
west, fossil valleys are filled with moving dunes, and to the east is
the Bilma Erg, one of the greatest sand seas in the Sahara. In the
view of the *caravanniers*, the Aïr is the last soft and restful place
before the Ténéré and Bilma, and is the traditional staging post for
the salt caravans of the central desert.

ℭℜ

SOUTHEAST from Djanet and the Tassili, along the Libyan-
Algerian border and then the Niger-Libyan border, and past both
the Erg de Murzuq, Libya's greatest sand sea, and the Djado Plateau,
is another of the Sahara's great massifs, the Tibesti, about 800 miles
southeast of Tassili.

Those caravans that ventured close to the Tibesti came down
from the Fezzan province in Libya to Tejéré, a dismal little place
tyrannically ruled, when Gustav Nachtigal was there, by a fierce
one-eyed sheikh. The terrain around Tejéré wasn't that difficult,
but the region was nonetheless treacherous. Most travelers who
passed through were heavily armed. During Nachtigal's stay,
Tejéré was subject to constant raiding—by Arabs from the northeast, by Tubu from the Tibesti, and by desert Tuareg. This war-
ravaged story has persisted to modern times; as late as 1941 the
Free French based in Chad noted, laconically, "tip and run raids
by nomads from the Tibesti against Tejéré," and in November
2000 fierce fighting was reported in the area between government
forces and Tubu insurgents.

The Tibesti, or the Tibesti Massif, or the Tibesti Mountains, "Tu"
or rock to its inhabitants, the Tubu, is no small thing itself, every bit
as massive as the Tassili. The mountains are mostly in Chad, but
stretch north into Libya and west into Niger. Depending on where
you draw the boundaries, they cover about 300 miles northeast to
southwest, and about 175 across, smaller than the Ahaggar but rival-
ing them in the ferocity of their demeanor. In effect, they are less a
mountain range than a massive rupture in the earth, formed when
lava streams forced their way through the planetary skin, leaving a
stratum of crystalline rock covered with sandstone. The sandstone
was then forced violently upward again; they now rise abruptly from
the surrounding plains, reaching to 11,204 feet at the summit of
Emi Koussi, the Sahara's highest point. Some of the volcanoes are
still active and emit a sulfurous smoke. The whole place is deeply
eroded, cracked with ravines and awful wells in the rock, unplumbed

and of unknown depth. In places the lava resembles the waves of a petrified sea, albeit a sea with swells reaching 500 feet or more. Once, in the Sahara's distant past, great rivers roared through these ravines, leaving scars still clearly visible. Three of these ancient river courses provided the secretive Tubu their way into the massif, and there they built their few isolated towns, among them the still-remote Bardai.

Over the centuries, outsiders have tended to avoid the whole massif. An Arab geographer, Muhammad Ibn Omar el-Tounsy, dismissed the whole thing as "Tubu Reshade country, a scorched region with steep bare rocks, offering only a miserable scanty vegetation."[3] Leo Africanus believed that the hazards of the Tibesti were rather human than natural, and he described the Tubu as a people who "are making continuall warre against the princes, and oftentimes spoil the merchants of all their goods, and as many of the people as they can catch, they kill with all pitie and compassion,"[4] laying on the irony pretty thick. Very few trails or caravan routes penetrated the Tibesti proper. The road was too difficult, the terrain too inhospitable, the people too dangerous. Even in modern times, travelers traverse the Tibesti with care; the few remaining Tubu are hostile to outsiders, and it is regarded as dangerous to travel without a Tubu guide.

Nachtigal, who eventually made his way to Bardai on the eastern side of Tibesti and was imprisoned there, had never intended to visit Tibesti at all. He had been on his way to Bornu, carrying impressive gifts from the Prussian government to the Bornu sultan (these gifts a nice mix of piousness, ostentation, and practicality: a velvet chair of state with gilded arms and legs; life-size portraits of King William, Queen Augusta, and the Crown Prince; a parcel of heavy guns with their appropriate ammunition; a number of Bibles in Arabic; a bronze pendulum clock; a gold watch and chain; a double telescope; half a dozen silver watches; a double-plated silver tea service; pieces of silk and velvet; a pound of attar of roses; a pound of geranium essence; rosaries; bracelets and necklaces of coral; a dozen burnoooses of velvet; a dozen Tunisian tarbushes; and a harmonium). But he got stuck in Murzuq, in the Fezzan, and his caravan to the south was put off for several months, perhaps a year. It was to pass this time productively rather than idle around a town already well known to Europe that he hit on the idea of visiting the Tibesti.

Almost everyone he consulted urged him not to go. Even the guide he hired, one Kolokomi, who earlier had accompanied Barth on his travels, argued vehemently against going: "Remember the warning, *sidi*," he told Nachtigal. "A man enters the country of the treacherous Tubu only if he has so much to answer for as makes his execution certain. The wickedness of those men is as vast as the desert."

Nevertheless Kolokomi promised to guide him to and from the Tibesti in return for three hundred German marks.

It started badly. In Zouar, gateway to the massif proper, he was met with a belligerent group of local notables, who demanded gifts, and to be fed. He eyed them dubiously. "They all squatted down in a wide circle in front of the tent, holding their lances, javelins and throwing-irons upright in their hands, and with long, broad forearm knives fastened to their wrists by leather rings," and began their interminable greetings. For a day or so thereafter, as Nachtigal put it, they appeared at frequent intervals "to renew their delightful efforts to improve their nutritional condition at my expense." Negotiations about "tolls" to pass through their valley began at sunrise and ended an hour after sunset, with Nachtigal, predictably, losing, after which the Tubu withdrew, setting up their camp in a nearby thicket, "a retreat which is characteristic of the habits of the Tubu, and harmonizes completely with the principle of isolation and secrecy in accordance with which they seek to avoid each other when on a journey."

The Tubu interrogated Nachtigal continually. Why was he there? In vain did his escort explain the foolish partiality of Europeans for pointless traveling about. No one believed this. No Christian had ever appeared in their country before, and no one wanted to see one there now. Anyone who sacrificed so much money, and ventured alone into their insecure country with its violent tribes, must perforce be following some venture of profit. And they wanted their share.

Nachtigal explained that he was carrying letters to their nominal ruler, Tertefemi, in Bardai, and they should read the letters to be sure.

It was not their practice, they said indignantly, to read the letters of others.

Well then, Nachtigal said, since you are more powerful, take what you want.

We are not robbers, they explained. Gifts will recognize our honor. So gifts there duly were.

As travelers do today, Nachtigal marveled at the wildness of the landscape, massive dark boulders piled one on another. The bleakness, the absence of life "filled me with an emotion of awe-struck horror, such as children might feel alone in a churchyard at night. On the vertical walls of the ravines there frequently appeared in the depths gray, red, white, violet, brown or yellow limestone under the colossal covering of dark sandstone. Here were rounded hills covered with immense blocks of stone, there gigantic cubes strewn one above the other, forming either larger horizontal stone surfaces, or, if the ground around were broken or crumbling, real colossi of columns and pillars."[5]

For weeks he and his companions wandered around this appalling landscape. Often, his Tubu guides, taking "shortcuts," seemed to lose their way, which Nachtigal interpreted, probably correctly, as some devious ruse. Many times they were near death from thirst. Most of the landscape was stony plains pierced by massive ravines and cone-like crags; there was some springwater at the base of the massifs, and gnarled thorn trees and squat dúm palms. Many villages were abandoned. Hidden among the ridges and folds of the rocks were primitive cave shelters, which gave some credence to the Tuareg dismissal of the Tubu as cave dwellers. These were "concealed in just the way that the secretive and mistrustful character of the inhabitants and their fear of unexpected attacks made desirable."[6] His notions of the character of the inhabitants were reinforced by the skittish nature of his guides, who tended to panic on seeing the footsteps of a single camel, fearing it was an outrider for a marauding band.

ℰↃ

THESE DAYS there are thought to be no more than eight thousand or so Tubu left in the Tibesti, the rest having migrated elsewhere. The massif is now the haunt of prospectors looking for the next "sure thing"—the Tibesti is supposed to be full of tungsten, tin, uranium, oil, those motors of a rapacious civilization alien to the few Tubu left behind, and from which they have so far benefited not at all.

ℰↃ

FARTHER to the southeast is the sandstone plateau called Ennedi, which is not as stark a landscape as the other Saharan massifs—the Ennedi don't rise up in sheer cliffs like the Ahaggar or Tibesti, but ascend gradually up long sloping valleys. Even in the interior, they are more open than the other massifs. Nevertheless, the peaks are intricately carved by the wind and ancient water into often bizarre shapes, and scattered here and there in the landscape are precarious balancing rocks, great boulders tipping a hundred-foot finger of sandstone.

The plateau is centered on the town of Fada, and the surrounding terrain is sand sheets with sandstone peaks ranging to a high of 4,756 feet at Mount Basso, the Ennedi's highest point.

The wind patterns in the region are extraordinarily steady, and their effects strikingly clear: The windblown sand has carved up the landscape with a precision that looks artificial. The prevailing winds start in the northwest, and are funneled in a ninety-degree curve between the Tibesti and the Ennedi, blowing southwest across the Djourab Sand Region of central Chad. Satellite pictures of the region show the trenches this wind has caused, as precise as the strokes of a comb. On the ground, the landscape is not nearly so neat; the parallel trenches can't easily be appreciated or traversed, and travelers frequently become lost in what seems to them a labyrinth. Just to the north is the Mourdi Depression and its natron lakes, Ounianga Kebir and Ounianga Serir, leftovers of something much greater.

The area is populated by a mix of Tubu, nomadic Arabs, and Buduma from the south, and even by the standards of the Sahara is unruly and anarchic. The French never really subdued its inhabitants; the Ennedi region was considered ungovernable even after independence, and the new government of Chad asked the French to stay on and run the province under military rule, which they did until they finally departed in 1965. Insurrections in the region are still common, politics continually on the boil.

∾

BY SAHARAN STANDARDS—and even by the slightly more elevated standards set by the other massifs—the Ennedi area has a relative abundance of water; and in some of the ravines there are even forests of acacias and dúm palms, dense but passable, cool relief from the hot desert sun, home to weaverbirds and other creatures. Wild game, too, is still relatively abundant; ostriches are still hunted in the region, and the occasional leopard has been spotted in the deep bush. The Archeï canyon, with its crocodiles, is here.

There is life in the Sahara, for those who think to look. And sometimes it thrives in places more inhospitable by far than the valleys of the Ennedi.

CHAPTER SEVEN

☙

The Tenacity of Life

THE SALT CARAVANS still assemble along the Tiguidit escarpment south of Agadez and head out for Bilma, 250 miles or so to the east. A few days out, they pass the location of the Tree of Ténéré, famous in Tuareg legend, for it was the first growing thing sighted by travelers heading in the other way, from the Bilma salt mines to Agadez and the Aïr Mountains. It grew, stark and lonely, the only tree for 150 miles, in stony soil with no water in sight. No traveler dared to cut it down, no matter how desperate for firewood, and after a century or so it took on an almost mythical stature.

During the winter of 1938–1939 a well was dug by French sappers near the Tree (still usually spelled with reverential capital letter). One Sgt. Lamotte, who supervised the digging and constructed the well, found the roots of this solitary acacia at 115 feet, all the way down to the distant water table, such as it was.[1] Alas, after a road, of sorts, was built past it, the tree, perhaps three or four hundred years old by then, was knocked down and destroyed by a drunken truck driver. The place where it had once grown, still marked on the maps as the "Arbre de Ténéré," is a junk heap of scrap metal, plastic, and discarded bottles, a gathering point for trucks that stop here to tap Lamotte's still-bountiful well. The trunk of the Tree itself was saved, and now lies in the Natural History Museum in Niamey, barely seen for the dust.

Nevertheless, the Tree still stands in Niger as a living metaphor for the toughness and tenacity of the Tuareg themselves, as well as a metaphor for the stubbornness and the resilience of growing things.

◈

GROWING THINGS have needed to be resilient in this place. Long ago, when the Sahara was still verdant, the not-yet-desert was lively, in all senses of the word. There were forests in the gullies and on the mountain slopes, massive stands of cypress and pine. The plains were grasslands, as lush as the American prairie in the time of the buffalo; reeds, papyrus, and water lilies filled the ponds and mosses lined the streams.

As the desert dried up and the water supply shrank, growing things retreated to a few specialized habitats. First the cultivated

The famous "Arbre de Ténéré." (Michael Taylor)

crops like millet disappeared, and then the forage, the tough wild grasses. Some grasses, shrubs, and trees survived in the upland plateaus, which precipitated some moisture, and in the wadis; salt-tolerant plants hung on to life on the periphery of former lakes. Saharan perennials, the shrubs and trees that survive in the wadis, have generally made their own accommodations with the climate. They have huge root systems but meager above-ground sections, usually protected by a waxy coating from evaporation and by thorns from herbivores. The acacia, the best known and most ubiquitous of these trees, has both tap root and lateral root systems to maximize its search for water; the tap root, as with the Tree of Ténéré, can descend to extraordinary depths. The thorny mimosa, a shrub, has similarly deep roots, and so does the prolific tamarisk, prized for its dense foliage and thus its shade.

As though to demonstrate that plants can grow anywhere, given even faint encouragement, along some Saharan tracks *cram-cram* grass seeds have implanted themselves and germinated in the small ridges thrown up by the tires of passing trucks. A thin row of brittle yellow grasses, long dead, can be found for miles in such places. They are what botanists call ephemerals: They can germinate within forty-eight hours of even the most meager rainfall, and sow seeds as little as two weeks later. These seeds may lie there, dormant, for years or even decades before the next generation emerges in a similar cycle. Some of these ephemerals form occasional pastures much prized by the nomads. When they spring up after the rains, they are called *acheb*. This is not dense foliage: Individual grass plants can be almost fifty yards apart.

In the massifs like the Ahaggar and the Tassili a few Mediterranean species of plants have survived, especially olives and tarout cypresses. A few wild olives can be found high up in the Ahaggar. These forlorn survivors have become something of an ecologist's pilgrimage, and botanists will trek the several days onto the highlands to photograph their greenery, pitifully shriveled and brown with weariness. In Ghat, a now-abandoned caravan town just over the Libyan frontier from the Tassili, the doors and ceiling beams of the houses were made entirely of cypress wood cut in the nearby mountains, but the only cypresses now to be found are high on the uninhabited Tassili Plateau, and no forests at all, just isolated individuals hundreds of years old, stubbornly clinging to life.[2] Only about 240 such trees are left, each carefully counted and protected,[3] gnarled old things that draw water through huge roots sunk deep in a Tassili ravine. Their seeds are unable to germinate for lack of water. They are the last of their kind.

❧

AS WITH THE PLANTS, so with the animals. In the Sahara's lakes and rivers of ancient days were fish, ancestral *tilapia* most likely, and crocodiles. Hippos populated its ponds and swamps: Cave paintings in the Tassili Mountains in Algeria depict the hippos perfectly, with their big bowling-pin teeth and curiously girlish eyelashes. Giraffes, and great herds of antelope, from addax to wildebeest, roamed the plains, and the same cave paintings show bands of hunters spread out over the savanna, running down the wild cattle. Herds of elephants existed on the fringes of the desert in

Cave paintings in the Tassili mountains. (Encyclopaedia Brittanica on-line)

Roman times, made extinct only in the Christian era. They were hunted by the Greeks, in the old days, who had learned what Alexander did with elephants on his Asian campaign; and of course Hannibal made use of them in his wars on Rome—he had been a tribal boy from the Libyan desert, and knew what elephants could accomplish. As recently as 1787 there were still elephants browsing on the foliage of a forest east of Timbuktu. The great African predators, especially the lions and leopards, hunted on the plains and in the mountains.

As the forests disappeared and the oases diminished, the wild creatures thinned out, some to the point of disappearance. Most of the early European travelers in the eighteenth and nineteenth centuries noted the presence of ostriches, gazelles, and other animals, sometimes in large numbers, deep into what is now stony desert. Jean-Auguste Marguerite, a veteran of the Franco-Prussian war who hunted ostriches in the bush near Ghardaia in Algeria, in the countryside between the two great Algerian *ergs,* in the period after the French conquest of the Sahara, compared the region to the prairies of America.[4] Today the grasses are gone and the landscape is grimmer, and both ostriches and vegetation have disappeared from the area within living memory. The hartebeest survived in Morocco up to the Second World War. There were lions in the Middle Atlas Mountains until at least 1922 and there may still be cheetahs in parts of northern Algeria. In the Sudan there are tortoises, sometimes as big as a man's chest, found even in regions void of any vegetation.[5] In the Aïr Mountains of Niger there are still jackals and foxes. The small Saharan striped hyena, lacking the sinister "laugh" of its savanna cousins, can be found in the dunes not far from oases. There are crocodiles and hippos in Lake Chad and on the desert's fringes, and dwarf crocodiles in isolated places elsewhere.

The Iherir Valley, at the Sahara's heart, has been registered as a Wetland of International Importance by the Algerians (as has another wetland, the swamps of Isskarassene, in the Ahaggar near Tamanrasset, which bizarrely gives arid Algeria as much acreage in declared wetlands as the United States).[6] Migratory birds rest here on their way to and from the Southern and Northern hemispheres, and birders have recorded a dazzling assortment of species passing through: herons, storks, ibis, bitterns, kestrels, and eagles, both short-toed and golden. Coots and moorhens nest in the region, and so do Barbary partridges. Most of these are transients. Hardly any birds make their lives in the deep desert. Even the carrion eaters are vanishingly few.

సు

DESPITE ITS LOSSES, and despite the vast stretches where nothing at all lives, there is still life in the Sahara, for nature is endlessly fecund, and evolution ponderously intelligent. Wild things have adapted to the desiccation in one of two ways: They have stayed the same, but with radically shrunken habitats; or they have adapted to aridity, their bodies (and their behavior) marvelously conserving what little moisture they can still find and their habits attuned to the cycles of heat. An animal that has not changed is the monitor, one of the planet's oldest lizards (unchanged for maybe 130 million years). Monitors can still be found lurking on the desert fringes, where once they roamed the whole desert. The modern monitor is five feet long with daggerlike incisors, razor claws, an intimidating hissing roar, and an omnivorous appetite. It can stand the high temperatures of the open desert, even in summer, one of the few living things to do so, which may be why it remains the same. As an example of behavioral adaptation, in the Tibesti Mountains there is a raven that has taken to sleeping during the day, sheltering his black feathers from the Saharan sun by tucking himself under a rock.

Most of the desert's creatures, though, are small, with dull colors and moderate water requirements. They live in burrows or holes, emerging only at night. Insects and small rodents are the most common.

The jerboa, a rodent that looks half mouse and half tiny kangaroo, is found in many places deep in the desert, mostly in Algeria and Libya. An inquisitive little creature, it can sometimes be spotted

Jerboa (National Geographic)

hopping through a camp at night. It "runs" on its hind legs and uses its long tail as a rudder, making sharp banking turns (almost right angles) in midair. It survives the scorching heat in closed burrows in the sand, where it can stay for days at a constant seventy-six degrees. It is one of the few mammals that never drinks water; the nomads say it drinks its own moisture, and indeed there are indications that the jerboa can actually recycle the moisture from its own exhalations.

The jerboa's greatest enemy is the fennec fox, a ferocious creature even though it weighs a mere two pounds, about the size of a large kitten. Its range is similar to the jerboa's, and it, too, spends its days underground in a burrow, sometimes a tunnel thirty feet long. Its huge ears radiate heat and its fur-soled feet provide insulation from the burning sand. It eats rodents like the jerboa, but also roots, from which it derives its moisture. The sand cat, or sand dune cat, is also small, and tunnels, spends the days underground, and preys on the jerboa. But it also eats venomous snakes and this curious fact, combined with the disconcerting way the sand cat has of erupting from its hidden burrows like some spectral jack-in-the-box, fills the Tuareg with superstitious wariness. It has large spreading feet that enable it to cross soft sand easily, and double earflaps that offer acute hearing—it can hear ultrasound and can locate underground prey with astonishing accuracy. A staple of its diet is the Saharan gundi, which live in a large part of the central Sahara—Algeria, northern Niger, northwestern Chad, northeastern Mali, and southwestern Libya. Gundis, curiously, seem actually to like the heat, and in winter they spend much of the day sunbathing, stretched out on warm rocks, flat on their stomachs. Confronted with a predator, usually a snake or a lizard, the little rodent lies motionless on its side with its legs stretched out, and stops breathing for up to a minute, appearing as dead as can be. Then the state of rigidity slowly fades, and normal breathing resumes.

A few predators maintain a precarious existence in the massifs.

One day in the winter of the year 2000, as a little caravan passed through the Taghouadji Mountains in the Aïr, a harsh screaming rent the air from the rocks above. It was just after dusk, and the travelers were supposed to be stopping for the night "soon," as the guides kept saying soothingly, and this high quavering screech came as a nasty surprise, erupting out of the dark like the cry of the damned, a reminder of why the desert folk believed so implicitly in djinn, for there was something otherworldly about the awful howling. But the Tuareg were unmoved. "Caracal," one of them said, "cat."

In the morning before they left they scrambled up to find the tracks, and there they were, in a sandy patch just behind a rocky look-off. The paw prints were huge, and suggested a beast the size of a lion. "No," said one of the Tuareg, "a meter at most, a meter and a half, including tail."

"Are they dangerous?"

"To us?" He looked surprised. "No. Birds and jerboa, small things only." He'd seen a caracal only once, he said, in the early dawn, on a dead run after some hapless prey, but though he'd never seen such a thing he'd heard they were capable of taking a low-flying bird in flight. He smiled slyly. "The most dangerous things here are much smaller than that. Things that get into your robes at night."

☙

SNAKES ARE FOUND in many parts of the Sahara except the hottest and most arid sand seas. The Saharan horned viper is the most common, and its close cousin, the sand viper, and even these are generally found relatively close to wadis or oases. In Egypt cobras do exist, and in southern Mauritania and Mali a dismal list of other venomous creatures: the puff adder, the white-bellied carpet viper, various kraits, and others. But the overall number of snake species found in the desert is quite small.

Encounters do happen. Only the previous day the small caravan had spotted a sidewinder twisting off across the desert, and had been glad to actually see it in time. It was a Saharan horned viper, a deadly creature that strikes at its prey from hidden burrows in the sand, erupting out suddenly, sinking its fangs into a jerboa or other small mammal, or into a passing ankle. The viper will rattle when alarmed or angry, but not like an American sidewinder with its purpose-built rattle. Instead, it makes the sound by rubbing the scales of its back against each other. Its venom is extremely poisonous. "There was in the caravan a merchant of Tilimsan known as al-Hajj Zaiyan," wrote Ibn Battuta in the fourteenth century.

> He had a habit of taking hold of these snakes and playing about with them. I had told him not to do this but he did not stop. One day he put his hand into a lizard's hole to pull it out and found a snake there instead. He grasped it in his hand and was going to mount his horse but it bit the index finger of his right hand, giving him severe pain. It was cauterized, but in the evening the pain grew worse. He cut the throat of a camel and put his hand in its stomach and left it there for the night. The flesh of his finger dropped off and he cut off his finger at the base. The Massufa told me that the snake had drunk water before biting him; if not the bite would have killed him.[7]

Travelers in the Sahara often exaggerate the hazards of snakes, however. Their populations are sparse, and they're seldom found far from water sources. A little prudence—such as not pitching a tent or camping in a wadi, where the snakes are more commonly found—easily enables the nomads to avoid them. And almost all Saharan snakes are dormant in winter, especially at night. Indeed, Ibn Battuta's anecdote more clearly illustrates the extent of human folly than it does the dangers of the desert's snakes.

Scorpions are a more pervasive problem. The poisonous vipers and krait infest the oases and waterholes and their environs, but the scorpions, which seem to be everywhere, can seldom be escaped entirely. All prudent travelers are careful when turning over a stone, and always peer under a pillow before retiring. Some Tuareg are said to be immune, but they seldom act that way.

Almost all chronicles of Saharan travel seem to mention scorpions.

In 1818 in Tejéré, on the northern fringes of the Tibesti Mountains, George Lyon, the young British explorer, was billeted with a family of Tubu. Three of the family's young children, he was told, had been bitten by scorpions. Two young boys had died.

"Where was this?" Lyon asked, uneasily.

"Oh, right here, in this room where you are staying," his hostess replied blandly.

Lyon turned over his sheepskin, and poked in the corners, but found nothing.

"You won't see them," the woman said. "They will drop from the roof sometime during the night."

A week or so later, he was indeed bitten. "I hastened with a lancet to cut to the bone and to suck out the blood; then Mr. Ritchie burnt a deep hole with caustic. The pain remained very acute for some time."[8]

A surgeon with Kitchener's army, on its way to Omdurman, reported that "hardly a day passed without somebody being stung, and though I myself was spared the pain of that experience, yet at different times I killed in all six of them that were carefully coiled up in my blankets."[9]

The author of *Desert Life* became obsessed with the devilish creatures: "During three or four months they always haunted our tents, so did they our thoughts. We usually found them when starting out in the morning, under the packages, saddles, and tent carpets. One was detected by a colleague in a pocket. Another stung the same man before lunch in his tent. One was caught during a meal on the back of a chair, crawling towards the sitter's neck, while he was just scanning to see whether any were about. My servant more than once turned them out of my bed, usually before I turned in, but once, at least, from under my pillow immediately after I had risen."[10]

In this, nothing much has changed. The small caravan that had seen the tracks of the caracal camped one night in the *erg* just to the east of the Aïr, and as the small fire of twigs and dung was dying down for the night, three ghostly pale scorpions, so colorless they looked translucent, were seen scuttling across the sand, heading for the packs. One of the Tuareg scooped them up between two sticks and tossed them onto the fire. After that, the party slept as uneasily as Lyon had, every small sound an imagined invasion of an army of deadly scorpions.

And "deadly" is not just a turn of phrase. Saharan scorpions can reach six inches and, unlike those of the Ténéré, are often a brilliant emerald in color. Their sting can cause paralysis, usually temporary, and occasionally death. Entomologists are unnervingly effusive about scorpions because they are among the oldest living unevolved creatures (they were apparently the same 400 million years ago as they are now), and point with glee to their intricate courtship dance and the hazards of their mating. The male scorpion is commonly killed and eaten after copulation, which a desert traveler can be forgiven for thinking serves him right.

And yet, despite their threat and the sleepless nights they cause, scorpions are not the desert's greatest pest. Other insects, not necessarily venomous or dangerous but omnipresent, are more pervasive and considerably more irritating. Lice torment all travelers in the Sahara; they were imported on and are transported by humans, and now infest most Saharan oases. In the oases, also, mosquitoes are a constant pest, and dangerous to boot, for they carry malaria. And ants: Sit anywhere on the sand, in almost any part of the desert, and you'll be swarmed by huge ants, the worst a curious silver variety whose nips burn the skin. Almost any bush or scrawny tree is covered with spiders and beetles, some of them unnervingly fast. In the western Sahara live beetles called *gan-gans*, which burrow under blankets at night, and although they're benign they have to be taken seriously—they could be scorpions. Worst of all are the flies. Everything is covered with flies—people, animals, piles of garbage near wells, water buckets, houses, camels, food. Any food left untended is soon smothered in a buzzing cloud of flies.

಄

THE MOST EXHILARATING of all the animals of the desert, perhaps because of their scarcity and perhaps because of their fleetness and natural grace, are the antelope. Three species are still found in the Sahara. A few Mendes antelope survive in Egypt and in high parts of the desert, and so does a small population of Dorcas gazelles, which were placed on the Endangered Species List in 1980. The Dorcas, which is only about two feet high at the shoulder, lives primarily in the Sahel and in parts of Arabia, though it has been found far into the desert's interior, for it can survive for long periods without water and, where plants grow, may live its entire life without drinking any water at all. Dorcases can run for many miles at high speeds, more than thirty miles an hour, and have been clocked at over sixty when panicked. Jackals and hyenas prey on them, but their real enemy is man. The Dorcas rather resembles the Springbok of eastern and southern Africa.

The most impressive of the antelope, however, and the most eagerly sought by visitor and nomad alike, are the fleet-footed addax, the desert's largest mammal, animals that have been spotted ninety miles from the nearest water, traveling over rough terrain at better than forty miles an hour. Addax are found only in isolated spots in the Sahara, elegant animals white in color with dark faces and spiral horns, not much more than three feet tall at the shoulder. The Tu-

Addax (National Geographic)

areg tell many stories about the addax. They are supposed to have a way of sensing desert grasses and bushes from fifty miles or more, and because grass is linked to water, a wise man watches where the addax are going. Possibly because of this, in the central and southern Sahara the Tuareg seldom hunt addax, and seldom eat them unless desperate hunger intrudes. Ibn Battuta wrote about addax in the desert south of Taghaza, in Mali, in the fourteenth century: "There are many wild cattle. A troop of them will approach so near that the people can hunt them with dogs and wooden arrows. However, eating their meat produces thirst and so many people avoid it. It is remarkable that if these cattle are killed water is found in their stomachs. I have seen the Massufa [Tuareg] squeezing the stomach and drinking the water in it."[11] In modern times, in Algeria, Mali, and Niger, the remaining addax are rigorously protected.

Sometimes, though, this protection is more in spirit than in fact. In the first year of the twenty-first century, in the shabby little oasis town of Telouess, in the south-central part of the Aïr Massif just below the Bagzan Mountains (their peaks looming overhead, black and jagged, as exotic as a wizard's castle) lived, albeit temporarily, a Nigerian functionary charged with helping to manage the Addax Wildlife Reserve, to the east of the massif, a vast tract of land de-

clared a World Heritage Site by the irrepressible UNESCO, in a
hopeful but probably vain attempt to prevent the disappearance of
the last few remaining animals. This personage—he declined to give
his name, out of a profound suspicion of outsiders and their purposes, but it later turned out to be Walid—was actually based in the
northern Aïr oasis of Iferouâne. He'd been there since the late
1980s, when the Niger government of the time had set up a rudimentary office to manage the park and to guide tourists into it, but
the Tuareg rebellions of the 1990s had intervened and addax were
for a few years furthest from the government's mind. As a consequence, Walid has languished there ever since, employed but un-
salaried, and has made his living by fixing trucks (the oasis is on a
tenuous route to the Ahaggar) and by helping out at the tiny air-
port, into which few tourists now fly but which sees the occasional
representative of Big Oil, needing outfitting and guidance into the
deep desert. His cousins were salt *caravanniers*, he said, among the
last of their kind, but made a good living. Walid had a small side
business refilling water bottles from the oasis's well and reselling it in
places like Timia as imported "European" mineral water.

The previous month Walid had taken a small group of German
eco-tourists from Iferouâne east through the Tamgak Mountains
and onto the *erg* that has drifted up against the eastern side of the
massif, where the sanctuary is located. Four Germans, three Tuareg,
and a string of thirteen camels had made the trip. The Germans had
wanted to pass all the way through the sanctuary down the east side
of the Aïr southward toward the Bilma track, but had not realized
how far it was, more than 250 miles, most of it through country
with no wells. So Walid took them into the desert for a few days,
and then took them back to their starting point.

"They were angry with me at first," Walid said with some asper-
ity, remembering their obduracy. "But if they died I would get nothing but trouble, so I refused. They had no idea how far it was."

Nevertheless, he said, the Germans soon forgave him, because
early in their venture they had a magical morning that made anger
superfluous.

"We left before light, at late moon, perhaps three in the morning, and at dawn we saw a pair of gazelles, then a few monkeys hurrying back into the rocks." The dawn was violet, the air still, but perfumed by some scent born in the high mountains. The sand was smooth, and turned golden as the sun rose, and the tourists just stared, mesmerized by the landscape. "We saw no addax that day, but the next we did, we saw one, and they got good pictures." For three more days they wandered, the black basalt towering on one side, the grand *erg* shimmering on the other, traveling in the morning, camping during the day, hunkered down, and traveling again into the moon. On most days they caught sight either of a gazelle or an addax, sometimes fleeting glimpses only, but real enough to be thrilling. Walid described what he showed his group, intense black rocks, sand like fine gold, the air still, the silence filling, as he said, all the emptiness between the ears. He was lyrical about this silence, and spoke of it as a living thing, a presence, a mistress of revelation. He would be a good warden for the national park, if it ever gets anywhere and the tourists start to come, and pay him to do what he would do anyway, at one with his beloved landscape, a fellow traveler over the desert with the antelope after which the park is named.

PART TWO

And the People
Who Live There

CHAPTER EIGHT

❧

First Peoples

TWO MILLION PEOPLE now live in the Sahara, in one way or another. This may seem a very small number for so vast a space, or it might seem a lot, given the starkness and aridity of the landscape they call home. Two-thirds of them live in cities or in oases scattered throughout the desert, from the Mauritanian Adrar in the west to the Egyptian desert to the east, from the Mediterranean hinterlands to the Sahel. All the countries of the Sahara—Mauritania and Western Sahara along the Atlantic; the Sahelian territories of Mali, Niger, and Chad; the lands that make up the Maghreb (Morocco, Tunisia, Algeria, Libya), and of course Egypt and Sudan—have oases, and though a good number of them are now vulnerable to resource degradation, overpopulation, and desertification, just as many remain verdant, sustaining life as they have for millennia. Of these oasis dwellers, many are former nomads, now become town-bound merchants, shopkeepers, date growers, goatherds, or worse. Some are relatively prosperous, but others can only find work as roustabouts on the oil rigs and kick up their heels in the grim taverns of the oases; they are poor, and easy prey for the more militant imams. Many dream of returning to the desert, nomads once again.

Perhaps a third of the 2 million Saharan citizens remain nomads, traveling with their flocks and their strings of camels and their tents with closely woven hangings and silver teapots, traveling wherever need and desire take them, relatively immune to politics with only tenuous connections to modern polities (though in the end they will very likely be no match for the binding ties of the modern bureaucratic state), and subject only to the exigencies of the desert's savage climate.

These ancient patterns persist, seemingly immutable. To the modern eye, they are deeply conservative, rooted in the past. But if you go back far enough they are the product not of endlessly accreting custom but of violent events: wrenching climate change, famine, forced migration, invasion, empire, and wars both holy and profane.

☙

IN THE BEGINNING, obscured by the swirling mists of time, were the pastoralists of this then-verdant Sahara, little Neolithic hunter-gatherers, putative cousins to the equatorial pygmies and the Khoisan of southern Africa, though this is still a hot debate in the academic journals of ethnography. Perhaps they developed separately, if from a common ancestor. It is now thought that "at least two early varieties [of the Negroid type] existed [in Neolithic times]: One developed within and around the Saharan region, whereas the origin of the other is traceable to tropical woodland and forest habitats."[1] In any case, no one doubts that these were the first people. What is disputed is that the *haratin,* the modern agricultural laboring classes of the Western Sahara, are their lineal descendants, though the evidence points to it. (Recent DNA testing has shown that the *haratin* are eerily similar to the equatorial pygmies, which implies that they might be remnants of the original inhabitants.)

Elusive signs of human activity in the Sahara can be traced very early, possibly as long ago as one hundred twenty thousand years, certainly as early as forty thousand years ago. However, the dating is erratic and uncertain. Saharan specialist Angela Close of the University of Washington has said, a little sardonically, that if you want a firm date for something by carbon dating, it is best to make only one test, because "the more [tests] you get the wider the scatter." The drier the desert, the less carboniferous material there is to date, and the less certain the dates that are essayed. These earliest Saharans, whose numbers and presence waxed and waned as the desert itself did, left behind spear points and crude stone tools. Later came middens, rudimentary camp sites, and, later still, cave paintings, but little evidence of settled life. This is not so surprising; the modern San ("Bushmen") of the Kalahari Desert at the other end of Africa live a life consisting entirely, in the modern jargon, of software: They have no possessions to speak of but a rich and varied repertoire of stories and a poetry that is inventive, sophisticated, and fecund. Perhaps the Saharans were the same. Their art is similar; perhaps their lives were too.

The first Saharan culture to be given a name, the Aterians, lived in a wide band in the central desert, from Egypt to the Atlantic, from the sub-Atlas to southern Mauritania and the Senegal basin. They, too, left little but a few stone artifacts, and then disappeared from the record.

In the deep desert, all the Saharan *ergs* are rich in relics of later Stone Age periods, containing fishhooks on old lake bottoms, artifacts, pottery, and tombs, and several traces of early agriculture have been found.[2] Barley and millet were apparently grown more than eight thousand years ago in the Ahaggar Mountains of southeastern Algeria. Cattle were domesticated at least seven thousand years ago, the proof in the rock art at Tassili n'Ajjer, north of the Ahaggar Mountains. Shortly thereafter cattle appeared around Darfur, east of the Ennedi Mountains (centered on El-Fasher on modern maps), and in the Aïr region. Skeletal remains indicate that the herders were negroid, and thus connected to the peoples of the Sahel-Sudan instead of to Egypt and the Maghreb. They came to be called "Nilosaharans," although their connection with the Nile remains obscure—they were a tall people who seem to have originated somewhere in the central Sahara and spread in all directions except north. Some Nilosaharans might have devolved into the Songhai empire, farther up the Niger River, and others were among the ancestors of the Kanuri people, who later governed another Saharan empire called Kanem-Bornu. There are also common linguistic roots with the Teda language of the Tubu, and the modern Nuer, who live in central Sudan.

చ్చ

IF YOU TRAVEL northeast from Agadez, that dusty little city in Niger lying at the foot of the Aïr, out into the Ténéré in the direction of the Bilma oasis and salt mines, and if you head into the dunes just after you get to the place marked on the maps "Arbre de Ténéré," you come to the massif of Adrar Madet. This is a stark and dramatic landscape, although unexceptional in this already stark and dramatic place. There you will find sandstone scarred with gullies and runnels, runoff from rains past streaked with red, rockfalls in a chaotic jumble, neither a tree nor a bush for sixty miles in any direction. But at the massif's foot is a perfect circle of rocks some sixty feet in diameter, part of what looks like a compass much larger in scope, almost two miles across. In each of the cardinal directions, a mile away from the circle, an arrow points away. The purpose of this artifact is unknown, and so is its provenance.[3]

It is presumed to be old, but if so, what was its purpose? And what if the circle isn't old at all, but a new artifact cobbled together out of old rocks by, say, the French in the early days of aviation, a guiding marker for the Sopwith Camels and other fragile biplanes that passed overhead? After all, to the north are the plateaus where the fiercest of the brigands were still said to be lurking in recent years and many stories are remembered from the early period of aviation history of unwary flyers touching down at oases to top up the tanks and to fill up with water, only to be set upon by Tuareg brandishing long swords, bent on plunder.

All skepticism notwithstanding, the stone circle of Adrar Madet appears genuine. Heinrich Barth, passing through the desert on his way to Bornu near Lake Chad around 1850, had noticed something similar, near Ghat, in the area of Tassili n'Ajjer, Algeria, "a circle regularly laid with large blocks of rock, at the southwestern slope of the cliff." Barth took the circle to "belong to the same period of antiquity" as the cave paintings and sculptures he had noticed in the area a few days earlier.[4]

Nor is Niger's circle the only sign of early construction in the Sahara. At Nabta Playa, eighty miles west of Abu Simbel in southern Egypt, a settlement has been found on the shores of a seasonal lake; the inhabitants, whoever they were, had hauled massive slabs of stone, weighing several tons each, to the lake's edge and stood them on end, possibly to mark the sun's zenith at the start of the rainy season. The megalithic stone circle is similar to Stonehenge in England, but at least a millennium older. The site included cattle and sheep graves, and thirty complex stone structures of still-unknown function. In one of them was found a 2.5-ton statue of a cow. The

Ancient stone circle at Nabta Playa. (NASA)

nomads who constructed it also developed pottery long before the people of the lower Nile, more evidence that they were more "advanced" than was earlier thought.[5]

Another circle, even larger than that at Adrar Madet, is in the desert near the El-Dakhla oasis in Egypt's Western Desert. This one is made of sandstone, thirty-five meters across and several feet high; nearby are more than a hundred smaller stone rings, all dating back twelve thousand years. Their purpose was supposedly a base camp for nomadic pastoralists, but no one really knows—why the effort, the expenditure of so much energy, on structures that were not practical but, presumably, symbolic? The people of El-Dakhla kept sheep, cattle, and goats, and possibly ostriches, since a large number of eggshells have been uncovered. They had begun to cultivate the wild grains that grew in the oasis, millet and sorghum. Flint tools in distinctive styles have been found, far earlier than those that later cropped up alongside the Nile.

The probability is that these circles, and the dozens of lesser ones elsewhere in the desert oases, were built in places of reliable water in a time of increasing desiccation. It is surely more than a coincidence that the first pharaohs came to power only a few hundred years after the western settlements like Nabta Playa dried up and had to be abandoned, in the birth of the modern Sahara.

A consensus is emerging that these places, and these constructions, were precursors of the much more elaborate civilization that soon emerged, the culture that we know as Pharaonic Egypt.

☙

HEINRICH BARTH was a scholarly traveler (prone, in his *Travels and Discoveries in North and Central Africa*, to long-winded digressions on the proper regional pronunciations of obscure Tuareg names), and his notebooks and sketches revealed an astonishing array of sculptures and paintings. The sculptures in the Ennedi region of southeastern Chad, he noted, were particularly interesting, because they showed the longhorn cattle of central Africa. "If we consider," he wrote, "that the sculpture described is close to a watering place on the high road to Africa, we are reduced to the conjecture that at that time [undated, but probably several millennia ago] cattle were not only common in this region, but even that they were the common beasts of burden instead of the camel, which we here look for in vain. . . . I have been assured that in 1847 or 1848 the well-known Tébu [Tubu] hajj Abérma traveled with oxen from Kano as far as Ghat in the month of December, the oxen being watered every second day."[6]

Gustav Nachtigal also came across a series of rock engravings in the Libyan desert, most of them involving cattle, with only one rather crude depiction of a camel. He speculated that the cattle dated from the time before camels had been introduced to the region, and that the camel had been added more recently by a Tubu boy. Only one human figure was depicted, a warrior carrying the standard Tubu lance, but bearing a shield divided into four quadrants, rather like a cross. This figure still exists, though it is crumbling now; the matter-of-fact Tubu hold no reverence for these engravings, and are wont to use the warrior's shield for target practice.[7]

Prehistoric paintings exist everywhere in the Sahara, from Mauritania in the west to Egypt in the east. Many are old, very old, reliably dated to thirteen millennia ago, and astonishing in all particulars, fluid, expressive, impressionistic, interpretive. Some are merely crude. And some are fairly new—Tuareg lads around many deep-desert capitals have been known to daub "rock paintings," which they will then show, for a modest fee, to the few noncomprehending tourists who do show up.

Some of the best are those that Barth discussed, in the Ennedi range in Chad. An hour's walk from the fading and somnolent town of Fada and a further thirty minutes' scrambling up a three-hundred-foot cliff, there is a ledge above the valley, about twenty feet wide at its best, a precarious perch for a long-vanished village of Stone Age hunters. On the overhanging cliff, behind where the houses had once been, are friezes of red cattle, people dancing, men on the hunt, animals fleet of foot running for their lives. Like other paintings in the Egyptian oases of Uweinat, which is on an old route that

Cave paintings in the Ennedi Mountains. (Maelstrom)

led from El-Dakhla oasis to Lake Chad, some of the figures are a
startling violet, others splashed on in impressionistic white. A speculative date for them is four or five thousand B.C.[8]

In Algeria's Tassili n'Ajjer, more than fifteen thousand drawings
and engravings record the climate changes, the animal migrations,
and the evolution of human life in the Sahara, from 6000 B.C. to the
first centuries of the present era. Among them are striking scenes of
hippopotamus, buffalo, elephant, rhinoceros, and giraffe and, in the
Wadi Djerat canyon deep in the Tassili, elegant depictions of what
seems to be the hunting of wild sheep called moufflon.

The best Tassili rock paintings are within an easy day's arc of
Djanet, in the rock outcroppings of Tin Taradjeli and Tin Teghert,
in the canyon of the Iherir River, and at Tasset, where there are prehistoric dwellings still occasionally inhabited by Tuareg herdsmen.
Tihodaine, across a dune field to the northeast, is one of the richest
sites in Algeria, the location also of ceramic shards dated between
8,500 and 9,500 years ago. At Tin Tarabine is a rock famous for its
giraffe, cattle, buffalo, and shamanistic rituals, as well as some curi-

ous imprints of human footsteps; at Tagrera, where rocks have been naturally sculpted into a formation once called "The Three Negroid Heads" and now simply called "The Three Heads," is an ancient City of the Dead, where fossils of human skeletons, prehistoric tombs, formations of unknown purpose in the shape of mush-rooms, and depictions of elephants have been uncovered.

Giant giraffes, incised into the black lava-like rock northeast of Agadez, are bigger than life. They were discovered only a few years ago, and their location is supposed to be known only to a select few for fear of looters and vandalism (though every Tuareg guide in Agadez will offer to take you there, if you wish). Their age is esti-mated at better than seven thousand years. Sketchy evidence of what might be harnesses in these and many rock paintings suggests that the ancient people who made them had attempted to domesti-cate not only giraffes but zebras and other savanna fauna.

The giant giraffes near Agadez.
(Cornell University Library)

The conventional dating of Saharan rock art, and the scheme used by the curators in the Tassili National Park, divides them into five loose groupings: the Large Wild Fauna Era (prior to 6,000 B.C.), the Era of Hunters (6000–4000 B.C.), the Era of Stockbreeders (4000–1500 B.C.), the Horse Era (1500 B.C. to first century A.D.), and the Camel Era (first century on). Henri Lhote, a French archaeologist who made a lifelong study of Saharan art, mostly in Libya and Algeria, broke them down into four groupings (if you ignore, as he did, the earliest phase of all), though his dates differ somewhat, predictably, since dating these paintings is a far from assured task.

The oldest of Lhote's groupings, until about 5000 B.C., he called the "round head" period, depicting human figures with bulbous heads, holding incomprehensible objects and symbols. Naturally this style, found at many places across northern Africa, has teased out a swarm of pseudoscientists and cultists, who take the round heads for space helmets and conclude that the awestruck locals were depicting arrivals from outer space.

The round heads disappear about 5000 B.C., never to reappear, and the second period, ending somewhere after 2000 B.C., is marked by a more naturalistic style, with thousands of splendid examples of hunting, celebrating, and everyday living.

The third period, from 1500 or so B.C. to about 500 B.C., is the most interesting, because it depicts apparently dramatic changes in the Saharan climate and thus in its societies. First the cattle disappear from the rock art, and then, eventually, so do horses. The presumption is that these disappearances were linked directly to increasing aridity in the region. The changes were consequently also political and human, for fleeting glimpses are seen of the upheavals that were sweeping across the desert; the Garamantes empire, which ruled vast swaths of the Sahara in the period, is shown sending horse-drawn chariots to attack fleeing herdsmen; but then the chariots and the horses and by extension the empire itself simply drop off the artistic landscape, just as they disappeared from the real one.

In the fourth and final period, around 500 B.C., writing appears for the first time. These messages from the past are in the Tifinagh script still used by the Tuareg nomads, but the language is unknown and their meaning is lost.

☙

ADVERSITY, the theory goes, force-fed human ingenuity. As the climate worsened, the Neolithic first people, who had essentially lived off the land as hunter-gatherers, were obliged to pay attention to the foodstuffs they had taken for granted, and began to cultivate them actively. In this way, the wild grasses were domesticated. As the aridity intensified and the lakes dried up altogether, places where farming was practical became fewer and fewer, mostly confined to the valleys of the Senegal and Niger Rivers and around Lake Chad, and, of course, the Nile. Radar scans of the sands underneath Nabta Playa, in Egypt, clearly show the skein of waterways that once nourished the landscape, now deeply buried with an overlay of blown sand.[10]

Filtering between the cultivators were nomadic herders, pushed southward by the same worsening aridity, their movement made easier by the retreat of the tsetse fly, that endemic African killer itself killed by the increasing aridity.[11]

The desertification process that began six or seven thousand years ago, then, meant that the Nilosaharan farmers, whoever they were, were scattered in a band immediately south of the desert and in ribbons along the Niger and Nile Rivers. A few, from the evidence of the cave paintings, remained in the deep desert, in the massifs and the oases, castaways of geological time, clinging to the last places where settled life was possible.[12] There were curious holdouts, themselves castaways on a climatic oasis, in the Tindouf Depression in the northwest desert of Algeria, just south of the Anti Atlas in modern Morocco. Possibly because of runoff from the mountains, the climate in this little corner remained more or less temperate and a small population survived to modern times.

By contrast, the population along the Nile doubled, and then tripled, and eventually reached a critical mass for a lasting civilization.

ᘓᘓ

F O R   A L L of the nineteenth century and much of the twentieth, it was a truism of Egyptian studies that the origin of the Nile civilization was to be found in migrations from elsewhere, probably the Near East or Mesopotamia. In this theory, the indigenous peoples were ruled by invading Semitic people from outside Africa. Thus, a more advanced people created the wonders of the Nile Valley, using the labor of the Africans to do so.

This was a theory rooted in the assumptions of its time. Africans, who were to the academics of Europe and the Arab world self-evidently savage and primitive, could not possibly have built or even caused to be built the magnificence of Egypt. The ancients, however, had no such preconceptions. Greek historians of the first millennium B.C. commonly thought Egyptian and Ethiopian (then defined as the "burnt people" or blacks of Africa) were synonyms, and there is at least one early Greek writer who asserted that it was Ethiopians, led to the Nile delta by the God Osiris around 3000 B.C., who founded the Egyptian civilization. Moses' wife, according to the Bible, was an Ethiopian. Khufu, the greatest pyramid builder of Egypt, was described by a contemporary as a "thick lipped and woolly haired black."[13] During the Twenty-fifth and Twenty-sixth Dynasties beginning around 720 B.C., Egypt, it is known, was governed by Nubian rulers.

The Egyptians themselves believed they originated elsewhere, in a land called Punt. The name came up in inscriptions dating to the third millennium B.C. Much later a curious queen, Hatshepsut, decided to see for herself. She mounted an expedition in 1500 B.C. and had the details of her journey inscribed on a temple at Dayr El-Bahri. Punt lies along the Gulf of Aden, in what is now eastern Ethiopia, Eritrea, and Djibouti.

In any case, the Western notions of African fecklessness have long been convincingly debunked. The dozens of Neolithic and Holocene-

era sites since uncovered have convincingly made the case for a precipitating force much closer to home, from the Western Desert and
the Sahel and not from the Middle East or Mesopotamia: It was the
desiccation of the Sahara that force-fed the emergence of a settled culture on the lower and middle Nile. The flowering of ancient Egypt,
by this reckoning, was a by-product of climate change, the Pharaohs-
to-be boiling out of the drying Sahara, with the annual flooding of
the Nile sustaining the cultures that did emerge. The environmental
refugees from the deep desert brought with them the knowledge of
agriculture necessary to a settled and urban civilization; the new river
dwellers then learned to harness water, with irrigation canals and the
machinery of sluices, and human ingenuity rose to the occasion.

A new theory also points to the desert origins of the ancient
Egyptians. It suggests that the pyramids of Giza were inspired not
by arcane religious symbolism but by the pyramidal rock shapes
commonly found in the Western Desert and used by the nomads as
route markers—not necessarily that the ancient architects copied
such forms, but that they had, after centuries of observation, come
to understand that the pyramid shape best resists wind erosion.
Were the pyramids cubes, they would long ago have vanished,
eroded away by the desert winds.[14]

❧

AROUND 3000 B.C., the conventional histories say, the
founder of the First Dynasty, King Menes of Memphis, unified the
kingdom of the Delta with the new kingdom of the Nile Valley,
thereby reaching the population density that made an advanced
technical civilization possible. After that, of course, things are well
enough remembered: thirty-odd dynasties and three thousand
years–plus of continuous indigenous rule. Thus was nurtured the
civilization that produced the Sphinx, the great pyramids, and the
Valley of the Kings.

CHAPTER NINE

୧୨

Empires of the Sun

FROM THE TOP of the Jebel al-Mi'ysrah, a little hill at its center, the Bahariya oasis in northern Egypt spreads out to the horizon—except to the west. In that direction, massive golden sand dunes loom; they have already engulfed part of the oasis, and their steady roll sometimes seems unstoppable. In the far distance to the south and east are the hills of the Black Desert, quartzite and dolorite laced with iron, whose eroded rocks cover the desert like a film of soot, hence its name. You can't see the whole of Bahariya—the oasis covers a depression of about eight hundred square miles—but you can see a number of small mud-hut villages with their attendant palm groves, apricot plantations, and rows of corn. The lake that once covered much of the depression floor has long ago seeped away, but springs remain. Some, like the one at Bir ar-Ramla, are much too hot to use for irrigation or livestock, but there are many others, such as the ice-cold Bir al-Mattar and the perennial gusher at Bir al-Ghaba, about ten miles northeast of the little village called Bawiti. Some basins hewn in the rock to catch water date from Roman times, others even earlier. The ruins of a Seventeenth Dynasty temple have been found buried in the sand, as well as tombs where birds were buried, presumably for religious purposes now unknown.

Bawiti today is small, overcrowded, and without any distinction. But at the height of the Middle Kingdom (2040–1786 B.C.), it was already famous, its grape wines not only consumed at Pharaonic tables but gracing the banquets of Mesopotamia and Phoenicia as well. In the Greco-Roman period (approximately 330 B.C. to about A.D. 400), the oasis's heyday, as many as twenty thousand farmers and artisans lived in Bahariya, the center of the empire's wine industry. Nearby, a burial ground, not used for two thousand years, covers almost fourteen square miles.

This was an important place, with pretensions beyond its stature, which reveals a fascinating story of local hubris: the tomb of a vizier, Gad Khensu Eyuf, who dared in his lifetime to represent himself in temples in the style of the kings.[1] Nearly one hundred mummies have been found in the oasis, including one eminent woman with gold-plated breasts.[2]

Under the Romans, there were roads from Bahariya to Siwa, or the Farafra oasis, through the Al-Sillim Pass and across the White Desert, a landscape unique even by Saharan standards, surreal wind-formed rocks of bizarre shapes, a blinding white in the glare of the sun. The roads closed when Bahariya fell into disrepair after the Roman occupiers left, and its population dwindled, but in any case El-Dakhla, Bahariya, Farafra, and Siwa, together with the Nile itself, represented the full extent of ancient Egyptian colonizing, well within the boundaries of modern Egypt. Perhaps because the people who had become Egyptians had fled the desert as the aridity closed in on them, they were, for all their magnificence, an in-turned culture. The deep desert was regarded as hostile, a barrier to be penetrated only in need, best left deserted. The rulers of Egypt traded with black Africa, and even sent convoys all the way across to the gold mines of Old Ghana, but after the Romans and later, after the Arab conquests had run their course, their focus was much more parochial: The scholars in the holy schools continued their explica-

Roman ruins at Volubilis, Morocco. (University of Kansas Library)

tions of paradise and the *fellahin* waited for the annual flooding of
the Nile as they always had, and life went on, paying little heed to
the Endless Desert beyond the borders. The Nile was the beginning
and the end of their universe, and became even more so as the Sahara continued its assault and the hinterlands became ever more
hostile: During the Greco-Roman period, the water table lay only
fifteen feet beneath the surface; today, in places where there are no
springs, wells must be sunk forty-five hundred feet to hit water.[3]

℘

THE PHARAONIC DYNASTIES fell into decay and dis-
array around the fourth century B.C., when Egypt was overrun by
the Persians. In 332 B.C. the Persian usurpers were themselves defeated by Alexander of Macedonia. Egypt welcomed Alexander as a
liberator, and he journeyed to the oasis at Siwa to "consult" the oracle of Ammon. To no one's surprise, the oracle found he was Am-

mon's son, as well as a relative through his mother of the last pharaoh, which gave him whatever legitimacy he needed.

When Alexander died nine years later it took his generals less than a week to carve up his divine empire. Egypt became the property of Ptolemy I, son of Lagus of Macedonia. The Ptolemies ruled for several centuries, but eventually their power faded and they became clients of the Romans.

Roman Egypt was a place of little importance. The Romans treated it like a backward provincial satrapy, and the main evidence of their passing was extensive vandalism of the ancient culture's monuments. In A.D. 640 Egypt was conquered by the invading armies of Islam and became a center of Islamic learning and culture under the Fatimids. Egypt rediscovered the vast hinterlands to the west, and from Egypt were launched the two waves of Arab invasion that changed the desert forever, and completed the process of Islamization of the entire Sahara.

It was also the end of indigenous rule in Egypt until modern times, for then came the Ottomans, the Mamelukes, the Europeans, the Ottomans again . . . Egyptians paid attention to Egyptian matters, and apart from the traffic in slaves from Sudan, once more turned their backs on the Great Desert.

⁊⁊

APART FROM EGYPT, the first organized state to be shaped by the Sahara and to map its byways was that of the still-mysterious Garamantes. No one knows, really, who they were; they were sometimes described as negroid in appearance and were possibly Nilosaharans, but may have had Libyan/Berber or Egyptian traces. They inhabited what is now Fezzan, in southwest Libya, and their empire, such as it was, lasted a thousand years or more until it was overrun by the Romans in 19 B.C.

Nothing is left in modern Libya of the Glorious Garamantes (their own description) except the ruins of their ancient capitals, a few rock paintings depicting the characteristic Garamantes four-horse chariots hunting the cave dwellers or "troglodytes" of the High Mountains of

Ethiopia (though "Ethiopia" in ancient writings simply meant "black lands"⁴), and a few enigmatic references, first from Herodotus and then from Pliny the Elder, who both described not only the chariots, much admired by the technologically minded Pliny, but also their peculiar "backward grazing cattle." Herodotus's enumeration of the tribes of Libya listed among the troglodytes a people he called Awjila, who presumably lived in the area of the modern oasis of the same name, between Siwa and Tripolitania.

Whatever their origins, the Garamantes certainly penetrated the deep Sahara very early, and their emissaries and traders routinely crossed the desert, traveling vast distances to do so. Pliny, in his *Natural History*, asserts that the Garamantes governed the whole of the eastern Sahara as far as Sudan, but his meaning (and the boundaries) is uncertain.⁵ In practice, their governance followed the ancient caravan routes from Fezzan to Bornu, already well known to traders. By 1000 B.C. Garamantian chariots were traveling from Tassawa in the Fezzan district to the Niger town of Gao, via the Tassili, the Ahaggar, and the Adrar des Iforhas, thereby pioneering some of the Sahara's most venerable caravan routes.

It was a Roman army, under the African Proconsul Lucius Cornelius Balbus, that finally conquered the Garamantes and annexed their country, which the Romans came to call Phazania ("Fezzan"). This conquest was an astonishing achievement: Not only were the Garamantians notoriously powerful and recalcitrant, but the culminating battle at Garama had to take place after a thirty-day march through waterless country from Ghadamès, the first time Roman armies had penetrated the real Sahara. After that, the everrestless Roman legions raided to the far corners of the former Garamantes lands, into what they called Agisymba, which is probably the Tibesti. The Garamantes were reduced from overlords to Roman escorts, an undignified fate for so glorious a military empire. Still, there are tantalizing hints that some of the distant Tubu of the Tibesti Mountains might be descendants of the Garamantes, or a Berber-Garamantes mix.

When the Vandals dislodged the Romans in the fifth century A.D.,

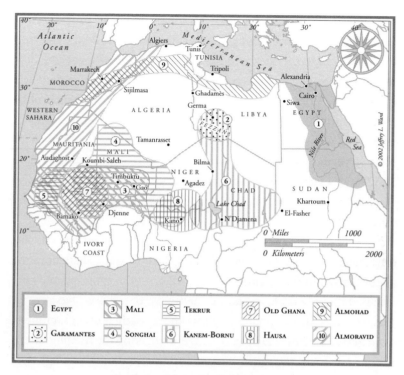

Territories of the ancient Saharan empires.

Phazania regained its independence. As Leo Africanus put it, "It hath a peculiar governor within it selfe, who bestoweth the revenues of the whole region according to his owne discretion."[6] Thereafter it was ruled by a succession of Arab and native dynasties, mostly independent of any central government, until subdued by the Turks and made part of the Ottoman Empire in 1842.

The ruins of the Garamantes empire can be found around Germa, in the Wadi al-Hayat, in Libya. The ancient capital cities, Garama and Zinchecra, are both near Germa. Zinchecra, the earliest capital, is on a bluff overlooking the wadi to the south. There are still signs of an old fort on the flat top of the promontory; dozens of houses and other buildings spill down the slopes. Zinchecra was occupied until about the first century A.D., after which the capital shifted a few miles away, to be closer to water as the population grew, and Zinchecra was used as a city of the dead. Garama, the second and last capital, was occupied as early as the fifth century B.C., long before it became the capital. The only clue to ancient glories is a massive network of water tunnels penetrating the rock and sand on both sides of the wadi, clear signs of a substantial settled population and intensive cultivation. The modern town of Germa is dilapidated, its old fort a ruin, most of its houses crumbling. There are paved roads, a single gas pump, a hotel, and telephone service to the outside world, but it is hard to believe that this area was once the center of an empire that dominated, and terrorized, a good deal of the Sahara.

℘

FARTHER TO THE WEST, there were no indigenous organized states or political confederations in the northern Sahara until the Arabs arrived in the seventh century A.D. The indigenous people were the Berbers, who lived in and on the fringes of the northwestern Sahara. As with the Garamantes, little is known of their origins. Hunter-gatherers (called the "Lybicocapsians") lived along the Mediterranean coast from Neolithic times, but about seven thousand years ago they were succeeded by (or evolved into) a people whose economy included raising sheep and goats. It is possible they came from Yemen, and brought the animals with them. Two thousand years after that, these "new" people developed a cattle-herding economy; the cattle might have been domesticated from local varieties, or brought in from elsewhere, like the sheep and goats. Subsequently, wheat and barley cultivation began. These early agriculturists are known as the proto-Berbers.[7]

Their own legends tell of a crossing from Egypt, Arabia, Yemen, Uzbekistan, Afghanistan—there are many versions. The Berbers are often classed as "Mediterraneans," a term difficult to define. Some Berber groups in the Moroccan Rif, middle Atlas Mountains, and the Jebel Nefusa of northwestern Libya include many individuals with fair skin, blue eyes, and light hair, particularly in their beards. Curiously, their blood types are northwestern European, and in some tribes of the Moroccan middle Atlas the frequency of Rh-negative blood is matched elsewhere only by the Basques. However, it is one of the curiosities of African historiography that "origins" of various African peoples are so often sought outside Africa. As with Egypt, this has something to do with the lamentable fact that outsiders could never quite bring themselves to believe that native Africans were anything but primitive, a notion reinforced to some degree by African scholars themselves after they became Islamicized. After that, it was always more noble to have an origin that placed your people closer to the epicenter of Islam itself, and any African prince of any standing had perforce to have come from the East.[8] Whatever their origins, the Berbers are now a wonderfully exotic mix of desert nomad, Phoenician trader, Arab invader, Andalusian, and Roman and black African genes.

Subsequently, North Africa and the Saharan fringe suffered successive waves of invaders: the Phoenicians, the Carthaginians, the Romans. In 428 the Vandals landed, and a hundred years later the Byzantines under Belasarius (533), and then the Persians under Chosroes (616). In later centuries, when the coast was infested with Christian pirates, the Berbers developed an aphorism: "The Indian ocean was blessed by God with spices; the Mediterranean cursed with storms and Christians." None of these colonizers had a lasting effect, and the Berber population beyond the Atlas Mountains was relatively unaffected by their fleeting presence. The Saharan interior would scarcely have noticed their appearance, their presence, or their disappearance.

∽

THE ARABS were different: They came to plunder too, but also to stay. Two waves of Arab invaders headed along the Maghreb coast. The first wave, which came mostly from Yemen in the seventh century A.D., was part of the astonishing flowering of Islamic culture, immigrants full of zeal for spreading Mohammed's newly revealed Word. But although many of the new arrivals intermarried with the Berbers, and with the leftovers of half a dozen kingdoms— Romanized settlers, Carthaginian and Phoenician remnants, Jews and Judaized Berbers—theirs was nevertheless primarily a military invasion and hardly penetrated beyond the coastal mountains, and thus had no great effect on the composition of the interior population or their way of life.

The second Arab wave, the invasion of the tribal confederation called Beni Hilal in 1050 and the subsequent rampages of another such group, the Beni Soleim, was mainly a matter of pillage. "It was an evil day for North Africa when, in the 11th century, the Beni Hilal poured out of Egypt westwards, along the coast," wrote the historian of North Africa Edward Bovill. "Knowing no home but a tent and abhorring any more lasting structure [they] systematically pillaged every town and destroyed every solid building they encountered. Cities, towns, aqueducts, dams, cisterns, and bridges went down before a savage horde far more destructive than any of the earlier invaders of the country. Land dependent on irrigation went out of cultivation and turned to desert. Even great expanses of forest were destroyed by the invaders and their herds, thus further aggravating the water problem by hastening surface run-off. Unlike the earlier Arab invaders of the seventh and eighth centuries, the Beni Hilal gave the country nothing."[9] This harsh judgment is not just a latter-day European opinion: As early as 1360 the historian Ibn Khaldun described the Hilal as "a plague of locusts," though he admitted their epic poetry was pretty enough.[10] One can trace the desertification of the north, its loss of forest cover and water sources, to the destructive effects of the Beni Hilal.

No part of the desert was unaffected by the Arab invasions, and their effects were felt far beyond the desert itself. Even the Nmadi, the hunter-gatherers of the Adrar in Mauritania, living as they still do in the most primitive way, fell into a vassalage under their newly Arabized neighbors. The gold and silversmiths of the desert blended almost completely into the Arabized tribes. South of the Sahara tribes like the Dogon, who now live high in the cliffs of Bandiagara, took up their refuge in that inaccessible place because of the invasions. Those among the Berbers of the coastal plains who resisted the invasions and the forced conversions to Islam were driven into the desert. As they fled, the leftover native Nilosaharans, who had been there since the verdant times, retreated to the Sahel, the Niger, and Lake Chad. The Buduma people who live on the shores of Lake Chad as fishermen but who until recently had a piratical reputation that made them much feared in the region are almost certainly modern descendants of these early refugees, and from the evidence of eighteenth- and nineteenth-century travelers the lives they were living until the latter part of the nineteenth century were very similar to the patterns developed so many centuries earlier in the deeper Sahara.

The Arabs—and the Muslim proselytizers—followed the retreating Berbers into and across the desert, until every part of the Sahara had its population of Arabs. Even here, though, nothing is as simple as it first sounds, and "Arab" has itself become slippery of definition. There are Arabs in the Sahara who assert a more or less pure Arab ethnicity—in the western Sahara, for example, the Beni Maghfar and Beni Hassan claim direct descent from the invaders, and Hassaniya, the Arabic dialect of the Beni Hassan, has become the common language of the region. But Arab doesn't necessarily imply ethnicity—it commonly refers also to the warrior or aristocratic classes, many of them non-Arab in origin. In addition, other Saharan groups, like the Kunta of the southwest, assert on thin evidence that they are Arabs because they claim descent from an earlier Arab conqueror of North Africa, 'Uqba ben Nafi. And some Berber clans distinguish themselves as "Arabs of the veil," because in their view their ancestors originally came from southern Arabia in pre-Islamic times.[11] Few inhabitants of the deep desert escaped conversion to Islam. The Tuareg resisted for many centuries (and succeeded in remaking Islam in their own idiosyncratic way), and the Tubu in the Tibesti gave up the fight only in the twentieth century, after more than a thousand years of often fierce resistance, but in the end, they all succumbed.

It is not too much to say that the swirling, restless, violent politics of the deep Sahara is still reverberating from the passing of the Beni Hilal, and that their brigandage still lives in the secretive heart of the nomadic clans of the Ahaggar and the Tibesti.

ᏋᎧ

ON THE SOUTHERN FRINGES of the desert were the greatest empires of Old Africa, whose stories are only now beginning to emerge in their fullness. The settled cultures along the southern rim date back as far as Egypt, and owe their flowering, at least in part, to the same grim fact of climate change: Adversity bred ingenuity, ingenuity bred technology and thus an increasing population, population bred organized politics, and the Sahara, in this progression, bred empire. These ancient African empires, so little known in the West, regarded the Sahara quite differently from the way northerners did. For the Egyptians and the legions of invaders from the north, the desert was a barrier, formidable and intimidating. For the empires in the south, it was both a protection and an opportunity. They grew rich trading first with the Egyptians and then with the Caliphates of the north, but also by remaining unknown, remote, and therefore unconquered.

The first of these kingdoms, as far as anyone knows, was Ghana, Golden Ghana as it was called, partly for its storehouses of real gold but partly because the kingdom glittered, in the estimation of its neighbors, as bright as gold itself. It is now generally called Old Ghana, to distinguish it from the modern nation cobbled together by Kwame Nkrumah in the 1940s, which is a long way to the south. The lesser-known kingdom of Tekrur, which was west and south of Old Ghana and reached the Atlantic, may be almost as old; at any rate, it was the first organized southern Saharan state to adopt Islam. At its height, sometime after the eighth century A.D., Tekrur traded extensively with the Zenaga Berbers of Morocco, mostly in gold and slaves. The Zenaga have given their name to the modern country of Senegal.

The earliest extant written reference to a kingdom of Ghana dates from the close of the eighth century.[12] At the height of its power, in the tenth century, Ghana's influence, centered on Koumbi Saleh just inside the southern border of modern Mauritania, reached east to the Niger floodplains southwest of Timbuktu and as far west as the

The ancient city of Djenne. (ghanaweb)

Senegal River Valley, an immense if thinly populated land, covering much of the modern countries of Mali, Mauritania, and Senegal to the southwest. Ghana adhered to the traditional animist African religions until near the end of its existence, though one of its eminent kings, Tounka, allowed Muslim merchants to build mosques in the tenth century.

Ghana grew rich, and so in tandem did Morocco, which sometime late in the eighth century founded a new town to be the northern depot of the gold trade. This was Sijilmasa, in the oases of Tafilalt, just south of the Atlas Mountains between the Drâa and Saoura Rivers,[13] and just to the west and out of reach of a militant kingdom founded in the ninth century by Ibn Rustem, a leader of the heretical Ibadite sect, which for the next hundred years or so tried to infiltrate this lucrative Saharan trade.

Koumbi Saleh, Ghana's capital, now just a ruin in the bleak gravel plains of southern Mauritania, was not the only city in the Empire of Ghana. It may not have been the largest, or even the oldest. Djenne, a trading city of some twenty thousand people on the Bani River in Mali, on the Niger floodplain, is probably older, but

even Djenne is relatively "new": Two miles away are the ruins of
Djenne-Djenno, Old Djenne, a major city that was mysteriously
abandoned almost seven hundred years ago and now is little but a
heap of eroded mud brick, glass beads, fragments of tantalizing
metal, scraps of pottery, and small statuettes. Old Djenne has been
dated to somewhere around 200 B.C., and was a thriving city by A.D.
300, when jewelry, copper objects, and decorative ceramics were being mass-produced. Old Ghana had a network of markets, a developed agriculture, a sophisticated art, an evolved politics, and a
tax-collecting bureaucracy before the Europeans emerged from the
Dark Ages, somewhere around the end of the first millennium.

❦

FOR GHANA, trouble started on the northwest frontier as
early as the ninth century.

Berber nomads had been drifting south from the Moroccan oases
since the Arab conquest several centuries earlier. By the ninth century these desert chieftains had formed themselves into a loose and
fractious confederacy that controlled at least part of the Atlantic Saharan caravan routes and terrorized the more settled citizens of the
kingdom, boiling out of the desert with their silver scimitars as long
as a camel's leg, killing the farmers, then the farmers' protectors,
then whole caravans of traders who had headed north across the
sands with their saddlebags of gold.

But the confederacy was short-lived: It had no unifying motiva-
tion except a sense of historic grievance and an ethos that glorified
robbery as conquest, and the clans soon fell to fighting among
themselves. In the tenth century the Ghanaian kings reasserted
themselves and once again took control of the oases and the caravan
routes, pushing the nomads back and subduing those who could be
subdued. The rest remained in the deep desert, out of sight, nursing
their anger, developing their legendary mastery of the shifting
sands, biding their time. Their raids provoked reaction, reaction fueled more anger, more partisans to conduct new raids, and the pattern repeated itself.

Eventually the tribes began to cohere once more, many of them into a new loose confederation called the Sanhajah, whose center was around Audaghost, in today's Mauritania just north of the northern frontiers of the Ghanaian kingdom, from which they staged devastating raids all the way across the desert, into the Anti Atlas and the fertile oases of Moroccan Drâa. They began to assert control over the western Sahara caravan routes and nibbled away at the frontiers of Ghana itself.

Early in the eleventh century this new confederation took on a more menacing form. A chief of the time, Yahia Ibn Ibrahim of the Jedala tribe, made a pilgrimage to Mecca and brought back with him an Islamic scholar from Morocco, Abd-Allah Ibn Yasin, with the determination to improve his people's rather hazy notion of Koranic correctness. Ibn Yasin, by all accounts, was filled with righteous zeal. At first, his teachings went well, and he succeeded in converting Tekrur's ruler War Jabi and many of his people, who were from the Tukulor tribe.[14] But Yahia's own tribesmen, the Jedala, found Ibn Yasin's austere asceticism "so repugnant that they burnt his house and drove him from the country."[15] The indignant cleric sought seclusion in some place now uncertain—it was said to be surrounded by water, and could have been the island of Tidra, near the Mauritanian coast. The curious and the furious and the dispossessed found him there, and his ideas, a more militant, puritan faith with little room for backsliders and apostates, spread rapidly. Still, many of the Berber tribes resisted, and when Ibn Yasin's scholastic choler finally boiled over he resorted to force. He was supported by a Sanhajah chief, Tilutan, whose partisans became known as the *al-murabitin*, the Almoravids, a name elusive of definition but that could be derived from the Koranic meaning of the root word *ribat*, which is very close to that of *jihad*.[16]

The Islamic notion of the jihad, holy war, the righteousness of forced conversions to the faith and the holiness of killing enemies of the faith, united the tribes as nothing else had been able to do. In the middle of the eleventh century they launched attacks in both directions, on Old Ghana and on the oases of the northern desert. After a few successful battles in the north, Ibn Yasin's troops prepared to pillage the area, but their leader held them back. For a while, they tolerated him and his increasingly tyrannical ways, but in the end they turned on him in fury. He fled, and took refuge with the ruler of Sijilmasa, who was called Wajjaj. Here he found both sympathy and something more practical: an order from Wajjaj threatening expulsion from Islam to all who refused to obey Ibn Yasin. Sure enough and soon enough, Ibn Yasin was back in the field, with yet another fanatic army, determined to destroy whoever opposed him. Within months he had ten thousand men under his command, then thirty thousand. Running out of conquests in the western and central desert, he yielded to an appeal to rescue the people of the Drâa from apostates and unbelievers. And before the north had time to draw breath, the Almoravids came pouring over the passes into the plains of Morocco, carrying all before them.

In 1057, Ibn Yasin was killed in battle,[17] but his movement was not slowed. In 1076, under their new commander, Abu Bakr, the Almoravids occupied the Ghanaian heartland, suppressing pagan practices, building mosques and schools, burning statuary, and smashing clay idols.

The Sanhajah occupation lasted only twenty years, but by that time the moral authority of the Ghanaian kings had been fatally compromised. Perhaps that wouldn't have mattered had not the Almoravids' raids and constant fighting also undermined the country's agriculture and thus its prosperity. Whatever the ultimate reasons, the empire began to break apart. Satellite kingdoms such as the Mande gradually began to assert their independence.

In Morocco meanwhile, Abu Bakr's cousin, Yusuf Ibn Tachfin, took over what was now the "home army," and after a string of victories refused to hand over power to his peripatetic cousin, who retreated glumly to the desert. Yusuf's army steadily expanded its base, winning victory after victory, positioning itself as the "champion of the masses, the liberator of the people from the cruel tyranny of corrupt princes," phrases with a nicely modern ring. In 1062 he founded Marrakech, and a year later he took Fez without resistance. More than twenty years later, in 1086, in another eerie precursor of the liberationist language of our own day, he "came to the assistance of the Spanish Muslims" and by 1102 the Almoravids ruled from the Senegal Valley to the Ebro River, well into Spain, and caused the flowering of the extraordinary Andalusian civilization.[18]

The Almoravids were succeeded by the purist Almohads, who destroyed Marrakech along with the Almoravid empire in 1147. The Almohads controlled all of North Africa for a brief but glorious time before collapsing from their own magnificence, deteriorating into the dynasties of the Hafsids of Tunis, the Abd al-Waidis of Tlemcen, and the Merinids of Fez.

In 1203, the Soninke natives of Ghana took back their kingdom, but it was not to last. In 1235 the Mande clan called the Keita, kings of Mali in the uppermost Niger Valley, assumed control of Ghana and incorporated what was left into their own, considerably more extensive and militantly Islamic, empire. It was called "the empire of the sun." Like Golden Ghana, the phrase had two meanings: Mali controlled the desert, but the link with the sun was meant to recognize its own material magnificence.

❧

SUNIATA, the first ruler of the Malian empire, was "of the country of Mema south-west of Timbuktu, of the Tungara tribe, emir of Malinke, kin to the Songhai of Gao."[19] He and his successors, kings of the Islamic Empire of Mali, systematically expanded their domains. They developed a new trade route from Djenne toward new goldfields that were being opened along the Black Volta and farther south still, into what is modern Ghana. They swept through Tekrur and reached the Atlantic. They extended their power beyond what had been the eastern frontiers of Old Ghana to the cities of Timbuktu and Gao, terminuses of the shortest trans-Saharan routes. They began sending caravans laden with gold across the desert to the central Maghreb states and to Egypt, all of which were then more stable than Morocco—for a century or so, the western routes closed altogether as the countryside deteriorated into brigandry.

The Niger River became Mali's east-west conduit. Soon, Malian merchants were trading south to the Gulf of Guinea, east to the Hausa city-states south of Agadez, and to the Islamic centers around the eastern Mediterranean and the Gulf of Arabia. Universities were founded at Timbuktu, Djenne, and Segou. Islam spread with the traders, and the Malians and then the Hausa converted en masse.

A map published in medieval Europe shows the extent of the kingdom, its lands sprawling from the coast into the still-hazy interior. "This Negro lord is called Mansa Musa, Lord of the Negroes of Guinea," the cartographer wrote. The capital of Mali was located at Niani (or Niani-Niani) on the Sankarani River in Guinea, a small and unimportant tributary of the Niger, but close to alluvial gold fields—this is where the golden rods of Ghana were supposed to be found. The little town, older than the empire, for it had once pledged allegiance to Ghana, remained the capital for some three hundred years. Mansa Musa, most famous of the Malian kings, succeeded to the throne in 1307 and took control of "the four large territories of the western part of Negroland: First, Baghena, formed out of the remnants of the kingdom of Ghanata [Ghana]; secondly Zagha, or the western Tekrur, together with Silla; then Timbuktu, at that time still, as it seems, independent of Gogo [Gao]. Jinni (Djenne), however, probably owing to its nearly insular character, seems not to have been subjected to Melle (Mali) at this period, although it was engaged in continual warfare."[20] Both Timbuktu and Gao surrendered without resistance, and Mansa Musa built massive mosques in both places.

Timbuktu, as a consequence, lost its independence, but gained much more. "And being thus well protected against violence offered on the part of the neighboring Berber [actually, Tuareg] population, and in consequence of the town increasing rapidly, it soon became a market place of the first rank, so that the most respectable merchants from Misr, Tawat, Tafilalt, Darah, Fez and other places migrated to Timbuktu."[21]

Mansa Musa made his *hajj* to Mecca in 1326. He took with him a massive entourage: Some reports, surely exaggerated, say he ordered sixty thousand of his subjects to accompany him. However, what most astonished the scribes of Alexandria and the merchants of Cairo were the hundred camels laden with gold that trailed after him. Indeed, he and his people showered so much gold on the local economy that the value of the currency was still debased a dozen years later.

Malian power was dependent on control of the Niger, which in turn meant they had to control the Tuareg, the Mossi kingdom to the south, and the Songhai to the east, who monopolized the commerce downstream. The Songhai had an independent monarchical tradition of their own that predated Mali, and the Mali kings kept only erratic control of the Songhai capital, Gao, which they first captured in 1325.

❧

THE SONGHAI ORIGINS are as obscure as those of the Berbers. They were very likely descendants of the original Nilo-saharans, but they too may have been from Libya, or even Yemen. The first of the rulers to come to outside attention was a king called Zá-Kasí, who ruled in the beginning of the eleventh century A.D., and was already the fifteenth king of the dynasty of the Zá. He was said to be the first Muslim ruler of Songhai.[22] After him, each new king was given three symbols of office: a ring, a sword, and a Koran, symbols that were said to have "come down from Egypt."[23]

A usurper eventually arose, named Sonni Ali, whose emotional appeal was to the traditional paganism of his people, which he set against the "false cosmopolitanism" of Islam. Ali reigned for nearly thirty years, beginning in 1464. Early in his rule his cavalry began raiding even to the Malian heartland, several times entering Niani. This was the beginning of that city's long decline; archaeologists picking through the bones of Niani now can trace how the city began shrinking in the fifteenth century until it was finally abandoned a hundred or so years later. Ali destroyed the Mali empire by his ceaseless warfare, and reigned in its stead, from his capital at Gao.

Sonni Ali, wrote Ahmed Baba, was "the great tyrant and famous miscreant, but a king of the highest historical importance for Negroland, and changed the whole face of this part of Africa by prostrating the kingdom of Melle [Mali]."[24]

While the Mali kings were defending their heartland against the Songhai, the Tuareg of the desert saw their chance and overran Timbuktu, which they had themselves founded a few hundred years earlier but lost to the Malian rulers. This impudent occupation didn't last. Sonni Ali, once he had consolidated his power, wrested it from the nomads with immense slaughter in 1488.

Ali died in 1492 (drowned, ironically, in a torrent in the town of Germa, in the Fezzan), and his sons, who were with him on a military expedition, "took out his entrails and filled the insides with honey, in order that it might be preserved from putrefaction." This proved, at least to Barth's satisfaction, that unlike Ghana and Mali, which had been conquered from the north, Songhai was influenced mostly by the east, particularly Egypt, for this technique of preserving bodies for later burial or mummification was known in Egypt from antiquity.[25]

In 1493 power passed to one of Sonni Ali's former generals, who became known as Al-Hajj Mohammed A'skia, and who was both a Mande (the dominant tribe of Mali) and a Muslim. A'skia wrested power from one of Sonni Ali's sons after a desperate struggle, helped, no doubt, by one stroke of good luck: Another contender, Mohammed Bánkorí, was on his way to Gao with a formidable army to contest the throne when he passed by Timbuktu and was induced by the local religious leader to give up his quest for material gain in exchange for a life of contemplation and study, much to the astonishment and fury of his army, which had expected bloody battle followed by rich spoils.[26]

A'skia had, by all accounts, a notable reign.

It is of no small interest to a person who endeavors to take a comprehensive view of the various races of mankind, to observe how, during the time when the Portuguese, having taken possession of the whole western coast of Africa and founded their Indian empire, that at this same time a negro king in the interior of the continent not only extended his conquests from the center of Hausa almost to the borders of the Atlantic, and from the pagan country of Mossi, in 12 degrees northern latitude, as far as Tawat [Tuat] to the south of Morocco, but also governed the subjected tribes with justice and equity causing well-being and comfort to spring up every where within the borders of his extensive dominions, and introducing such of the institutions of Mohammedan civilization as he considered might be useful to his subjects.[27]

When A'skia undertook his hajj to Mecca, the most distinguished men of all the tribes under his command accompanied him on his great journey, with fifteen hundred armed soldiers, one thousand on foot and five hundred on horseback. He took with him three hundred thousand *mithqal*, but behaved so generously he was obliged to contract a loan for one hundred fifty thousand more. He founded a charitable institution in Mecca for the people of Tekrur, his birthplace. The great one abdicated in 1528.

Songhai's seizure of the Taghaza salt mines close to the Moroccan border upset the balance of trade and in 1591 provoked retaliation from the Sa'adi dynasty of Morocco. A force of four thousand soldiers, many of them Spanish recruits from Andalusia under the generalship of Judar Pasha, was dispatched by Sultan Abu Yusuf Ya'qub al-Mansur (self-described, in a fit of immodesty, as "The Golden One"). This army crossed the Sahara and sacked Gao, Timbuktu, and Djenne.

The four thousand invaders faced an army of up to one hundred thousand men, but in reality numbers meant little, for the Songhai military were no match for the better-armed Moroccans. At the time of the invasion, the Songhai kings were spending most of their military appropriations on horses bought from the merchants of the Maghreb. Songhai horsemen wore coats of mail, and occasionally brass helmets, but the Songhai army never mastered firearms (a cannon, a present from a Portuguese ambassador, was found in the capital's treasury rather than in its magazine, and was never deployed).[28]

The sultan's army, having looted the Niger cities of what gold they could find and thousands of slaves, hastily returned home to Morocco to defend their ruler against revolts provoked by his fiscal mismanagement. The few men he left behind, no matter how well armed, couldn't hold together an empire. Indeed, they were unable even to control the network of trade routes within West Africa that brought gold and other produce to the Niger cities. The main beneficiaries of the Moroccan conquest were therefore the nomadic Tuareg, who filled the vacuum the Moroccans left behind. In the years that followed they were able to demand tribute from the remaining garrisons.

None of this benefited the ancient city of Timbuktu. The constant warfare between the Moroccan invaders, raiding bands of Tuareg, and armies from the Bambara and Fulani tribes shook the government of the town, and it deteriorated into virtual anarchy.

With the fading of Songhai, the domination of the western Sudan by the black African kingdoms of Ghana, Mali, and Songhai, which had persisted for at least five centuries and in some places twice that, was at last ended. Only little kingdoms remained, most of them lost to history and with small claim to glory.

క⁊

THE EASTERNMOST and last of the empires of the southern Sahara was Kanem-Bornu, which flourished first east and then west of Lake Chad under the Sayf (Sef) dynasty, lasting in various forms from the ninth to the nineteenth century. Rumors of its great wealth were current in Renaissance Europe, and at its height it controlled a good deal of the trans-Saharan caravan traffic, as far as the Fezzan in Libya. It survives now only as an emirate and province of the Nigerian federation.

The empire began, or so the legends say, with the people called Sao. The village of Gaou, a small hillside town in the modern country of Chad, is supposed to be the ancient capital of the Sao people. The Sao no longer exist, but have left behind artistic traces in the form of terra-cotta heads and figures and decorative bronzes. If they were giants, as the legends say, there is no sign of it in Gaou; the gaily painted wattle-and-daub houses of the present inhabitants are, if anything, tiny rather than merely small.[29] The Sao were supposed to have originated in the Nile Valley; possibly they were related to the Nuer of the Sudan, and other Nilotic people.

Sometime around the ninth century, another people, salt traders, began moving into the area, perhaps also from the Nile Valley, perhaps via the Tibesti, intermarrying with the Sao, who eventually disappeared. These newcomers were Zaghawa, of whom nothing is known except that they were "a Sudanese people," which means they could have been from almost anywhere. In a short while a new people called the Kanuri emerged, founding the state of Kanem, east of Lake Chad. The first capital was at Njimi, northeast of the lake.

Kanem's original wealth derived from a settled and productive agriculture and from mining salt at Bilma, several hundred miles to the north. Its location made it a nodal point for trade among North Africa, the Nile Valley, and the sub-Sahara. By the eleventh century, massive Kanem caravans were crossing the Fezzan to Tripoli, mainly to exchange slaves for horses, which were needed for the cavalry contingents that formed the backbone of the empire's military power. Kanem had no gold of its own, and relied instead on "black gold," an ample supply of slaves seized from the leaderless and kingless tribes to the south and west. The trade in salt, copper, cotton, and slaves brought the Sayf kings to the attention of Muslim merchants, and by 1200 Islam was the dominant religion. Soon, Kanem not only traded with the Fezzan but owned it, and had set up diplomatic missions in Tunis and Cairo. The ruler of Kanem once sent a giraffe as a gift to the sultan of Tunis in a year not recorded, causing something of a sensation.[30]

In the late fourteenth century, when the Kanuri were driven out of Kanem by raiders from the dimly remembered Bulala tribe, a new capital called Ngazaragamu (or Birni Ngazaragamu) was built, and the new state called Bornu was created. The empire languished there, dormant, until it was roused again in the sixteenth century, pushing out the interlopers and retaking Kanem. Under the greatest of its kings, Idris Alawma (1571–1603), the empire, now given the double-barreled name of Kanem-Bornu, was expanded and consolidated; Alawma developed a cavalry force strong even by Kanem standards, complete with chain mail, quilted armor, and iron helmets, and had a small force of musketeers trained in Turkey. It was Kanem-Bornu, alone of the old empires, that later resisted the jihads by the nomads called Fulani in the eighteenth and nineteenth centuries. The capital was sacked at least once by Fulani holy warriors, and a new capital was created at Kukawa, but the state was not overthrown.

One of its more eminent rulers, el-Kanemi, was in power when the Clapperton-Oudney expedition reached Lake Chad, the first Europeans to do so. They knew little of Kanem and even less of its ruler, but he was not so ignorant, having diplomatic missions at many places in Islam. He knew, for example, about British rule in India.

௲

THE FINAL Saharan political force before the modern era was the Fulani theocracies. They were not empires, but rather a series of overlapping and intersecting fundamentalist statelets, short-lived usually but far-reaching in their effects, driven by a righteous militancy as uncompromising as it was violent. Jihad was their operating principle.

There is nothing inherent in desert life that encourages holy wars. It does seem clear from the evidence that the harsh Darwinian environment of the Sahara has nourished uncompromising politics and uncompromising religions, and that sometimes this is expressed in the fundamentalist religious outbursts that we know by the shorthand jihad. But equally often in the Sahara it has been expressed in an excessive individualism bordering on anarchy—the fissiparous Tuareg and especially Tubu societies are evidence in chief for this view. On many occasions the nomads of the deep desert embraced the more radical incarnations of Islam and that led them to jihad; on just as many others they resisted, even rejecting mainstream Islam for a very long time and adhering (as they still do) to practices that are eccentric, bordering on heresy. The Tuareg generally were and are devout enough, but they remain convinced that the One Way has several paths for the righteous to follow, a tolerant view of devotion that was the very opposite of fundamentalism.

Still, if jihad wasn't invented in the Sahara, it rooted there, as tenacious as an acacia, and in the centuries after Islam came to North Africa wars of religion occasionally boiled up in the desert, as ferocious and unpredictable as djinns.

In the southern Sahara, the foremost practitioners of these very focused wars—charismatic fundamentalists waging righteous war on the recalcitrant—were the people called Fulani, once nomadic pastoralists thinly spread over much of the southern Sahara, cousins to the Wolof of Senegal.[31]

The Fulani theocracies, which came into being in the chaos that followed the disintegration of the ancient empires, terrorized everyone in the Sahara in the seventeenth and eighteenth centuries. They even outdid the Tuareg in their ferocity and tenacity in battle. Their apparent predisposition for holy wars may partly be due to their own long tradition of Muslim asceticism, but also to their close connection with the disaffected of the desert. It was this formidable combination of fundamentalist clerics and an available corpus of armed and dangerous nomads that made the Fulani jihads so effective.

The precipitating event for the first of the most recent wave of Fulani jihads was the arrival in West Africa and the Sahel of a mystic and militant version of Islam, the *tariqah*, which held that the forced conversion of pagans was for the glory of God and an urgent duty on the faithful. The *tariqah* spread through Fulani society like a desert storm in the late seventeenth century, setting off a flurry of localized jihad movements that were only a taste of the agitation to come. In 1790, a Fulani holy man, Usman dan Fodio, who was born in the northern Hausa state of Gobir, now in Nigeria, began to preach sedition against the ruling class, whom he accused of being little more than pagans. Usman was an ascetic who had studied under Jibril Ibn Umar, a radical cleric of Agadez, by whom he was admitted to the Sufi order. Usman was also a scholar of eminence, an author of texts in Arabic and Fulbe that are still widely read in the region. He is now most famous for having founded a new political entity known as the Sokoto Caliphate, which brought the independent-minded Hausa states under one ruler for the first time in history.

For a time Usman's activities were tolerated by the Gobir sultan, but when his followers started to arm themselves, the ruler turned on Usman and issued a declaration still remembered in the region: Among other things it forbade the conversion of sons from the religion of their fathers, and proscribed the use of turbans and veils. More pointedly, it insisted that Usman alone, and not his followers, would be allowed to preach the Word of God. In 1804, apparently with some reluctance, Usman allowed himself to be declared *imam* of the new caliphate, and jihad was declared.

That the Gobir peasantry thought themselves grossly overtaxed by their overlords no doubt added to Usman's popularity, and the armies of the jihad swept through Hausaland and engulfed Adamwa; Nupé; Yorubaland to the south; the four old Hausa kingdoms of Kano, Katsina, Zaria, and Daura; and dozens of small tribal chiefdoms in what is now northern Cameroon and southern Chad. Only the armies of Kanem-Bornu, secure against Lake Chad and trained in battle against the warlike nomads of the central Saharan mountains, were able to resist.

The Hausa kingdom of Kano, founded in 999, had been converted to Islam in the 1340s, when scholars from Mali set up centers of learning there, many of which still exist. But in Usman's view the residents of Kano were backsliders and apostates and he overran the city in 1807. He also took Kano's commercial rival, Katsina, to the northeast by the Niger border. In the fourteenth and fifteenth centuries, Katsina had been so successful that it briefly replaced Timbuktu as the chief West African center of Islamic studies, and "[became] the chief city of this part of Negroland, as well in commercial and political importance as in other respects; for here that state of civilization seems to have reached its highest degree, and as the Hausa language here attained the greatest richness of form and the most refined pronunciation, so also the manners of Katsina were distinguished by superior politeness from those of the other towns of Hausa."[32] The libraries of Katsina were full of Hausa stories, written in *ajami*, a script derived from Arabic.

Usman took the town in 1812 after a long and bloody siege. "[He waged] an unrelenting war against the town for seven years before he at length reduced it by famine; and the distress in the town is said to have been so great that a dead vulture (impure food which nobody would touch in time of peace) sold for five hundred *kurdi*. Afterwards the town declined rapidly, and all the principal merchants migrated to Kano."[33] The only sign of the city's former glory now is at the festival of Durbar that ends Ramadan, when the nobles carefully unpack their ancient finery, get themselves up on horseback, and charge around the playing fields north of town, faded ghosts of the glorious cavalry of the elder days.

At the end of Usman's campaign in 1814, two major military encampments, Sokoto and Gwandu, emerged as the twin capitals of a new theocratic Fulani empire.

But Usman's purist version of Islam soon lost its way in the sophisticated atmosphere of commercial Kano. The commanders of the jihad, Usman's younger brother Abdullahi and his son Muhammed Bello, who were both eminent scholars as well as military commanders, had become the viceroys of this new empire, but their hearts were obviously not in the militant mullah business, and before Usman died in 1817 he was already warning of backsliding. After his death the standards once again declined, the people seduced by the softer life of the Hausa, and the Hausa tongue, forbidden by the theocrat, returned as the language of state. "The Fulbe [Fulani]," Barth reported soon afterward, "marry the handsome daughters of the subjugated tribe, but would not condescend to give their own daughters to the men of that tribe as wives. As far as I saw, their original type has been well preserved as yet, though by obtaining possession of wealth and comfort, their warlike character has been greatly impaired, and the Fulbe in Kano have become notorious for their cowardice throughout the whole of Negroland."[34]

Most visitors, however, found the Fulani very much up to reputation and Bello, particularly, an impressive figure. He received Hugh
Clapperton courteously, though clearly astonished at the visitor's notion that he had somehow "discovered" Bello's already venerable
realm, and said he would be happy to establish cordial relations with
England. He gave Clapperton a diplomatic letter to George IV, a
missive very much king-to-king in tone, and more than a little con-
descending about Clapperton himself ("Your majesty's servant came
to us, and we found him a very intelligent and wise man; representing in every respect your greatness, wisdom, dignity, clemency, and
penetration").[35] Clapperton confessed that he had been quite out of
his depth in discussing theology with the great man.

In 1818, another Fulani cleric called Ahmadu Hammadi Bubu, a
disciple of Usman's, launched a jihad of his own in what is now the
Macina region of Mali, aimed at the forcible conversion of the Bambara and Fulani pagans. The local Bambara chief called on his ruler,
the king of Segou, for help, but to no avail. Bambara was only a pale
imitation of its former glorious Malian self, and the Segou army was
crushed. A new theocratic state was set up that included Segou,
Djenne, and Timbuktu, and Ahmadu had the great mosque at
Djenne destroyed, for its opulence violated his fundamentalist view
of what an Islamic place of worship should be. The Tuareg were
summarily ejected from Timbuktu and seethed in the desert, waiting their chance for revenge.

Timbuktu itself, in the center of all this turmoil, struggled on. In
1844, the year Ahmadu died, the Tuareg drove out the invaders after a battle fought on the banks of the river, in which a large number of Fulani were slaughtered or drowned. This victory was of no
avail either, and "only plunged the distracted town into greater mis-
ery; for, owing to its peculiar situation on the border of a desert
tract, Timbuktu can not rely upon its own resources, but must always be dependent upon those who rule the more fertile tracts
higher up the river." The Fulani still controlled the hinterlands of
Timbuktu, and had only to forbid the exportation of corn "to reduce the inhabitants of Timbuktu to the utmost distress."[36] Ah-

madu's theocracy persisted a while longer, and he was succeeded in turn by his son and grandson, Ahmadu II and Ahmadu III. The third of the line was finally crushed by an army of another radical cleric, Al-Hajj Umar, in 1862.

In 1854 yet another jihad, the third of the nineteenth century, had been launched by this same Umar, who was seduced by the new puritanism of the Wahhabis in Arabia, still the dominant sect of Saudi Arabia. Umar, also known as Umar Tal, was a Tukulor leader who established his new polity between the upper Senegal and Niger Rivers. In modern terms, his realm covered parts of west and central Mali, upper Guinea, and eastern Senegal. It was he who named the region Macina, after an early emirate. Umar, whose most famous book was called *Book of the Spears of the Party of God*, preached meditation, self-denial, and blind obedience to rulers, meaning mostly himself. The *griots* of Senegal still somewhat sacrilegiously compare his life to that of the Prophet himself, glorifying his victories and citing the thousands he killed and sold into slavery as proof of the divine character of his mission. Some of the earlier jihads had used Islam more as a mobilizing force than as a goal in itself, but Umar's was different. He forbade dancing and the use of tobacco and alcohol, banished charms, and prohibited pagan ceremony and the worship of idols; in the areas under his control he appointed Muslim scholars to enforce *Shari'a*, Islamic religious law, even among non-Muslims.

His earlier career had been scholarly and contemplative. So widely admired was he as a learned man that the eminent Muhammed Bello, by then the emir of Sokoto in Nigeria, offered him his daughter Maryam in marriage. He settled for a while in Cairo, and on a visit to Jerusalem he succeeded in curing a son of Ibrahim Pasha, viceroy of Egypt, of an unspecified ailment, which began his reputation as a magical healer who was the confidant of djinns. Partly as a result of this incident, he was appointed the West African caliph of a relatively new activist brotherhood, formed a community of his own, and in 1852 "came into conflict," as the historians put it, with nearby Bambara chiefs. This was perhaps not so surprising: To prove the sincerity of his mission and the purity of his zeal, he once put to death three hundred Bambaran hostages, thereby developing a parallel reputation for cruelty as well as scholarship. A jihad was launched northward through the gold-bearing valleys across the upper Senegal, then east down the river toward Gobir, where he was eventually repulsed. After 1859 he sought to enlist the Fulani of Macina in taking on the Bambara kingdom of Segou, but they refused. He conquered Segou anyway, and continued down the Niger until he was able to assert control over Timbuktu in 1862. This, too, was short-lived. The old established Muslim towns and Fulani communities regarded Umar's people as upstarts, considering his activities less a jihad than a civil war, and Umar's army was ejected from Timbuktu with great slaughter. In the battle that followed, his forces were defeated by an unlikely alliance of Tuareg, Moors, and dissident Fulani. He took refuge in a cave, but its entrance was detonated by a massive bomb and he was killed. It was 1864.[37]

∽

MOST OF THE FULANI of Senegal, Mali, Chad, and Nigeria have settled down now, their nomadic ways forgotten, their holy wars barely remembered (though the embers are still alive, and there have been recent reports of a rising militancy in the northern Hausa towns). In Chad and Nigeria they intermarried with other tribes, becoming farmers or traders; in Cameroon they have become a modern political force. Only in the southern Sahara, in a rough triangle from Agadez to In'gal and Aderbissinat, do the nomadic and pastoralist Fulani remain, fiercely attached to their herds of zebu cattle, independent, scornful of settled ways, contemptuous of people who make their living by making things. These people are the only Fulani to have resisted Islam; they took no part in the infamous Fulani jihads. They call themselves the Wodaabe, people of the taboo (that is, those who adhere to the old ways). The Islamicized city folk, on the other hand, refer to them as Bororo—"people who live in the bush and don't wash."

In August and September the rains briefly come to In'gal, west of

Galloping camels at the cure salée at In'gal. (United States Peace Corps)

Agadez, and leach to the surface a quantity of subterranean salt; and each year thousands of Tuareg and Fulani herdsmen make their way to the oasis for the *cure salée*, the salt cure. Their beasts eat the fresh salty grass, while the men and women celebrate with camel races, dancing, singing, feasting, and rites of seduction. One of the highlights of the festival is the *gerewol*, a Wodaabe ceremonial that includes, among other things, a male beauty contest that lasts for hours and involves long bouts of preconcert preening, dancing, and face-pulling, for the benefit of the female *sélectrices*, or adjudicators. Wodaabe men are somewhat obsessed with their own physical beauty, even—it is rumored—to the extent of urging their wives to sleep with a more attractive man in order to conceive a more attractive child.

The host of the annual *cure salée* is the sultan of the Aïr. It is, still, one of the grand festivals of Old Africa, and has been thus for more than a millennium, since the first nomads wandered over the dunes, refugees from those long-ago northern invasions, marking out the first routes through the otherwise trackless wastelands. The Sahara has preserved many grim traditions, but there are also many that are less melancholy, and that the joyous *cure salée* has persisted into modern times is a triumphant affirmation of the human ability to adapt to the harshest of environments.

CHAPTER TEN

❧

Route Maps

ALTHOUGH THE WHOLE (by then) ramshackle edifice of Saharan trade essentially collapsed in the late nineteenth century with the theoretical ending of slavery and the introduction of Western ways, and then suffered another blow with the introduction of reliable diesel engines, for millennia before that there was a network of caravan routes across the desert and a substantial traffic in commodities and human beings, as the traders of the Mediterranean and the Middle East did business with the rich and sophisticated empires of the ancient Sahel.

For more centuries than records exist, travelers from the *Bilad as Sudan,* the Land of the Blacks, have been heading out into the Great Emptiness on their perilous journeys, from the trading centers of the Sahel, from Kano or Bornu or Bilma, from Agadez or Gao or Timbuktu or Koumbi Saleh. Some of them made for Cairo and Leptis Magna, others for the Fezzan and Tripoli, or Algiers, or Fez or Zagora and the perfumed gardens of Marrakech, or perhaps Mogador (now Essaouira), on the Moroccan coast. At the same time merchants from the north—most from the African littoral but others from Arabia and Mesopotamia—would take their trade goods to sell in the marketplaces of the Sahel.

Caravan routes have always depended, obviously enough, on the desired destination and on the available water. Egypt was for millennia the nodal point, the place from which trade was done—from the Egyptian ports of Herakleion and Menouthis you could reach Mesopotamia, the Ottoman redoubts, Rome, Carthage, and Tripolitania. Egyptians traveled southeast to the Indian Ocean and the Horn of Africa, and thus to the Land of Zanj and across to Asia. And of course they went into the desert. For at least a millennium before the Christian era, there were trading cultures across the Great Thirstland, all the way across to the Atlantic, that drew merchants hungry for profit.

Four primary land routes made their way from Egypt—at first from Memphis and Thebes, and later from Cairo—to the interior of Africa. Two plunged southward to Darfur in western Sudan and two headed generally westward to the Fezzan province of modern Libya and to Tripolitania.

One of the southern routes went along the Nile, through Nubia, Kush, and Meroë and thence to the Sahel. The other, more direct, was a route where the oases were few and the going grim, even for the Sahara: west of the Nile along the *darb al arbain*, the "road of the forty [days]," also known in ancient times as the Slave Route, through the Kharga oasis, the Selima oasis, and El-Fasher and thence to Lake Chad and central Africa. The third route passed through the oases of Kebir in southwestern Egypt and Al-Kufrah in eastern Libya to the Fezzan town of Zouila (another nodal point for travel south to Bornu or north to Tripolitania, though Murzuq later supplanted Zouila in importance). The fourth headed west along the coast, then angled southwest to Siwa on the edge of the Qattara Depression, and thence farther southwest to Zouila/Murzuq.[1]

As old as Egypt's routes was the Garamantian "Chariot Route" from the Fezzan southwest across the desert, via Djanet (near Ghat), the Ahaggar and Adrar des Iforhas Mountains to Gao, on the Niger

River in southern Mali. This could have been how the ancient Egyptians reached the goldfields of Old Ghana. It is called "chariot route" because in caves at many places along the way, from the Fezzan to Gao, there are rock paintings depicting the Garamantian four-horse chariots.

West of the Tibesti Mountains a skein of routes threaded from oasis to oasis. They started at Tripoli, Tunis, and Algiers along the coast, Fez and Sijilmasa in Morocco, Ouargla in Algeria, and Murzuq in Libya, heading for the Kanem-Bornu towns around Lake Chad; for the Hausa trading cities of Kano, Sokoto, and Katsina (in modern Nigeria); for Gao and Timbuktu; for Djenne and Niani, all of them in modern Mali; and for Koumbi Saleh, the capital of Old Ghana, now in Mauritania—anywhere gold was to be found, and ivory, lion skins, and slaves. Not all of them were used all the time. Routes were sometimes abandoned, either because the wells dried up or because an area became embroiled in warfare, as happened in the far west, or simply because some other route was thought to be easier.

Caravans from Kanem-Bornu on Lake Chad or the Hausa trading towns generally passed through Agadez or through Bilma (and occasionally both). The easiest crossing, easy enough even for pack-horses until recent centuries, passed north through Agadez and the Aïr massif, thence through the eastern reaches of the Ahaggar and the Tassili n'Ajjer to Ghat, then to Ghadamès and so to Tripoli, but there were many other subroutes and alternatives. One popular alternative from Agadez was to join the lateral (eastbound) branch to Bilma, which merged with the major northbound route from Lake Chad at the Bilma salt mines. From Bilma south there was a virtual highway across the Erg of Bilma to Bornu, reaching Lake Chad at its northwest corner. North of Bilma caravans would have passed the Djado Plateau, the Tummo Mountains, Gatrun, and Murzuq. Apart from the *darb al arbain* and the Chariot Route to Gao, this was perhaps the oldest route to and from the north. It was certainly well established by the ninth century.

In the glory days of the Sahelian empires of Ghana and then of

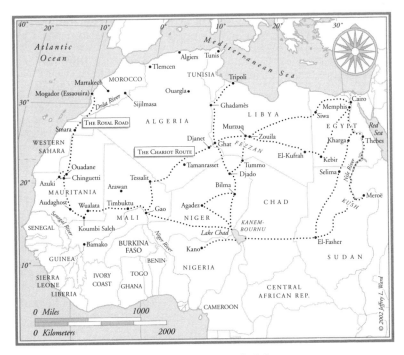

Ancient caravan routes in the Sahara.

Mali, between the eighth and the fourteenth centuries, traders from the western Mediterranean seeking gold preferred what came to be called the Royal Road for reasons now obscure—possibly it was because of the sheer volume of gold that was carried northward to the burgeoning Moroccan trading cities. The key destination was Koumbi Saleh, which controlled the richest goldfields; the nearby town called Chinguetti was the main victualing point. In medieval times caravans, some of them massive, left from Chinguetti on an almost prescribed schedule laden with Ghanaian gold, heading for Mogador (now Essaouira in Morocco). The caravans passed through Ouadane in the Adrar Plateau region, making a leisurely curve paralleling the Atlantic coast.

From Koumbi Saleh and Chinguetti there was also regular traffic eastward through Walata to the Niger River towns of Timbuktu and Gao, and since there was a well-traveled route from Gao to the Hausa towns and to Lake Chad, this had the effect of extending the

Royal Road all the way eastward across the Sahel. In one sense, therefore, this Royal Road could also be described as a Great Circle Route, because from Lake Chad there was regular traffic to Egypt. It is also possible that this route is older than the Christian era, and the Pharaoh's minions could just as easily have come this way looking for gold, in the Elder Days.

It was a curiosity of this network of "highways" that few of the northern termini of the caravan routes were actually on the coast. Marrakech, Fez, Sijilmasa, Tlemcen, Ouargla, and Ghadamès were all inland towns. The reason was simple enough: to keep the commerce, and therefore the profits, out of the hands of Christians, who traded up and down the coast in vessels from European ports.[2]

Sijilmasa, which dominated the Tafilalt oasis in southeast Morocco (near modern Rissani), was such a town. Sijilmasa was civilized, urbane, cosmopolitan, with lush gardens and gracious houses, built because the city was an important destination for slaves from the south and for gold from Ghana (Sijilmasa's mint produced coinage for countries all around the Maghreb, even including dinars for the Umayyads in Spain, beginning early in the tenth century). Already by the ninth century the town had several hundred thousand inhabitants, and was one of the major political and cultural capitals of the Maghreb. It was not just a commodities market, but a stock market too. Ibn Battuta noted in 1340 that a certain family of brothers, one of them resident in Sijilmasa, two in unnamed places in the Sudan (the south), and two in Tlemcen, were kept abreast of current prices and trend lines by the brother in Sijilmasa, where prices were set. Ibn Battuta seemed to approve of the town, which he said was "a very beautiful place, with an abundance of dates."[3] The merchants at Sijilmasa also had a hand in the salt trade, whose customers were generally in the south and in the Sahel; most of the salt mined at Taghaza, some twenty days down the road toward Timbuktu, was controlled by Sijilmasa trading houses.

The city had, like many Saharan towns, a turbulent history. It was founded in 757 by Kharijite Muslim schismatics, just one hundred years after the Prophet's successors struggled to assert leadership over all Islam. For 200 years, the Kharijites built monuments, organized the water resources of the oasis to create a rich agricultural base, and accumulated great wealth through trade across the Sahara with Old Ghana. Control of the city was fiercely disputed by a succession of outsiders, first the Fatimids of Ifriqiya (modern Tunisia) and then the Umayyads of Cordoba in southern Spain; these two groups alternately controlled the city in the second half of the tenth century. The Arab author Ibn Hawqal, writing late in that century, maintained that half the tax revenues of the Fatimids came from Sijilmasa. (In the last decade thirty-two gold coins from Sijilmasa were unearthed in Aqaba, Jordan.) The city was overrun by the Almoravids in 1055, sacked by the Zayyanid dynasty of Tlemcen in 1235, destroyed again in 1363. Internal feuding damaged its reputation as a safe haven for commerce, and by the time Leo Africanus arrived in the early years of the sixteenth century, it was already in substantial decay. Nevertheless, it was rebuilt by Maulay Ismail (1672–1727), and ruined again in 1818 by Tuareg from Ait Atta. That was essentially the end. Now there is nothing left: The desert and the weather have finished the work human dissension began.

∽

SIJILMASA was eminent but far from alone as a northern entrepôt. Others were to be found in the northern provinces of Algeria, serving as the gateways to the Algerian Sahara—these were generally farther into the desert, more rough and ready, with a tougher, more raffish reputation. Of the cluster of such towns—El-Goléa, Ouargla, Ghardaia, Touggourt—Ouargla was for centuries their chief.

The town has a spectacular setting, an oasis of palms in a massive dune of white sand almost surrounded by jagged cliffs. The perimeter wall is penetrated by six gates; inside, there is an arcaded marketplace, bordered by date-palm groves and fruit and vegetable gardens irrigated by numerous wells tapped from a deep aquifer.[4] Today it is an oil town, rough and rowdy, and at night it glows bright orange from the wellhead burn-off. Still, it is one of the oldest settlements in the Sahara, founded by the Ibadiyah, or Mozabites, a Muslim heretical sect, in the tenth century. Only melancholy ruins of that period remain, but it is still possible to wander among the rubble and ponder the swirling schisms and doctrinal quarrels that drive the pioneers into the desert to form their community of brothers.

After only a hundred years in their desert fastness the heretics who founded Ouargla fled northwest to nearby Ghardaia, chased out by forces bent on holy war, and the abandoned Ouargla site was settled by nomadic Berbers, Tuareg, and black Africans from western Sudan and the Sahel, many of them outport traders of the Hausa kings. For the next five hundred years the town maintained a somnolent independence, dozing in the desert heat, animated only by the arrival of trading caravans from Zinder and Kano. It called itself, without much conviction, the Oasis of Sultans, and for a while it was the "puffed-up capital of a microscopic kingdom."[5] The Turks captured it briefly, but found it of little use, and drifted away to more important conquests, but not before perpetrating their own small versions of hell: "Many M'Zab [Mozabites] inhabit the city, but none are found in the Beni-Braham quarter, all of those who lived there having been massacred in one night in 1652."[6]

Ouargla remained autonomous under its Berber chieftains until the French scooped it up with the rest of Algeria in 1872. But the French hold was tenuous, and the surrounding tribes continued to be dangerous (as, indeed, they still are, for Ouargla needs continual policing by the secular rulers of modern Algeria faced with Islamicist uprisings).

The Flatters expedition arrived in Ouargla on February 25, 1880. "What a magic spectacle," wrote Captain Frédéric Bernard, traveling with the expedition. "It is an immense plain of white sand, dazzling beneath the rays of a fiery sun. A chain of strangely jagged cliffs close it in on all sides, forming a reddish backdrop for a grandiose half-circle of 800,000 palm trees." Much of the town, he reported, was in ruins. Most of the extant houses were one-story affairs. Small triangular windows punctuated the whitewashed walls, seemingly at random. In the middle of a tortuous labyrinth of streets sat a small fort,

the *ksar*. Behind its high walls, square towers, and a moat full of stagnant water, an animated market opened each morning at dawn and
continued until it became too hot to trade. Flies coagulated on the
raw meat. The place reeked of pestilence. Perhaps it was to cover
these odors that many oasis dwellers stuffed scented things in one
nostril—flowers, an orange peel, an onion.[7]

                                    ℰℐ

TO OUTSIDERS, perhaps the most exotic cities of Saharan antiquity are those that served as the southern termini of these same
caravan routes: Koumbi Saleh, Timbuktu, Gao, Agadez, and
(though not in the desert, nonetheless connected, for it was a great
trading city) Kano in northern Nigeria.

The most westerly of these cities was Koumbi Saleh, Old Ghana's
capital, which is about thirty miles or so inside the southern border
of modern Mauritania. Nothing is left of it now except a few unim-
pressive ruins and the camps of resident archaeologists in a landscape that is bleak and featureless. Already several hundred years old
when the first Arabs arrived in the seventh century, by the middle of
the eleventh century Koumbi Saleh was divided into two towns, a
stone-built one inhabited by the Muslim traders and a mud-built
one of the locals, in which the king had his walled palace. Their centers were five miles apart, and the considerable population was supported by the produce of surrounding farms, which were irrigated
from wells. The court displayed "many signs of power, and the king
had under him a considerable number of satellite rulers"; he was
said to be an adept of the African religions.[8] Judging from the archaeological evidence, the capital contained better than twenty
thousand people.

Several other towns along the Royal Road prospered on the trade
that Koumbi Saleh made possible. Chinguetti, in later centuries the
"hub" of the traffic of the western desert, and the main staging post
for caravans, dates back to the thirteenth century, as do some of its
existing houses and mosques. It was once, as one of Islam's holiest
places, called "the Seventh Mecca," and there are still more than a

thousand ancient manuscripts in the town's dank and ill-lit library. Alas, an ocean of sand is bearing down on the city, and the oasis is split in half by ever-increasing dunes, some of them already more than two hundred feet high. In the hinterlands of Chinguetti, farther up the Royal Road is Audaghost, now only a massively picturesque ruin but once the center of the Almoravid empire at the close of the first millennium and the stronghold from which the warrior monks launched their fiery crusade. Nearby is Ouadane, a crumbling town of rock within a landscape of massive boulders and cliffs, which was founded in 1147 by Berbers and has been stubbornly clinging to life since, the waves of conquest and jihad leaving it untouched, but also undeveloped.

After the tribal confederations fell apart in factional and religious animosity in the eleventh century, Koumbi Saleh was abandoned; and after the successor empire of Mali was itself overrun by the Songhai in the mid–fifteenth century, the western Sahara deteriorated into an anarchy remarkable even by the standards of desert nomads. No chieftain governed, no prelate held sway; caravan traffic virtually ceased for centuries as the Western Desert nomads preyed upon any unwary traveler, seemingly for the sheer anarchic thrill of falling on an enemy and putting the men and their possessions to the sword. It wasn't until the coming of the French in the 1870s that it once again became safe for caravans to set out from Chinguetti for the north.

One town on the Royal Road is a great curiosity, a "historic" town that is either a monument to folly or one man's failed attempt to elevate his people to matters spiritual and aesthetic. Smara, or Asmara, or Es-Semara, the Forbidden City, was built in the Sequiet El-Hamra lowlands of Western Sahara over a period of years in the 1830s, founded on a crossroads in the middle of fractious and warlike tribes of Moors, on a caravan route all but abandoned for being much too hazardous for any but the best-armed and -equipped soldiery, put together out of nothing by the Sheikh Ma' el-Aïnin, who had been to Marrakech and fallen in love with its gardens and nearperfect architecture. He was determined to reproduce this harmonious expression of God's will among the godforsaken people of the remote desert over whom he had the misfortune to rule, the bandits of the Anti Atlas to the Rio de Oro.

In the middle of the desert, el-Aïnin caused to appear two kasbahs, a massive mosque, fountains, gardens, houses inlaid with cool mosaics in the turquoises and creams of the Almohads, all set down to astound the wandering tribes by something miraculous, a miragecity glowing golden under the sun, a city-on-a-pedestal, face to the silent desert. Fragments of the city still existed as late as the 1930s, but there is nothing left now but a ruined mosque.

ço

TIMBUKTU was never supposed to be a town, only a market, or so the story is told in Arawan, which was a town first and whose residents needed a market closer to the Niger, the Great River. The original market was presided over by an old woman of fierce and chastising ways, hence *Tin' Buktu* in Tamashek, Place of the Old Woman. A camel market first, then a general market, then a market town, then a great emporium, Timbuktu became a seat of learning, home to one hundred thousand prosperous citizens.

Fabled Timbuktu! Its university was founded seven hundred years ago, and had more than twenty thousand students in its glory days; it is still operating, though shrunken now in stature, funding, and real estate. One of the scholars of Timbuktu, Ahmed Baba, author of *A History of Songhai*, had a library of sixteen hundred books, one of the glories of Timbuktu's scholarly and pious community, and one of the most substantial in medieval Islam. "Here," wrote Leo Africanus in 1510, "are great store of doctors, judges, priests, and other learned men, that are bountifully maintained at the king's cost. And hither are brought diverse manuscripts or written books out of Barbary, which are sold for more money than any other merchandise."[9] He also described great groves of trees, even forests, nibbled on by wandering elephants.

The arts flourished; jewelry of rare delicacy and great age has been found in ruins in the neighborhood. The country became wealthy, so wealthy that the kings were profligate with money, as though it were in inexhaustible supply, and the city's reputation, inflated beyond reason, was such that across the desert and in Europe it became a metaphor for remoteness and exoticism. In the late thirteenth century, the Malian king Mansa Musa had built a tower for the mosque Djingereyber, and a royal palace, the Madugu; the mosque still stands, though the palace is long gone. Indeed, there are three massive mud-built mosques in Timbuktu, to which the faithful have come to pray since 1340, and they still look out over this exotic city, slowly decaying as the desert sand expands inexorably southward.

When Ibn Battuta visited in 1353, he found it the focal point of the Saharan trade. Merchants from Wadan, Tuat, Ghadamès, Augila, and the cities of Morocco gathered there to buy gold and slaves in exchange for the Saharan salt of Taghaza and for North African cloth and horses. In 1591 al-Mansur's Moroccan raiders took Timbuktu hoping to capture the gold trade and instead began its gradual decay. They may have been emissaries from a high culture, but they killed or exiled most of the scholars, equating learning with disaffection, as conquerors are wont to do. Thereafter the city was repeatedly besieged and sacked by a rolling roster of enemies—the Bambara, the Fulani, and the Tuareg—until the French took it in 1893 and restored a semblance of order.

Estimates for Timbuktu's population in the eighteenth and nineteenth centuries vary from fifteen thousand to more than fifty thousand. Some of the confusion, doubtless, was caused by the fact that arriving caravans were obliged to stay in the town when the Niger and its tributaries swelled during the rainy season and overflowed the plains, whereupon it became impossible to move about, and they built temporary houses for themselves. Ten or even fifteen thousand inhabitants were thus added to the town in a month; but when the water subsided, they dispersed.

René Caillié was not impressed when he first visited the city in the early part of the nineteenth century. In European imagination, the metropolis of Timbuktu rather more resembled an opium-inspired fantasy than a real city; tales of its spires and minarets, its mosques and centers of learning, seemed to rival those of Byzantium and Rome. By then the reality was more mundane. What Caillié saw was a typical desert town, low-built of mud, crumbling, its inhabitants scratching a living on the edge of the Great Emptiness, the roofs and minarets of gold conspicuous by their absence, its libraries meager and its countinghouses virtually empty. It was shabby, a metropolis only of mud, and in the precarious position of being entirely dependent on Tuareg goodwill. But his scathing reports were simply disbelieved in Europe, which preferred the legends to Caillié's first-hand recounting, and he was branded a charlatan.

There are now no forests and fewer trees than there used to be, as the desert closes in. Only a few scraggly shrubs are left, rapidly being cut down for firewood. In the old days, the Tuareg would never have cut down trees; they needed them for shade when they grazed their stock, and in the wadis the trees grew unmolested. Tuareg settled in town don't need shade, they need fuel. Families share ovens to conserve wood, but still the trees disappear.

Today, Timbuktu is a melancholy, crumbling ruin with fewer than twenty thousand people calling it home, unable to cope with the desert's inexorable advance. UNESCO has declared the city a World Heritage Site, a part of the cultural patrimony of the human species and therefore worth preserving, but has given the community no money for preservation. Small salt caravans coming south from Taoudeni still arrive in winter, but there is no gold to offer in exchange, and trans-Saharan commerce no longer exists. Timbuktu will, very likely, not last much longer. It will become just another ghost town, another place abandoned to the drifting sand, another desiccated reminder of a once-glorious past, a weary place with a violent and extraordinary history, a part of the Sahara's long, long story.

ço

EAST OF TIMBUKTU is Gao, the Songhai capital on what is called the Niger Bend. Gao was, and is, one of the most frequented hubs of Saharan traffic. From Gao the caravans would head north-

Timbuktu today. (Marq de Villiers)

ward, through Tadmekka in the wildly beautiful Adrar des Iforhas Mountains, to Tessalit, but from there the route branched in several directions, depending on the final destination—Sijilmasa and Fez or Tlemcen, near Oran on the Mediterranean coast, or to El-Goléa and Ouargla and so to Algiers or Tunis, or to Egypt itself.

Gao, originally called Kawkaw or Ga-gao, is older than Timbuktu, and was first mentioned in 872 by the Arab writer Al-Yaqubi, who merely noted that it was a great kingdom, the greatest he knew below the desert. It was probably founded by Nilosaharan fishermen sometime in the seventh century.

Gao was annexed by the Songhai in the eleventh century, and Songhai rule lasted until 1591, when al-Mansur's troops poured across the desert in search of gold and captured both Gao and Timbuktu (a mission fiercely opposed by his courtiers, who pointed out the uncertain nature of the destination, the inhospitable terrain over which he must pass, and the "perils and terrors" of the desert, by which they meant the Tuareg). The stories say al-Mansur dispatched only four or five thousand men, but his son, when he succeeded him, aghast at the empty treasury, said "23,000 men had perished"[10] in the escapade, an exaggeration no doubt aimed at persuading the population that taxes must perforce go up. Despite the nay-saying at home, Mansur's invasion was enough to put an end to the Songhai kingdom.

The town was wrecked several times over the centuries, but remains an important archaeological center (the tombs of the A'skias, Songhai's rulers, are in the town) and a still-important transportation hub. A road passable by four-wheel-drive vehicles now reaches from Gao into the northern Malian desert, but camel caravans still assemble in the market, beside the crumbling little Hotel l'Atlantide, with its "bar" and crates of aging Fanta, and wander north through the shanties of some no-longer-nomadic Tuareg and into the dunes, this close to town smothering in a depressing film of torn plastic bags discarded by water sellers. Piles of garbage lie in the lee of dunes, carelessly heaped up.

The road is one of the most beautiful anywhere in the Sahara. Outside Gao the water is still bountiful from the Niger floodplains, and the camels that traverse it have plenty of provender. This is the valley of Tilemsi, threading its way through hauntingly beautiful mountains. To the west the stark red Jebel Timétrine, to the east the golden rocks of the Adrars—Adrar Hebjane, Adrar Timajjalelene, Adrar Tirarar, a landscape clean and potent.

Tessalit, in northeastern Mali, is the last town of the Adrars. In classical times, the caravans paused here, usually for a week or more. Those traveling north waited to gather their strength, because ahead lay the Tanezrouft, and it would be a dozen terrible days before reaching the first well. The Tanezrouft lacks everything: There is neither water, nor vegetation, nor any landmarks, and the place is still uninhabited, except by roving bands of Tuareg. Caravans used to push through it with all haste, hoping against hope that no calamity would strike them. Groaning trucks make the crossing now, but with no less trepidation.

For those heading south, Tessalit seemed like paradise; many a traveler arrived in town in a delirium of thirst, their *guerbas* dry, their camels stumbling, their throats swollen and raw from sand. Tessalit's reputation is benign; it is said to be one of the desert's mysteries that somehow the moochers and layabouts who are thick on the ground elsewhere have passed the town by—here, after all, was a perfect opportunity for extortion, because people crazed with thirst would give everything they owned for a draft of water. Perhaps the thought of the dreaded djinn of the Tanezrouft kept the venal away; or perhaps contemplating the awful emptiness intimidated lesser spirits. Whatever the reason, the people of Tessalit had an apparently well-deserved reputation for generosity, and travelers stumbling into the marketplace could often find water waiting, or camel's milk at knockdown prices, or even a beer, the Malians being rather less than devout in such matters.

☙

AGADEZ, the capital of the Aïr region in Niger, was a dusty village in antiquity, but grew rapidly in the twelfth century and then again in the fifteenth, when it became the seat of a sultanate of the Kel-Oui Tuareg. Heinrich Barth, as so often, was the first European to visit the town. "For what can be more interesting than a considerable town, said to have been once as large as Tunis, situated in the midst of lawless tribes, on the border of the desert and the fertile tracts of an almost unknown continent, established there from ancient times, and protected as a rendezvous for commerce between nations of the most different character, and having the most various wants?"[11]

By the time Barth got there, however, the city was already beginning its decline—the streets and markets were almost empty, "which left upon me an impression of a deserted place of bygone times, for even in the most central and important quarters of the town most of the dwelling places were in ruins. Some meat was lying ready for sale, and a bullock was tied to a stake, while numbers of large vultures, distinguished by their long naked neck of a reddish color and their dirty-gray plumage, were sitting on the pinnacles of the crumbling walls, ready to pounce upon the offal." The town was built on a flat plain, "interrupted only by hills of rubbish, deposited there by the carelessness of the people." The people were not true Tuareg, and wore their hair long "in a way which is an abomination to the Tawarek,"[12] speaking a curious mixture of Berber and Songhai.

In the intervening centuries, however, Agadez had become a major metropolis of the central desert, no longer just a key way-station on the cross-Saharan routes but a destination in its own right. There were several significant mosques, and the *medina*, the scholarly community, attracted the eminent of Islam from as far away as Arabia and Marrakech. Agadez was the home of one of the oldest schools of Arabic in Africa—the tutorials it still runs have been offered, unbroken, since the Word of the Prophet first came to the city, somewhere in or before the twelfth century. At the time of the European Renaissance, scholars from Agadez were already rendering Fulani and Hausa into written languages, using an Arabic script, and translating the Koran into many of the vernacular languages of the Sahel. The town's wealth was still primarily in trade, especially slaves and the gold hauled up on caravans from Gao, but it became a center of manufacturing too, and weapons and jewelry from Agadez were prized all over the desert—as, indeed, they still are. The sultan's palace, which stands in the center of Agadez, a seat of power as it has been for five centuries, housed a bureaucracy that governed all of the Aïr Mountains, controlled the trade routes to Gao and the south, governed access to the Bilma salt mines (and thus exerted a controlling interest over another of the cross-Saharan trade routes), and, as well, fielded armies that occasionally made common cause with the Tuareg rulers in the Ahaggar.

Like many of the other Saharan cities, modern Agadez is clay-

A street in Agadez. (Marq de Villiers)

built and sand-buried, the dun color of the surrounding dunes. It is also, like many other modern Saharan towns, a curious mixture of ancient trades and new ones (skilled camera repair people cater not to the rudimentary tourist trade but to the Tuareg's curious fascination, in defiance of Muslim custom, with photographs of themselves). The filmmaker Bernardo Bertolucci shot *The Sheltering Sky* partly in Agadez, and if you are so inclined you can poke about "the Baker's house" in which Debra Winger languidly succumbed to her Berber lover, provided you offer a small consideration to the old woman who lives next door and has custody of a key.

∽

UNLIKE TIMBUKTU AND AGADEZ, the third great city of the Sahel, Kano, has never lost its commercial importance. Perhaps this is because it is in Nigeria, an African powerhouse, but perhaps also the Hausa, an energetic people, have retained their entrepreneurial instincts. They were the greatest trading culture of Old Africa; Hausa traders could be found in every oasis town of any consequence. It was founded, according to tradition, in the year 999, and by 1400 it was already the most muscular city in this muscular culture, containing almost one hundred thousand people, its walls eleven miles in circumference, pierced by the Thirteen Gates of local renown; its black and brown and white humanity ebbing and flowing; its markets crammed with vendors and traders and sharp dealers in dyestuffs, textiles, leather work, nuts and dates, salt, and slaves. Visitors could hear a dozen languages in a hundred yards—Tamashek, Arabic, Hausa, Bambara, Mossi, Peul, Diawara, Wolof. Caravans set out from Kano every week for Lake Chad, Agadez, and Gao and thence to the coast—Kano was not in the desert, but it was very much of the desert, a key destination for traders and merchants from a dozen countries, including Egypt and old Mesopotamia.

The other major towns of the Hausa—Katsina and Daura—were for most of history subordinate to the commercial powerhouse of Kano. This was not to say they were unimportant—Katsina was a seat of learning and scholarship, and Daura, while a bit of a backwater, was at least symbolically important. It straddles the caravan route from Agadez to Kano, and was the spiritual home of the Hausa people, venerated for its legendary role in the Hausa beginnings. It was founded by a queen, the *magajiva* Daura, sometime in the ninth century, and was ruled thereafter by women for some hundreds of years (the senior princess in the household of the Emir of Daura even now holds the title *magajiva*). In the declining years of the queens, it is said, the Bayajida, a son of the King of Baghdad, killed Sarki the fetish serpent at the town's well and married the reigning queen. Their six grandsons and a son of Bayajida's other wife, a princess of Bornu to the northeast, became the Seven Rulers of the Hausa *Bakwai*, the seven true Hausa kingdoms. Sarki's well is still there, and women draw water from it every day for the daily chores of Hausa life.

In 1824, when Hugh Clapperton first reached Kano, the city was known to Europeans by name only, but Kano certainly knew of Europe: The city still had thirty to forty thousand inhabitants, more than half of them slaves, and the markets sold calicos and cotton prints from Manchester, French silks and sugar, beads from Venice and Trieste, sword blades from Solingen, and all manner of imported goods. Kano was well used to foreigners, many of them much more eminent than an itinerant Englishman. Clapperton was disappointed that, although he dressed in all his naval finery for a ceremonial arrival, the town paid no attention to his splendor or his person. He poked about, buying himself an English-made cotton umbrella in the market and observing sardonically that the Kano butchers were every bit as wily as their English counterparts ("for they make a few slashes to show the fat, blow up meat, and sometimes even stick a little sheep's wool on a leg of goat").[13]

Kano's Kurmi market is still there, still a center for craft work and manufacturing, including gold, silver, and bronze; fabrics; and leather work. Outside the market's gate on Kofar Mata road are the Kano dye pits, which have been there for eight centuries and more. You can still find men on that same open terrace with their hands and arms stained indigo, dipping fabrics into the vats, just as they have done for so very long. The Blue Men of the desert, the Tuareg, when they are not wearing Chinese synthetics, are almost certainly using *tagelmousts* made from Kano cottons as protection against the scouring Saharan sand.

∾

THE TRANS-SAHARAN ROUTES are now many fewer than they were. Egyptians still go to Siwa, and into their own Western Desert—there are excellent highways along the coast to Libya, down the Nile to Abu Simbel near the Sudanese border and to Farafra and El-Dakhla oases—but hardly anyone any longer penetrates the deep Sahara, and those very few who do so tend rather to travel the coast road to Benghazi or Tripoli in Libya before venturing southward. There is still some traffic through Libya from the south. Much of this edges past the Tibesti Mountains to the east and one way or another passes through or close to the El-Kufrah oasis before heading to the coast. Some truck and bus traffic, halting and erratic, heads through the desert on the ancient route that passes through Murzuq and thence past Djado to Bilma, or to Zouar in the western reaches of the Tibesti before heading south.

In Algeria, a good paved road leads into the interior through In'Salah and thence to Tamanrasset, but the road past the Ahaggar to Agadez is often treacherous—still passable, but only with a fair amount of digging and heaving. Another road heads southwest from El-Goléa to the Tuat oases, but there it stops, and doesn't penetrate the deep interior. An east-west Algerian highway also parallels the wadi of the Drâa; it is much used by military vehicles keeping a watchful eye on the uncertain Moroccan border just to its north.

In the south, Agadez and Gao can be reached from their national capitals, Bamako and Niamey, via good paved roads. The road from Bamako to Timbuktu is erratically passable depending on the season, and there are a few minor roads into the desert—to Tessalit north of Gao, for example—but only sandy tracks suitable for camels or four-wheel-drive vehicles penetrate the deep desert.

West of the Tamanrasset-Agadez route—nothing. For a thousand miles—a distance as great as from Paris to Moscow—there are no roads worthy of the name at all, until you get to the coast itself, where there is a highway of sorts that edges down the coast from Morocco, though not yet all the way to Nouakchott. Western Mali and most of Mauritania is accessible only by camel, and only the nomads who live there venture into its interior.

The traders have gone, and so has much of their traffic. No more gold is hauled across the desert on the swaying back of camels. No more slaves stumble across the intolerable sand. Trucks carry fuel and commodities, belching buses carry people, and only salt is left of the ancient merchandise. Salt is still carried by caravan, all that's left of the glory days.

CHAPTER ELEVEN

✑

White Gold, Yellow Gold, Black Gold

THE MARKET at Mopti in southern Mali is arranged around a deep basin set into the banks of the Bani River at the southern end of the city, a few miles before it joins the Niger. The market is remarkable for many reasons, not the least of which is that its methods and commerce have changed hardly at all in the last five hundred years, or perhaps a thousand.

The *pirogues* that ply the river are still made just out of town, by Bozo craftsmen segregated in their own boat-building village; they are still made in the same way, hand-hewn boards stitched together on frames nailed up by Bozo-made spikes. Their design is identical to that noted by Arab travelers in the twelfth century—long, needle-nosed, with a shallow draft but very stable, deck cabins roofed with arching boughs covered with thatch (occasionally tarpaulins, now). Similar but smaller pirogues act as ferries, carrying families to and from the pottery-making village on the far side. These boats travel from the upriver towns of Segou and Segoukoro to Mopti, and from Mopti east, downriver to Timbuktu and Gao.

The marketplace at Mopti. (Marq de Villiers)

In the dry season Mopti's market spills down the cobbled sloping sides of the basin itself. Everywhere there are pirogues, hundreds of them. And off to one side, spread over an area sixty feet long by as many wide, are great slabs of Saharan rock salt, brought by camel caravans out of the deep desert, traded in the markets of Timbuktu and Gao, and brought upriver to Mopti, whence they will make their way to the refineries and factories of the capital, Bamako. The salt slabs weigh 220 pounds each and are stacked in bundles of four or five, tied with cord and piled on sticks laid on the cobbles. They are the color of dirty cream, flecked with gray.

A merchant saw a stranger staring at the salt slabs, and came over to find out what he wanted. "You want to buy some?" he asked in French.

"No, what would I do with them?"

"Turn them into money," the merchant said, grinning. "That's what they're for."

"Where do they come from?"

He shrugged. "The Tuareg bring them in from the desert," he said. "I don't care to go and see, myself. What does it matter? They always come."[1]

Salt slabs at Timbuktu. (Marq de Villiers)

∾

THEY ALWAYS COME, and they always have. These slabs, brought two to a camel from the salt mines at Taghaza or Bilma (which means "salt" in Tamashek), have been a staple of Niger River commerce since the days of Old Ghana and Tekrur, nearly two thousand years ago. They were one of the commodities that fueled the rise of the old Sahelian empires.

When Ibn Battuta's caravan paused in 1353 at the dreary little town of Taghaza, in Mali, on its way across the desert to Timbuktu—a town, he pointed out with some astonishment, whose very houses and mosque were built of slabs of rock salt—he was at one of the nodal points of the Saharan trade network. He wasn't impressed. "It is a village with no attractions," he groused. Not only were its houses built of salt, "there are no trees, only sand in which there is a salt mine. They dig the ground and thick slabs are found in it, lying on each other as if they had been cut and stacked there. A camel carries two slabs. The only people living there are the slaves of the Massufa, who dig for the salt and live on dates brought for them from Darah and Sijilmasa, camel meat and *anli* [millet], which is imported from the land of the blacks."[2] Taoudeni, about a hundred miles south of Taghaza, was worse: nothing there but grim slaves who lived in salt houses and ate salty food and drank salty water and breathed salty air; nothing to eat but the desiccated flesh of camels that had died along the way. For centuries merchants from Mali made the trip with their packets of gold dust, and hauled away the slabs (so rough that they tore at the hide of a camel) to Walata. There, Battuta reported, it was sold "for eight to ten mithqals, and in the city of Mali for 20 to 30, sometimes 40. The blacks trade with salt as others trade with gold and silver; they cut it into pieces and buy and sell with these. For all its squalor, quintals of quintals of gold dust are traded [in Taghaza]."[3]

Caravans from Timbuktu were still, in the 1990s, fetching salt from Taghaza for resale in the market of Mopti. At Bilma in Niger, the more easterly and perhaps the more famous of the Saharan salt mines, only a few families are left to dig out the salt, meager inheritors of a trade as old as antiquity.

Heinrich Barth was in Kano, in Nigeria, in 1850 when a salt caravan arrived from Bilma: "Salt is the only article carried by this caravan. The form of the largest cake is very remarkable; but it must be borne in mind that the salt in Bilma is in a fluid state, and is formed into this shape by pouring it into a wooden mold. This pedestal or loaf of salt (*kantu*) is equal to five of the smaller cakes, which are called *aserim*, and each *aserim* equals four of the smallest cakes, which are called *fotu*. The bags, made of the leaves of the dúm palm in which these loaves are packed is [*sic*] called *takrufa*. But the finest salt is generally in loose grains; and this is the only palatable salt, while the ordinary salt of Bilma is very bitter to the European palate, and spoils every thing; but the former is more than three times the value of the latter."[4]

For all his careful descriptions, Barth neglected to say what this "very remarkable" shape was. But since the caravans still travel the same triangular route, and the Bilma salt merchants still quarry the salt in the same (or similar) shallow pits, and still dilute it with wa-

Salt cakes. (Marq de Villiers)

ter from the same wells in the same oasis, and pour it into molds, these molds are no doubt unchanged from the ones Barth saw. The small molds, Barth's *fotu,* look like nothing so much as ingots of gold. Some of the larger ones resemble, more than anything, a head-stone in a Christian cemetery, slabs about four feet by two, a few inches thick, often curved at the top, with a hole through which a binding twine can be threaded. Others are the same shape as the or-ange traffic cones that mark off construction sites on Western high-ways. Sometimes they bear the mark or device of the merchant's agent, in the same way that a Burgundian wine will carry the logo of a *negociant.* But there are also more fanciful shapes, and Barth might have seen these too: crescents and half moons and broken stars, made with apparent whimsy but carefully measured to stan-dard weights.

These days Bilma's bitter salt is not used for human consumption at all. Taghaza salt is fine grade, but Bilma's is used strictly for live-stock. The Tuareg prefer it to the synthetic diet supplements for sale in town; they believe camels grow strong because of it.

In classical times, when somewhere around three thousand tons were being exported from Bilma annually, a slab of salt traded for a bar of gold, as it did in Taghaza; now the same slab, maybe about fifteen kilos, will be sold to passing *caravanniers* for fifty cents. They, in turn, will take it to Zinder or Kano, and sell it there for three dollars. The profit margins are slimmer in modern times because salt is much more easily obtained and the competition is fiercer, but the profit still makes the trade go round.

℘

THE REAL REASON salt reached such eminence as a trade good in the Sahara, and the reason the northern merchants were so eager to take it south, to the Land of the Blacks, was its neat complementarity with gold: Salt was in very short supply in the Sahel, though it is a necessity for human life; gold, on the other hand, a commodity irrelevant to life, was in very short supply in the north. As a consequence, there was a seemingly insatiable hunger for salt in the south, and a similarly insatiable hunger for gold among the northern kingdoms and caliphates, and among the merchant houses of Europe. Indeed, salt and gold were intertwined from the beginning.

That there was gold across the desert was well known to the Maghreb by the close of the eighth century; indeed, only a decade or two after the Arab conquest of North Africa, sometime between 730 and 750, the new overlords sent an expedition across the desert to attack this already renowned place called Ghana and seize its wealth. The attack failed, and most of the troops died, but enough returned to make it clear that Ghana itself wasn't the real source of the gold—most of that came from a mysterious kingdom called Wangara, somewhere far to the south. Wangara has never been identified but probably overlapped Senegal, Guinea, and southern Mali, and seemed to have endless amounts of gold; what they didn't have at all was salt, which is where and why the Saharan salt trade was institutionalized.[5]

Two-thirds of the world's gold supply in the late Middle Ages came from west African mines, and for generations these mysterious goldfields of Africa took on an almost luminous eminence in the

European imagination. Africa was "the gilded place," the home of rulers who lived in golden palaces and sat on golden thrones and ate their meals from golden dishes. By an odd historical coincidence, there is such a society in Africa—the Ashanti, "the people of the golden stool"—but they live far away from the putative Wangarans, around Kumasi in modern Ghana, some eight hundred miles to the south. Still, it is theoretically possible if unlikely that people from what is now Ghana did travel and trade as far north as Koumbi Saleh, for it is now known that intra-African trade patterns were much more widespread much earlier than historians had until recently thought. An example is the Tuareg copper mine in the hinterlands to the west of Agadez, which sold copper to many far-flung places, among them Benin, on the Bight of Benin near the Niger delta, which needed copper for its now-famous brass and bronze jewelry, money, and architectural plates. Benin's artisans often covered the columns of their palaces with brass plaques, and decorated their towers and roofs with massive coiling brass serpents. Perhaps the rumors of the towers of gold and cities of brass to be found "in the Wangara country" were really mutated reports of refulgent buildings many hundreds of miles farther on, reports growing in the telling as travelers passed from the Niger to the Maghreb, Egypt, and beyond. These legends may have surfaced briefly in the *Thousand and One Nights*, in which the "City of Brass and the Cupola of Lead" are said to be found somewhere in a land unknown, in the depths of the Sahara.

Ibn Battuta, in his stopover at the salt mines of Taghaza, noted that "the business done at Taghaza, for all its meanness, amounts to an enormous figure in terms of hundredweights of gold dust." An anonymous Arab writer in the twelfth century, two hundred years before Battuta, left this account: "In the country of Ghana is gold, treasure inexpressible. They have much gold, and the merchants trade with salt for it, taking the salt on camels from the salt mines. They travel in the desert as upon a sea, having guides to pilot them by the stars or the rocks in the deserts. They take provisions for six months, and when they reach Ghana they weigh their salt and trade it against a certain unit of gold, and sometimes against double or more of the gold unit, according to the market and the supply."[6]

The exotic place from which the gold came, and the mysterious people who mined it, the Wangarans, gave rise to a number of colorful legends. Some were merely fanciful—beautiful young women, naked as the day they were born, were said to draw up the gold from holes in the ground by means of birds' feathers smeared with tar— but other stories were rather less lovely. For example, a number of medieval writers, no doubt copying from each other, speculated that the reason the Wangarans wanted salt so badly was that their lower lips hung down over their chests, red and glistening, and would be subject to putrefaction in the tropical climate were they not regularly sprinkled with salt.

The actual trading was effected by a system of "dumb barter," not unlike the Dutch auctions of the present. Merchants from the north never did the actual deals themselves. They picked up agents in Koumbi Saleh or Audaghost, and when they reached the Senegal River they beat their drums to let the natives know they were there. The practice was for the traders to lay their merchandise in heaps on the ground, and retire. The next morning "they would find a certain quantity of gold dust placed against every heap, which, if they think sufficient, they leave the goods; it not, they let both remain until more of the precious dust is added. These traders in gold dust are supposed to be devils, who are very fond of red cloth, the favorite article of exchange."[7] This practice was well established, both in Ghana and in neighboring Tekrur, and indeed elsewhere in Africa.

In reality, the goldfields were not that well hidden; it was just that the rulers of Old Ghana and Tekrur, and later Mali, made sure that the merchants didn't wander about in their territory, and thus kept their mines secure. The main gold-bearing strata were alluvial goldfields in the western Niger floodplains, around the Tinkisso tributary in Guinea, and somewhat richer mines to the north in the upper Senegal Valley, between the Senegal and Faleme Rivers. Wangara, it is now known, was one name for the Mande people of the Niger basin.

In the centuries that followed the Arab conquest, the gold traffic became well established along three main trade routes. Sijilmasa and the Almoravid powers in Morocco traded mostly with Tekrur, whose boundaries were west of Old Ghana to the Atlantic; Tekrur had been converted to Islam very early and was thus better known in Morocco than Old Ghana itself. Ghana's trade was much more commonly with Ouargla and what is now the Algerian littoral, and generally passed through the Niger River town of Gao. However, Ghanaian traders also dealt directly with Egyptian merchants via the Niger and Lake Chad and the Nile. The Malian empire later inherited all this trade,[8] and the town of Audaghost benefited greatly from all three routes.

The trade was rigorously organized. The rulers of Old Ghana levied steep duties on gold coming into their country, and also on consignments leaving it, and the king made sure that nuggets of gold, as opposed to mere gold dust, were reserved for himself, largely to prevent a slump in the price.

Mansa Musa, the most eminent of Mali's rulers, also closely controlled the mining of the precious metal. To do the actual extraction, he tolerated the existence of a number of "pagans," whom he exempted from the otherwise universal tax on unbelievers. The reason he employed pagans was simple: Mining was forbidden to believers, because the process of bringing gold out of the earth was thought to involve a number of magical operations and demanded a system of beliefs that were anathema to Muslims. (There is ample evidence elsewhere in Africa that gold production almost ceased after a society converted to Islam.)

The gold of Ghana and Tekrur was generally fairly close to the surface, and most mines were not much more than forty feet deep. Since each shaft generally yielded only a few grams of gold (the famous Ghanaian "rods of gold" notwithstanding), there would have had to be somewhere between 240,000 and 480,000 shallow shafts operating at any one time to meet the demand, a considerable mobilization of manpower.[9]

Gold is still being brought to the surface in Senegal in the way it was when Mansa Musa was alive. The miners work from shafts thirty or forty feet deep, less than three feet in diameter and about six feet apart, connected at the bottom by lateral tunnels. The ore is mined with short-handled picks; the men work in tunnels less than three feet high, half filled with water. Ore is floated to the shafts in calabashes and pulled to the surface by women. Women generally wash the gold, and guard it until it is collected by itinerant merchants who sell it in town.[10] However, its position on the world's gold markets is greatly diminished. Richer, deeper, and more productive goldfields in South Africa, Russia, and Canada have supplanted it, and modern mining techniques have made its alluvial seams largely superfluous. The rods of gold of Old Ghana, once legend, then reality, have receded back to the storybooks.

ᔆ

SALT WAS PROFITABLE, gold was more profitable still, but no commodity was more abundant and profitable than slaves, and slavery was always a mainstay of Saharan commerce.

No one knows the number of hapless captives who stumbled along the Saharan caravan routes from the African savanna to the slaving warehouses of the north. Their numbers were certainly in the many hundreds of thousands, and perhaps millions. In the eighteenth century, Arab caravans brought as many as five thousand slaves annually from the Sudan to Tripoli alone; slaving raids deep into the savanna "cleaned out" entire villages and, typically, returned with ten or fifteen thousand captives. For much of the last millennium the slave trade dominated all commerce, even gold, for there seemed an inexhaustible hunger for slaves all through the Maghreb, the Levant, and Arabia; and slaves from central Africa were even forced to walk across central Asia to Tashkent and Bukhara in the days of Tamerlane the Magnificent, in the fourteenth century. Black slaves were found all over the Hellenic and Roman worlds; and for centuries after the Arab conquest of North Africa there were flourishing slave markets in dozens of desert towns, with "warehouses" in places like Sijilmasa, In-'Salah, Ghadamès, and Zouila.[11] Until well into the nineteenth century perhaps half the value of all Saharan traffic was in slaves.

The attrition rate on the trans-Sahara crossing reached as high as a third, and sometimes even a half, of the captives. Many thousands left their bones in the sand or on the stony plains—grisly markers that go back into deepest antiquity, for the glorious Pharaonic civilization depended on slave labor, and blacks of the Sudan and Nubia rounded up in slave raids or captured in the chaotic aftermath of tribal warfare were transported across the desert to make their meager and despised but necessary contribution to the even running of society.

Eyewitness reports of slave caravans across the desert left many a grisly portrait. Dozens of them remark on the unnerving silence of the passing throng: the grumbling of camels, and the plodding of human feet, but never the crack of whips, never screams from the victims or curses from the slavers. There had been no need for whips, for the poor benighted slaves knew that laggardliness meant certain death. If one stumbled and fell, the other slaves would try to support him, or the slave masters would cut off his head and there would be an open neckband in the chain, a horrid reminder to the weary. Most of the wells on the other Saharan slaving routes were surrounded by skeletons and the bones of humans and animals. This was due mostly to children fallen by the wayside dragging themselves to the nearest well only to find the caravan gone. Many slaves also died when the wells were found to be clogged and took too long to clear.

From the Niger River, Mali, Bornu, the Hausa towns, and Sudan, the slave trade dominated life in the villages and petty kingdoms of the interior, keeping their pastoralist societies in a constant state of chaos and decay.

တ

THERE HAD ALWAYS BEEN slavery in Africa, but the Arabs brought to the trade a new thoroughness and energy, unsurpassed in its rapaciousness until the mercantilist economies of the West turned their attention to Africa. Once the first phase of Muslim conquest was over, none of the newly "protected" subjects, such as Jews, Christians, or Zoroastrians, could any longer be reduced to slavery, and slaves had to be sought elsewhere. Most were simply seized in punitive raids, but many were bought by Arab slavers from local chiefs, usually in weaker, less tightly knit societies incapable of defending themselves, like Nubia, Ethiopia, and central and western Sudan.

In the mid-1800s a typical raiding party returned from Sudan to Murzuq, in the Fezzan, a thirty-day journey across the empty desert: "They had brought with them 800 lean cripples, clad in skins and rags, between 2,000 and 3,000 Maherries [*mehari* camels], and about 500 asses: 180 of the mounted Arabs, and about 300 foot, were still left behind in the Negro country; nearly 1,000 camels, and many captives, had died on the road, besides children. The death of the latter was not included, as they were not considered of any importance."[12]

A slave was worth much less than a good camel, which was a fair approximation of their relative value. A "good black slave" was about half the price of a good piebald, brindled, or white camel, and considerably less than the tawny reddish-buff racing camels, so prized for their speed and endurance. An Ethiopian called Kafur, who later became regent of Egypt (945–966), was once a slave, picked up for a mere 18 dinars, a paltry sum.[13] Still, there were many exceptions, for talent was expensive and market economics were brought to bear on the slave trade.

Women were always more valued, and therefore dearer, than men by one-third or even one-half; young women, in turn, were more valuable still, for they could be concubines as well as toil for their masters. In medieval times, trained dancing girls had price tags between one thousand and two thousand dinars—for that, you could get a dozen camels or more. A female singer was sold in an aristocratic circle in 912 for thirteen thousand dinars.[14] Men, on the other hand, were prone to violence and sudden rages, which made them uncertain goods.

Slaves were occasionally well treated, and manumission was relatively common. But they were also subject to random violence and arbitrary punishments. On the one hand, a Tuareg who mistreated his slave was badly thought of, and any slave who was discontented with his master merely had to cut the ear of the camel of the man whose slave he wished to become. As the master was responsible for his slave's action, he had to give the slave in compensation for the damaged camel, and in the process lost face.[15] On the other hand, the Tuareg were known for their quick tempers, and might stab a slave in a moment of anger; for this, there was no punishment necessary. In the Tibesti region, "masters occasionally cut ligaments of their feet or toes, or drive thorns into the soles of their feet to make it impossible for them to run away."[16]

The institution is deeply rooted in the life of the desert. As late as the 1950s, the nomadic social hierarchy of sheikhs or sultans, drum group leaders, nobles, vassals, *haratin,* and slaves, the same hierarchy that Ibn Battuta had encountered, the same hierarchy that the British explorer Mungo Park and the German Heinrich Barth found, had barely changed in a millennium. The English traveler Robin Maugham was told in the 1940s by a slave in Timbuktu: "Though I know that I am free, I also know that I still belong to my master. I know that when the French leave the country, my master will take me again," which almost certainly happened.[17] Most upper-caste Tuareg of the Ahaggar and Tassili n'Ajjer regions still had slaves to take care of flocks and herds and to perform various domestic tasks in the 1960s. A cynic in Timbuktu said in 1998, "Yes, they freed the slaves in 1968, but not all of them have been told yet."

The *haratin* are the settled side of the nomads, tending to Tuareg gardens. Whether they are slaves is a semantic point. They are certainly lowly vassals with few rights. They are born to their role, and there's not exactly a free labor market for gardeners in the oases. They are generally darker than the Tuareg, but usually have Berber, not negroid, features. They work as sharecroppers. Their "pay" is one-fifth of what they produce, plus whatever they can conceal, which is sometimes substantial. Nevertheless, they are generally malnourished; the "general torpor of oasis life," which the early Europeans noticed so disapprovingly—most oasis dwellers seemed to spend most of the day sleeping and most of the night gossiping—was almost certainly caused by continuous malnutrition.

Upper-class Tuareg, certainly, had—and have—little interest in doing the kind of labor appropriate for slaves or *haratin*. They are still fond of quoting the proverb, commonly but quite wrongly ascribed to the Koran, that "when the plough enters a house, so does the condition of the family become vile."[18] The Tuareg work with camels, but domestic or agricultural work is completely unacceptable.

That there are still slaves in the Sahara is not even a secret. The Sudanese government has been using slave labor in its campaign against the pagan south. In Niger and Mali and Mauritania, the Moors and the northern Tuareg have never given up their ways, and while they seldom use the word *slave* openly, the practice remains. Mauritania officially declared slavery illegal in 1980, but at the time there were an estimated one hundred thousand "haratin slaves" in the country and best estimates are that the numbers have barely changed. There are, reportedly, still slave markets in the Adrar area, northeast of Nouakchott in Mauritania.

Indeed, in parts of the desert slavery is still the natural order of things. Those few slaves who escape, either by running away or by dint of a soft master and a hard education, find only incredulity when they tell their stories. Moctar Teyeb, a Mauritanian slave who came to America in the 1990s, was briefly a hit on the talk show circuit, but the media were soon bored with him and nothing very much was done, except among impoverished exile groups, who were all too frequently written off in the larger society as cranks. A report that up to fifteen thousand Malian children, many of them from impoverished desert families, had been working as slave labor in the plantations of the Ivory Coast was issued by the Save the Children Fund in the summer of 2001, but received virtually no publicity.

In some places, little effort is made to hide the reality. Tuareg in the desert towns of Agadez or Timbuktu will point out the round huts of the slaves as casually as though they were pointing out the mayor's house, or the post office. These round huts, usually made of reed mats hung on bent poles, can be found in every vacant space, tucked up against the town walls, lining the road to town rubbish dumps.

Life in the desert changes, but slowly.

CHAPTER TWELVE

❦

Adepts of the Uttermost Desert

NOMADIC MOVEMENTS are by definition, of course, fluid, and their mobility makes them hard to track over time. Nonetheless, if you were to draw an ethnic sketch map of the Sahara today, the patterns you would find are not very different from what they became in the centuries after the Arab conquests.

When the invaders came, some of the Berbers remained where they had been for so long, along the northern fringes of the desert, and they still live there, in the High Atlas and all along the littoral. But many of the Berbers fled into the deep desert. Those who were to become Moors drifted west and south, into what is now Mauritania, where they are still to be found in the western quadrants of the desert. The proto-Tuareg and Tubu are now thought to have taken a much longer and more circuitous route to the forbidding mountains—the Ahaggar, Aïr, and Tibesti—where they presently find themselves. They probably settled where they are now after being deprived of their first refuge, the hinterlands of Lake Chad, where they for some centuries dominated the ancient empire of Kanem before dispersing once again, whether through restlessness or harassment is not known.

Many others live in the desert too, some of them fairly recent immigrants, like the Arabic-speaking Bedouin of the Egyptian desert and the Chaamba in the M'Zab and the northern part of Algeria. True Arabs, long-ago colonists, are by now in every corner of the Sahara, and by some accounts are today an absolute majority of the population, although the numbers are unreliable, as are the definitions of Arab. The *haratin,* the laboring classes, are also found in every Saharan oasis. Scattered throughout the desert as well is a sampling of the bewildering fecundity of black Africa: Hausa, Mande, Bambara, Dogon, Wolof, and many others. Descendants of the original Nilosaharans are found throughout the south.

Over the centuries a good deal of ethnic mixing has taken place—the Chaamba, for example, intermarried with Arabs; the Moors with the Wolof, Tukulor, Bambara, and Mossi to the south;

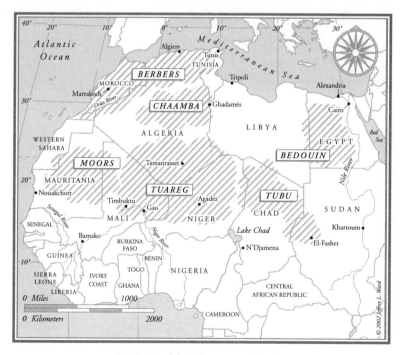

Territories of the Saharan nomads today.

the Tubu with the Hausa tribes of the Lake Chad region; and the southern Tuareg of the Aïr region with an assortment of Sahelian people, mostly the Hausa of Nigeria but also the Fulani and Bambara, as well as the Malinke, the successors to the people of ancient Mali. Nevertheless, the ethnic identities of all the main groups remain strong, and many of the Saharan tribes are hyperconscious of their own exclusive racial stock. The Tuareg especially consider themselves a superior people, and have a finely developed sense of the color of men, dividing them up into white, *abyad*, the color of Europeans and town dwellers on the north coast (white people are prone to illness and trickery, but are clever artificers); red, *ahmar*, the color of the Arabs and Berbers, though not of the Tuareg; yellow, *asfar*, a light bronze, again defining Arabs and Berbers, but including the Tuareg; brown, *asmar*, the color of the deep-desert dwellers and Sudanese Arabs; green, *akhdar*, dark bronze found among some desert dwellers who are mixed with southerners; gray, *azreq*, the color of the Nigritians (usually defined as someone south of the Niger river); and black, *assuad*, usually characterizing the Wolof and their cousins from Senegal, who are a dark ebony in color. There is no doubt which of these many shades the Tuareg deem best: Yellow is definitely better.

☙

IN MODERN TIMES, the most significant ethnic groups of the deep desert are the Chaamba, the Moors, the Tuareg, and the Tubu.

The Chaamba speak a language akin to Arabic, and seem to have arrived in the northwestern Sahara from Syria sometime in the fourteenth century. They settled in the M'Zab, their headquarters in the town of Metlili, only a few miles from Ghardaia, then chief town of the M'Zab region. Metlili soon became a fortress, the political and commercial center of Chaamba life, "at once their market, storage place and arsenal, their caravan terminus, raiding base, place of refuge and repose. It grew famous too as a haven for refugees and troublemakers from all over the northwestern quarter of the desert, and such recruits and their assimilated descendants helped to make the warlike Chaamba even more dreaded than they were at first."[1]

The Chaamba have long regarded themselves as the hereditary enemies of the Tuareg, which is fairly predictable since a good deal of Tuareg energy has historically been diverted to thievery from Chaamba herders. The Chaamba gave as good as they got, and for centuries it was the Chaamba who controlled the caravan routes south from the M'Zab; like the Tuareg, they made raiding into a high art and a basic part of desert life, with its own war chiefs and arcane rules. The French used this antipathy in their conquest of the Sahara, when they recruited Chaamba into the *Spahis,* their mobile desert fighting force.

The Chaamba are light-skinned, patriarchal in social arrangements, and, if possible, even more quarrelsome than the fractious Tuareg in their political arrangements: What confederations did exist were loose and functionally inert. Their nomadic range used to extend from Libya to Mauritania, and from the M'Zab southward to In'Salah, but it is now much more circumscribed. Most families keep a town house in Metlili, but are seldom there. In a nice modern gloss on their nomadic past, most of the cross-Saharan trucking and buses tend to be owned and operated by Chaamba.

೧ನ

THE MOORS, like the Tuareg, are descendants of Berbers. Why they are called Moors is rather harder to explain. The word was first used by the Romans, from the Latin *Mauri,* describing the inhabitants of the Roman province of Mauritania, then comprising the northwestern portion of modern Algeria and the northeastern portion of modern Morocco, a long way from modern Mauritania. The word was later used by the English to describe the former Muslims of Spain, of mixed Arab, Spanish, and Berber origin, who created the Andalusian civilization in Iberia and after the reconquest of Spain, completed in 1492, fled to North Africa as refugees.[2] The Moors are now found from the Wad'Noun in Morocco to the Senegal River south of Mauritania and from the Atlantic coast to the

Adrar des Iforhas Mountains in Mali. Many of their ancestors made up the troops of the Berber Sanhajah, who founded the Almoravid movement and empire in the eleventh century.

The Moors may be ethnic cousins, but they're generally looked down on by the Tuareg, for a variety of more or less obscure reasons, among them that they are more heavily bearded. The Tuareg view is that the Moors were too timid to properly resist the Arab invasions, and contaminated their blood by intermarrying with the invaders and adopting Arab customs, including patrilineal descent. The Moors also, according to Tuareg lore, intermarried rather too freely with southern blacks from Old Ghana. It is, thus, predictable that the Moors of Mauritania are extremely blood conscious.

Their society is still dominated by castes rather loosely associated with race, but the hierarchy is based on lineage, occupation, and access to power as well as simple skin color. About half the Moorish population is *Bidan*, or white, the other half *Sudan*, or black. The light-skinned Bidan Moors dominate the country—Mauritania is the only country, anywhere, actually governed by nomads. The real rulers are the noble castes of warriors, usually Arabs, reinforced by men of letters, the *marabouts*. Other Bidan Moors are vassals in the classic feudal sense, paying tribute in return for protection. Below them are the black Moors, who are either "servants," often a euphemism for slaves, or freedmen. Quarrels between these various factions constitute modern Mauritanian politics.

As with the Tuareg, there are also artisan classes, who are regarded as both indispensable and insignificant. In addition, in the bleak landscape north of Walata in eastern Mauritania there still lives a remnant group of early Berber nomads who call themselves Nmadi, whose culture has been degraded to the point where they have neither house nor tent, but live behind windbreaks and survive by hunting. Though the Moors, ethnic snobs at the best of times, generally disdain them, each Nmadi has a personal patron among the Moorish upper classes, who will lend him a camel for the annual hunt and give him victuals for the winter. In return his patron is provided with the skins of antelopes or dried meat or leather thongs. The Nmadi have no slaves or vassals, which makes them further suspect in Moorish eyes.[3]

∞

MANY STORIES are told in the desert about the wiliness and resourcefulness of the Tubu, who have often used their extraordinary homeland with extraordinary skill to escape their enemies. A lone Tubu was said to have once evaded an Arab slave-raiding party by burying himself in sand with only a gourd-full of air, until the raiders left. A Tubu can live, at least according to Tubu lore, for three days on a single date, on the first day eating the skin, the second the flesh, on the third the pounded stone.[4] These are hard men, even by Saharan standards, though they have now fallen on times harder than themselves.

The Tubu (Toubou, Tibou, *Tubu Reshade*, "the People of the Rock," the Teda), the wild men of the Tibesti, are sometimes considered cousins to the Tuareg and have often been regarded by travelers as "more a legend than reality, a race of ghosts called the Tubu, flitting among the rocks like the *moufflon*, and disappearing into extinct craters."[5] The Tubu continued to renounce Islam until recent times, despite centuries of proselytizing and a dozen or more savage jihads launched by a variety of fanatical clerics. Tubu men still keep a Y-shaped dagger, the *muzeri*, strapped to their wrists at all times, even while sleeping, and are said to be able to cut down a gazelle from sixty-five paces with a sidearm throw. Their women wear daggers strapped to their hips.

Once, they were a vigorous people, and much feared. Great raiders, they held sway over a huge area from the Nile Valley to the Niger Bend and from the heart of the eastern central desert (including the Fezzan) southward far into the Sudan. Their history is obscure. Herodotus's reference to the Garamantes hunting the "Ethiopian cave-dwellers of Troglodytes" could have referred to the Tubu in their Tibesti refuge (for there are still ancient homes to be seen in the shelter of overhanging rocks walled up with stone), but where they came

A Tubu woman. (Klaus Daerr)

from before that is unknown. It is also possible that the Tubu were not hunted by the Garamantes but are instead their descendants, intermixed with Berber or Tuareg blood, and that the "Troglodytes" were some now-vanished people. The Tubu blood-grouping is strikingly similar to the Berber, but they have also blended far into the south-Sudanese surroundings, and their language is utterly different from Berber. They are black, much blacker than their putative "cousins," the Tuareg, and whatever their origins have clearly mixed over the centuries with the central African black cultures. One of the three noble Tubu clans, the Arna, believe they came from the north, and were the people to import the camel to Tibesti.

The Tubu form, if anything, an essentially apolitical and almost anarchic society. Tubu political alliances are few. At least in theory, allegiance is paid to the Dardai, whose insignia of office is a pre-Islamic green turban called the *kadmul*, but Tubu confederations, like those of the Chaamba, are even looser and more fractious than those of the Tuareg. Their extreme individualistic ethic prevented their uniting even in the face of invasions. The Tubu system of blood feuds was so entrenched that it had complicated and elaborate formal codes. Blood revenge was, and is, a continuing hereditary obligation with no time limit. "In retribution for a murder, the murderer himself must be killed together with one of his descendants or at least a relative. Only payment of the blood price can put an end to such a feud [but] it is sometimes materially impossible to settle a feud by payment, even when both parties want to."[6] Sons inherit the right to their mother's camel brand, and can call on her clan for help in times of trouble or blood feud.

Some of the feud rituals are arcane even by desert standards. When a man has killed another in legitimate blood feud, and if he gets away without being killed himself, he will stop to catch a goat (anyone's goat will do), sacrifice it on a pile of stones, cut out a piece of intestine and pull the opposite ends over his feet like some bizarre form of hobble. He then jumps up and down until this intestinal "sock" breaks, whereupon he is magically freed of pursuit. Nevertheless, to be sure, he will draw a line across his trail, which line signifies the continuation of the feud: Cross this line and I'll kill you too.[7]

The Tubu glory days are long gone. They were harassed first by the Turks in the days of Ottoman rule of the Maghreb, then by the Senussi Islamic militants in the wars of the early twentieth century, then by the French and the Italians. The French bivouacked troops in the Tibesti region during the Second World War, and in their push to drive the Germans from Africa, stripped the Tubu of whatever meager resources were left to them. In the last fifty years, most of the Tubu converted to Islam, and although they still pay lip service to their traditional leader, the Dardai, and though clans still exist, the social structure is in decay. Some say there are no more than two hundred thousand or so Tubu left, and very few of them in the Tibesti. No census takers venture into the deep massif; unwary travelers are still occasionally murdered.

Bardai, the primary town of the Tubu, has decayed as well. Travelers think it a wretched place, poverty-stricken and charmless. So poor are the Tubu who live there that it has become the custom for pairs of men to share even the *tagelmoust,* the face veil, by taking turns wearing it.

❧

OF ALL THE TRIBES of the desert, though, there is no doubt that the Tuareg are the dominant presence.

The Ahaggar and the Aïr gave the Tuareg an extraordinary combination of remoteness and survivability, places from which to "raid and plunder between Ouargla and the Sudan." Tuareg roamed the desert freely, secure in the knowledge that the hidden canyons of the great massifs represented a refuge from their enemies.[8] Their lives were fine-tuned and intricate: The desert came to be home, and they the masters of it. They took to breeding camels up there in the rocky fastnesses, and submitted to no man's control, not even the Mali kings, greatest emperors of antiquity. They became what in their own eyes they remain: adepts of the uttermost desert, the *Kel-Tamagheq,* sand-riders and camel-masters.

❧

MOST OF THE TUAREG were nomads, but they also had towns—a few—and even small states with more-or-less organized politics. A group of Tuareg founded Timbuktu about nine hundred years or so ago, on the very borders of the empire of Mali. One of the successor states to the old empires was the Tuareg-controlled Takedda, centered on the modern town of Azelik, west of the Aïr Massif, in Niger. Takedda seems to have been named from the Tuareg word *teguidda,* meaning spring; but while the spring still exists, the town has long fallen into ruin. Nothing very much is known of Takedda's history, but its importance was due largely to the copper seams that surrounded it. Mansa Musa knew of this mine, and once said it was his most important source of revenue ("special and un-equaled," in his own words), its copper sold "to the pagans" for *mithqals* of gold. Ibn Battuta stopped at Takedda on his way home in 1352 but found little to say of it except to note that it lived by trade, and that its merchants "travel every year to Egypt," and "live in luxury and ease." Takedda was absorbed by the sultanate of Agadez sometime in the sixteenth or seventeenth century.[9] Subsequently, for the two hundred or so years before the colonial era, the primary center of Tuareg influence was the Algerian town of Tamanrasset, west of the Ahaggar Massif.

Tuareg politics were limitlessly quarrelsome and unstable; their way of life was fiercely libertarian, and they never took kindly to sultans telling them what to do. Their society was essentially feudal in makeup. There were lords and vassals and slaves. Politics were also complicated by kinship affiliations.

The Tuareg were rather loosely organized into "drum groups," so called after the hemispherical drum set outside the tent of all important chiefs, whose function, naturally enough, this being a warrior society, was to call the men to battle. Inside the drum groups, things were rigidly hierarchical and, while perhaps not harmonious, at least orderly. In the classic feudal manner, the nobles offered protection to their vassals, and when they were off raiding, which was frequently, they left behind their herds of camels "not only to be tended but to be used, if the vassals wished, for trade or domestic purposes."[10] Other drum groups were fair game. Camel raiding and short bloody skirmishes between groups were a routine part of desert life. When there were no caravans to pillage, there were always other Tuareg, who could be overcome with the proper combination of guile, bloody-mindedness, and ruthlessness. "Provision," said a Tuareg proverb, "is from tillage, inheritance or quarreling." Blood feuds were commonplace, settled by the spilling of more blood or with payment of blood money.

Drum groups were formed into loose associations or confederations, at the head of which was a chief called *amenoukal,* the most powerful being the *amenoukal* of the Kel Ahaggar, who was elected by the assembled chiefs of the drum groups. But these confederations were not always stable, and they had no divine sanction; the nomads were far too independent to allow themselves to be easily led. The *amenoukal*'s authority, as the French were to discover to their cost when they tried to bind the Tuareg with treaties, was only nominal.[11] Eventually, European power prevailed, and when the leader of the Ahaggar Tuareg, Aitarel, died in 1900, the French managed to install a "client" (aka stooge) as the new leader. Moussa ag Amastane was set in place after a series of sharp raids into the Ahaggar, including a massacre of Tuareg at the little village of Tit, near Tamanrasset, which later became a place of pilgrimage for rebel nomads.

In 1912 many of the Tuareg joined in the Senussi revolt, an Islamic revivalist crusade of Sufi origins whose intentions were to drive the "Christians" into the sea and free the land from their moral pollution.

In the end, the Tuareg of the Aïr never gave in; they merely retreated deeper into the massifs that protected them. Rennell Rodd, writing in 1926, said they had "migrated eastwards further and further into the recondite places of the Fezzan mountains, which they now leave only to raid Aïr or Kawar [Bilma] in company with rascals like the northern Tébu and the more irreconcilable Ahaggaren, who have refused to submit to French administration."[12] Tuareg revolts were still an ongoing menace in parts of the Sahara, especially Mali and Niger, well into the 1990s.

‽

THE TWO GOATHERDS who had stopped the Toyota Landcruiser as it skirted the dunes of the Ténéré were not citified Tuareg, wage earners, but nomads of the open desert, whose "home," if they reckoned they had one at all, was in the deep gullies of the Aïr Massif, the traditional refuge of the Kel-Oui Tuareg, the agglomeration of Tuareg clans centered in the region. They were dressed in leather sandals made from camel skin and robes called *gandoma* that sometimes swept the ground as they walked. These were not the traditional indigo color of the Tuareg—the color that sometimes sweated off onto their skin, which led to their being known around the desert as the "Blue Men"—but were in this case white. Around their heads and across the lower part of their faces was a *tagelmoust,* a twenty-foot length of cloth, the traditional indigo in color.

Tuareg men. (Marq de Villiers)

The *tagelmoust* was designed expressly for desert life, for protection against the sun and the blowing sand. It is, however, much more than a sand screen in Tuareg life. The women don't wear it, for example, but only the men, and they wear it even when there is no sand to screen. Though customs are eroding and laxity is setting in, the *tagelmoust* traditionally is kept in place even at home, and when a man drinks tea the cup is passed under the veil, keeping the mouth covered. Sometimes, the other hand is used to screen the mouth from the view of visitors. The higher the Tuareg's social status, the more likely he is to remain covered when meeting strangers. Among certain groups veiling is almost total, when eating, when sleeping, even in battle.[13] In certain clans, it is said, the Tuareg man keeps his veil in place even when making love to his wife. The Tuareg have long forgotten the reason for this *tagelmoust*. It must be right, they say, for it was the fashion of their forefathers.[14]

Only the eyes of the herders could be seen, and it was impossible to tell how old the two men were. The skin about their ankles was pocked with small blisters, a normal state after the *harmattan* has blown.

In addition to carrying a staff, each man had strapped to his waist a long-bladed broadsword in a scabbard. Presumably the blades were sharpened on one side only—among the Tuareg the *takouba*, the double-bladed sword, has always been restricted to nobles, and whoever these men were, they weren't nobles. Nevertheless, their sword hilts were worked in black leather and stone, with a pseudocross motif dominant. This cross has been the object of much academic curiosity centered around whether it is a Christian symbol. When the first European explorers encountered the Tuareg, with their medieval appearance and what looked like a St. George's cross on their saddles and swords, they assumed that the nomads had been Christians driven into the desert by invading Arabs in the seventh and then again in the eleventh centuries, a fanciful notion not without some plausibility. Indeed, the Arabs referred to the Tuareg as "Christians of the Desert," and the Arab word from which Tuareg is supposedly derived means "the abandoned of God." Another theory is that the cross was introduced into the Sahara as a purely decorative device from Spain by the returning Almoravids in the eleventh century, or perhaps later. Still others believe the whole connection with Christianity is spurious, and the Tuareg crosses evolved spontaneously, without reference to a crucifixion. The cross is a simple geometrical form, after all, and the Tuareg's admittedly freewheeling adaptation of Islam has almost no shared beliefs with any Christians, no matter how far they have wandered from Holy Scripture.

Even the name Tuareg is not as simple as the Arab explanation implies. The Tuareg don't use the word much themselves, but when they do they assume it derives from Targa, a district of the Fezzan in southern Libya that was the supposed original homeland of many of the Tuareg groups, Tuareg being the plural of Targi, "someone from Targa." The Tuareg call themselves Imohagh or Imajughen, "the noble ones," and their language is called Tamashek. Sometimes, indeed, they simply call themselves Kel Tamagheq, or Tamashek speakers. The written script, even more confusingly, is called Tifinagh.

There has also been speculation, on even thinner evidence, that the Tuareg are Jewish at root. They have, at least, been traveling in the company of Jews for many centuries, because the metalworking artisans who traditionally accompany the Tuareg are, plausibly in their own minds, ethnically different from the Tuareg and of Jewish origin, dispersed over the Sahara in the fifteenth century from southern Morocco.[15] The Tuareg, who disdain physical work other than tending to livestock and banditry, cherished these smiths, who were in old Tuareg lore thought to be "older than memory, proud as the crow, mischievous in mind." Tuareg nobles employed groups of smiths who traveled with them and were considered part of the family, though they camped slightly apart. The smiths were not treated as slaves and could shift allegiance to a new patron whenever they wished. The smiths' work has over the centuries accreted to itself a depth of arcane symbolism and a body of legend whose origins are often obscure. A Tuareg smith once said to the photographer Angela Fisher, who had been looking at a tiny padlock he had been working, "For you this is as small as my thumbnail, for me it is huge. Look, there is the ant, the hyena, the jackal, the horse's hoof, the moon, the stars and the sun, the good eye, the woman, the devil's eyebrows, the laughter, that is our life."[16]

Tuareg tradition supposes them to descend from the legendary queen Tin Hinan, "she of the tents," said to be from the Tafilalt oases in Morocco. However, legendary queens were common among the Aïr people, just as they are among the Saharan Berbers, and, indeed, among many sub-Saharan Bantu tribes.[17] It is also prudent to be cautious of "legends" in the Sahara. For example the French, who ruled most of the Sahara in the latter part of the nineteenth century, were fascinated by the Ahaggar Tuareg. They excoriated them for their all-too-apparent cruelty and violence, but running through all the French commentary is a rich vein of romanticism, and legends were attributed to the Tuareg that were never part of their tradition. One of these was of the beautiful young Queen Antinea, said to be originally from Atlantis, who lived in the Ahaggar and murdered young men when she could seize them. That this "true story" derived directly from Pierre Benoit's 1919 novel, *L'Atlantis,* never seemed to trouble anyone, and when in

1925 archaeologists announced the discovery of the tomb of a young woman who had been buried with what they called "royal honors" (unspecified), she was promptly and popularly translated into the redoubtable Antinea. Whether she was, in fact, the traditional matriarch of the Tuareg, Tin Hinan, is of course unknown, but in any case a royal tomb was, indeed, found at Wad' Abalessa near Tamanrasset, dating from around the fourth century. Even the formidable anthropologist Henri Lhote, an otherwise meticulous observer of Tuareg ways, was not immune to the legend. In 1928, in a remote cave, he discovered a rock painting of a woman whose breasts had been slathered with white paint, and claimed her as "Antinea, siren of the unforgettable Ahaggar."[18] The tale would not be worth mentioning—it is, after all, a colonialist invention—except for the surprising fact that versions of the Antinea legend began to reverberate among the Tuareg themselves, and variations on the theme could still be heard in the desert in the 1990s.

೧೦

IF THE TUAREG consider themselves adepts of the uttermost desert, as indeed they are, they also have developed over the centuries another reputation. To the merchants and *caravanniers* of the Saharan trade, the Tuareg also became the ferocious and unruly Blue Men, predators of the desert. When the French colonialists first got to the Sahara in the middle of the nineteenth century, the Ahaggar Tuareg ruled much of the desert from the oasis towns of Tamanrasset and In'Salah, trading in ivory, gold, and slaves, supplementing their income by extracting protection money from passing caravans. The Flatters expedition, sent to reconnoiter a railroad route across the desert, was therefore perceived as a threat to this way of living; the Tuareg answer, a raiding party of tribesmen armed with medieval weapons, was at once sent to eliminate it. The sheer ferocity of their response, and their appearance out of the deep desert where seemingly no man could live, only embroidered their legend among the French, and earned them a reputation for invincibility—apparently well deserved. Indeed, the French during their occupation of the desert through the last half of the nineteenth century and the first half of the twentieth seemed to spend most of their time fighting off the Tuareg, and seizing their seemingly endless array of weapons.

That the Tuareg were ruthless and prone to violence is not just a European opinion, or a product of simpleminded colonialist ethnography. As early as 1350 the indefatigable Arab traveler Ibn Battuta described the Tuareg as "a rascally lot"; and his contemporaries were fond of saying that "the scorpion and the Tuareg are the only enemies you meet in the desert."[19] The anthropologist Henri Schirmer pointed out that "with the Tuareg, the idea that man is free and a brigand is so inseparable that the same verb (*Iohagh*) means both 'he is free' and 'he pillages.'"[20]

A Tuareg guide in Timbuktu, Mohammed Ali, was once asked about his people's reputation for banditry. Their poetry, it was said, celebrated thievery—it was an opinion widely put about in the desert. But Ali was offended. The sagas celebrate daring, he said, somewhat defensively. It is the action, not the result, that is admired. A Tuareg would take by force, but never by stealth. "And stealing from thieves is not thievery," he said.

This is somewhat disingenuous, the counterpart of the urban Tuareg's suave dismissal of their tribesmen's current banditry in the high hills as a fight for liberty and independence—the Tuareg know the cant of Western liberalism as well as do the Berbers of Morocco and Algeria, who have recently issued declarations about "shrugging off Arab colonialism." The truth is rather more severe. One of the obstacles to peaceful settlement of the Sahara has long been the hostility of the Tuareg. "Established in the oases throughout the Sahara, these fanatics and brigands were accustomed to scan the whole desert, and as soon as they spied a caravan to fall upon it to rob and massacre," the normally equable *National Geographic* complained in 1905.[21] In more modern days, nomads don't slot easily into authoritarian nation-states or, for that matter, into societies that try to count votes every few years, and they are constantly at odds with their national governments.

The early Europeans who blundered through the Sahara in the eighteenth and nineteenth centuries left many a vivid portrait: "They were large men, with an imposing walk, who marched straight at us with a real disdain of danger," Lt. Gaston Cottenest remarked after a sharp skirmish with a marauding band of Tuareg.[22] Heinrich Barth, one of the first Europeans to visit Timbuktu, remembered his party's wariness of the Tuareg as they ascended from Kabara (the Niger River port village of Timbuktu) to the town itself: "The path was thickly lined on both sides with thorny bushes and stunted trees, which were being cleared away in some places, in order to render the path less obstructed and more safe, as the [Tuareg] never fail to infest it. It was from the unsafe character of this short road between the harbor and the town, that the spot bears the remarkable name of 'Ur-im-mán-des,' 'he does not hear,' meaning the place where the cry of the unfortunate victim is not heard from either side."[23]

He described Tuareg nobles "swaggering through the market-place," brushing aside lesser mortals, "pushing aside the blind and the halt,"[24] followed by a retinue of retainers and slaves, all imbued with their masters' impenetrable arrogance. The nobles often rented weapons to their serfs, which they would wield on their masters' behalf, usually in exchange for a share of any loot that might be seized.

The nomads' favorite targets were the caravans that plied the desert. Large caravans might depend on their size to barge through, while small ones might try to sneak by unnoticed. But most caravans took the precaution of purchasing a *ghefara*, or "pardon," from the Tuareg before passing through their territory.

Tuareg methods were usually devious, showing nothing of the daring Mohammed Ali so celebrated. They seldom just fell on an unsuspecting caravan, or burst over the dunes in a charging run. Instead, "operating in small groups of from three to twenty men, they first attached themselves to the caravan, protesting their friendliness, making themselves useful, all the while seeking out the most vulnerable members, the small merchant and, especially, the *kafir* or unbeliever, men who might be concealing wealth, men whom no one would protect. Each man calculated the odds, reasoning that were the Tuareg allowed to cut out one of their members, murder him and make off with his camels, then the rest could leave in peace."[25] It was this same deviousness that had given Tamanrasset, for example, its unenviable reputation for intrigue, since Tuareg scouts tended to hang out there, waiting for their moment.

෴

THERE ARE STILL armed Tuareg bands in the high hills, especially around the Djado Plateau in northern Niger, just as there are still nomads in the open desert, free and unfettered. But modernity has caught up with the Tuareg too. Mohammed Ali once recounted a story of an oil prospector whose name he didn't know but whom he called "the Texaco man," who had spent some time out in the desert with a Tuareg clan. The Texaco prospector left a large sum of money in his tent when he went away for a few days. Everyone had known of this money, Ali said. Everyone in the desert was talking about it— it was one of the tales told when caravans met. All the money was still there when he returned. But the point wasn't the honesty of the desert nomads. The point was that the nomadic Tuareg, whose legends celebrate that they are "afraid of nothing," are afraid of money. They need and covet it like everyone else in modern society, but they despise it, too, because money is a symbol. Money implies the end of self-sufficiency, the end of nomadism for a settled life in the cities, where there is sickness and filth and poverty. Money is corruption, the killer of tradition. The Tuareg want to keep their culture alive at all costs, and they haven't survived for so long in the desert by being soft, but Ali believes money is winning. Since the droughts of the 1980s that decimated their camel herds, many of the Tuareg have taken to the towns or become poverty-stricken goatherds, and it is sometimes hard to see in the desperately poor people who cluster around the desert towns the fiercely independent Tuareg of legend.

෴

THE DESERT NOMADS who fled the invading Arabs also fled the Islamic proselytizers who were so much a part of the invasion.

Of the various groups, the Moors converted to Islam earliest, just as they intermarried with the Arabs more than the Tuareg did. The Tubu were the last to convert, and resisted until well into the twentieth century. The Tuareg, for their part, resisted Islam for a long period, converting slowly over several centuries until almost all clans professed Islam by about the fifteenth century. Even so, instead of adopting the whole creed, they grafted it onto their own already ancient matrilineal traditions. As a consequence, they depart from Muslim orthodoxy in several subtle and not so subtle ways. Among the most obvious to non-Tuareg is their use of joyous music during their devotions, a frivolity frowned on by the devout elsewhere, and the extraordinary freedom of their women.

More interestingly, many among the Tuareg don't regard Mohammed as the only, or even the most important, prophet. This is not new backsliding on their part, but a tradition of long standing. Heinrich Barth, who had stumbled into some convoluted, and sometimes dangerously heated, religious disputes in Timbuktu 150 years ago (when unorthodoxy was hazardous to life, and Christians were routinely killed), had once pointed out to his hosts, rather tactlessly, that the local Muslims acknowledged Musa, Aisa, and many others as true prophets, "and that they seemed to acknowledge the superiority of Aisa by supposing that he was to return at the end of the world." The Sultan of Timbuktu in return accused Barth of being a *kafir,* or unbeliever. Barth, of course, hastily denied it, but his point, derived in many other conversations with eminent Tuareg in his six years in the desert, remained that the Tuareg had adapted Islam, not adopted it; many of their own traditions had merely been given new names but had otherwise remained unaltered.[26]

Travelers told varying stories about the degree of devoutness of the Saharan nomads. Ibn Battuta, dubious as he was about what he considered their scandalous morals, never doubted their punctiliousness in prayer. Nor did Hugh Clapperton or even Archibald Robbins, who was not exactly an apologist for nomadic ways. On the other hand, George Lyon, traveling on a caravan in the Libyan desert in 1818, found that his companions "were not very scrupulous in their religious duties; no one, or at most only one or two, ever praying at all; and as for Mukni [his caravan leader] and his followers, they seemed to give themselves very little trouble about it. The only devout person amongst them, was one of our camel-men, who roared out all day, as loud as he was able, verses from the Koran, and charms against the devil; yet, in spite of his sanctity, he was the greatest rascal in the kafflé [caravan]."[27]

These "charms" are still very much in evidence among the Tuareg of the twenty-first century, also in violation of Muslim convention. Women commonly wear a fertility symbol called the *khomissar*; older women frequently hang around their necks an arrangement of camel's teeth whose therapeutic abilities are thought to be manifold. In earlier days some of the Tuareg nobles wore as many as twenty amulets pinned to the chest to ward off evil and disease. By wearing, or sometimes swallowing, a sacred text, deep-desert Tuareg believed they were protecting themselves against illness and even against violent death. Certain charms were believed to make a man (and his camel) bulletproof, a belief that persisted into the twentieth century despite ample evidence to the contrary. So effective were charms and amulets believed to be that the desert proverb "After death they hung an amulet on him" is the equivalent of the Western folk homily "to close the barn door after the horse has left." A belief in the malevolent spirits of the desert, the djinn, is still widespread. And the devil to the Tuareg is not a figure of purely theoretical malice, but a malevolent trickster who frequently leads men astray in the desert, and leaves them there to die.

In the grim ecosystems of the Sahara, there are many causes of misfortune, and it pays people to be extra careful; consequently a series of complicated beliefs and taboos has grown up around many everyday activities. It might be something as simple as a stranger expressing admiration for a child, or a horse, or any other possession that is the most certain evil. The remedy is to pass over the object a finger wet with saliva; or alternately to employ the Hand of Fatima, sewn on the clothes or tattooed on the skin. It is also regarded as dangerous to take a knife or scissors directly from anyone else (which is only prudence, perhaps); the weapon must first be placed on the ground, after which it is safe to pick it up. Smearing a layer of damp gunpowder around the perimeter of a room keeps evil spirits, *iblis*, away. This is important, for *iblis* were a constant menace, especially it seems in the Libyan desert. "If the woman of the house is delivered of a male child, this precaution prevents *iblis* and the devil's children, or imps, from coming into the room to tease or injure him; or, what is worse, to make him squint."[28]

When the first Europeans appeared in the desert, they were regarded with the utmost suspicion—perhaps they, too, were the devil's imps? With greater acquaintance, this fear faded, though others took its place. The Tuareg considered the soft Europeans so vulnerable to disease that for much of the age of exploration, which meant for the eighteenth and a good deal of the nineteenth centuries, Europeans were forbidden to sojourn in the Fezzan capital, Murzuq, except in the three winter months, when there was no threat of malaria. This was not because of concern for their welfare, but because of the conviction that the disease best reproduced inside white people, whose pale and water-rich bodies seemed somehow unfinished, and they therefore made things worse by their presence.[29]

℘

THE TUAREG differ even more fundamentally from orthodox Arab societies in their treatment of women. The most obvious symbol of the difference is that Tuareg men are veiled, but the women are not. Tuareg women can divorce their husbands without difficulty, while for a husband, divorce is hedged around with so many restrictions as to be practically impossible.

Tuareg, of course, see nothing unusual in any of this.

One day in late May, a wedding took place in Timbuktu. The afternoon before the evening festivities, the family was relaxing in a tent, anchored to a dune north of the city. No trees were nearby to cast shade, and in the Tuareg style ventilation was provided by a simple canopy of black cloth, tied to poles and floating a foot or two above the tent; this simple device caused convection currents to

A Tuareg family. (Marq de Villiers)

draw in a small breeze to keep the tent itself manageably cool. Inside, the tent was meticulously maintained: Rugs on the sand, pil-
lows for sitting, gear stowed neatly around the periphery, weapons
hung from loops, a silver tea service on the floor. The smell of mint
filled the air; mint tea is a ritual of hospitality among the Tuareg, as
it is elsewhere in the desert.

Ahmed, a young *caravannier* who plied the route between Timbuktu and the salt mines of Taghaza, was getting married that night,
but the family seemed remarkably unhurried about their daily rituals
and untroubled by the preparations necessary for the nuptials. The
bride was with her family, getting her hands and arms smeared with
henna in traditional patterns in preparation for the ceremony itself.
Ahmed himself lounged on a pillow. His sister, their parents, and as-
sorted uncles crowded in on the other side. The young woman was a
living evocation of a phrase from Angela Fisher's *Africa Adorned*, in
which she referred to "the strange wild beauty of the Tuareg women,
unveiled and free, with their startling blue eyes and fair skin burnished to old ivory by the Saharan sun, evidence of their Berber ancestry."[30] Earlier in the day she'd been dancing in the sand with her

mother and other women, their feet shuffling, singing an ancient love song, a dozen women in black or green robes, along with giggling children and one old man, dreamy in a white robe with sky-blue *tagelmoust,* who was keeping time by beating the sand with an ancient sword. The young woman was in a green robe, loosely draped; her skin was like caramelized cream. Her eyes were not blue but deep black, bold and mischievous. Around her neck she wore a single strand of blue beads and a *khomissar,* the fertility symbol. When she stood straight her head covering, kept in place by a silver pin, trailed down her back.

Tuareg women—young and old, vassal and noble—look and act like aristocrats. They seem not just independent but occasionally overbearing: They leave their husbands and return to their parents on the slightest pretext. All matters of inheritance pass through the female line, which is one reason the men find divorce so difficult, and many Tuareg men preferred to delay marriage until after their mid-twenties, contenting themselves with non-Tuareg concubines.[31]

The Tuareg are good-humored about outsider astonishment at their ways, amused that anyone would find them extraordinary. One of Ahmed's uncles, the same Mohammed Ali who made his living as a guide based in Timbuktu, asked about the religious sanction to take more than one wife, was at first evasive. It is the job of the mother to teach the writing of the language, Tamashek, to her children, he said, but a man must school his sons too, in the ways of the tribe, by which is meant a knowledge of the rituals and traditions, familiarity with the Koran, and a deep, practical knowledge of the desert and its caprices.

"It's why," Ali said, "a man should have only one wife. You can't educate your children properly if they live in too many tents."

"How many children, on average?"

"Only five, no more. The life is not easy."

But after a moment's reflection, he amplified the issue of one wife. After all, by long Islamic custom a man was "entitled" to four wives. But to the Tuareg, where the women are hardly submissive, this is altogether too difficult.

"You can have four wives, but only if you treat them all equally, and fairly," Ali said. He laughed. "And it's not just that you think you're treating them equally—they must think so, all four of them. The thing is impossible."

Traditionally, women were held in such respect that they were seldom molested, even during bloody raids by rival drum groups, and rape was vanishingly uncommon, and when it did happen, punishable by death. "Men and women toward each other are for the eyes and for the heart, and not only for the bed" was a common Tuareg aphorism. After marriage, a Tuareg woman was expected to keep a number of male friends who were encouraged to visit her tent even when her husband was away.

In a society with unsubmissive females and males so often away for extended periods, there were many curiosities of belief. Gustav Nachtigal found that "no Tuareg doubts for a moment that a child can 'sleep' in the womb for years, or even forever. This pious faith gives a frivolous wife a welcome and convenient pretext for representing to her husband in a respectable light any increase in the family that may have taken place in his absence. The embryo of the child was conceived before he set out on his long journey, but God then neglected to waken it on time to effective life, to birth. In such a case, indeed, a husband may be unable completely to suppress his doubts, but against the possibility there is absolutely nothing to be said."[32]

℘

WELL INTO THE EVENING of Ahmed's wedding feast, goats were still being slaughtered for the grill. At midnight, the air was still smoky, still aromatic from the grilling goats. In the desert or on caravan, the Tuareg seldom eat meat, not even camel, but this is not to say they don't appreciate it. "The highest act of love for a courting Tuareg was to kill a camel. 'I cut out a steak from the most tender part and stuck it on the end of my lance,' the *amenoukal* of the Ahaggar Tuareg remembered of his youth. 'To offer a very red steak, still steaming with life, to the woman one adores, what a beautiful expression of love.'"[33]

The Tuareg are a slender people, but not thin; the older people sometimes look desiccated, but they are wiry and tough in the fiber. "Unless a man is reaped by the sword," the saying goes, "he lives forever in the desert." Tuareg elders in their nineties are common enough to escape comment. Day to day, their diet is spare, but nutritious enough, made up mostly of dates, camel and goat milk and cheese, and millet, with occasional meals of camel or goat meat. In the Mauritanian desert, Archibald Robbins found his captors subsisting almost wholly on the milk of the camel, which they sometimes warmed on heated stones. Traditionally, the Tuareg wouldn't eat birds or their eggs, and still don't.[34] Pack food called *zummita*, taken on the caravans, is not much more than lightly salted cakes of millet, moistened either with camel's milk or water, and seasoned with a smidgen of rancid fat. It is eaten sparingly: Taken at dawn, a handful does a fullgrown Tuareg for the better part of a day. To accompany this, there are sometimes sheets of spiced and sun-dried camel's flesh, beaten so thin it looks like lace, carried at the camel's side like meaty doilies.

In need, the Tuareg will do as needs must. The roots of desert plants are sometimes ground for "coffee," and so are date nuts. In dire straits nomads will occasionally dig up anthills to retrieve the reserves of grain and seeds.

Water-rich outsiders still find that imitating Tuareg eating habits is very hard. René Caillié, trying a native diet, wrote in his journals: "I have since been told that my eyes were hollow, that I panted for breath, and that my tongue hung out of my mouth."[35] Barth himself noted that "it is indeed very remarkable how quickly the strength of a European is broken in these climes," and François Lamy, who helped pioneer the French Sahara regiments, once tried to cut his intake to the Tuareg level and nearly starved. Archibald Robbins and his companions found it just as difficult, and would do almost anything for a bite of meat, however small, and however peculiar. "We thought it no great crime to steal a little water from a goat skin, as we were nearly choked. After this Mr. Savage [the master of their shipwrecked vessel] recollected that early in the morning a wen or sore had been cut out of one of his master's camels; and we concluded to cook and eat this excrescence. A little fire remained, mixed with sand, into which we put our delicious morsel, and before we had half roasted it, we saw Mr. Savage's mistress approaching, and ate it down, almost at a mouthful, knowing that this was the only method we could take to secure it."[36]

It is still not uncommon for Tuareg on caravan to eat nothing more than a handful of dates during the day, with a little *zummita* and milk at night, and seem none the worse for it, even over an extended period.

಄

THE SETTLED ARABS of the Fezzan (who themselves frequently drank pure fat, butter or oil, and, not unnaturally, "complained continually of bile"[37]) tell stories, half admiring and half contemptuous, of the Tuareg and their ways. One such was of a man who was sent on an errand from Ghat to Ghadamès, a journey of some eighteen days. He was given sufficient provision to keep him the whole way "but which, devouring [it] at a meal, and girding his loins with a belt, he mounted his camel and performed the journey without other sustenance."[38] This almost contemptuous disregard for the hazards of desert life seems ingrained in the nomads, and has been reported by almost every Sahara traveler. Typical was the story Gustav Nachtigal reported when his party seemed lost, deep inside the Tummo Mountains at the fringe of the Tibesti. For three days they traveled without finding any new water, when they were down to their last ten liters (for ten men, camels, and two dogs), their guide, Kolokomi, took his turn after all the others. He took only a small mouthful, cooled his mucous membranes with it, then spat it out. He was not thirsty, he said, but Christians, People of the Water, it was well known, were not able to endure privation, and should drink their fill. He didn't need water because he was Tubu.[39]

The Tuareg feel the same, and so do the Moors. They can survive in the desert, in places where no others can live. It is a basic part of their self-regard.

CHAPTER THIRTEEN

❧

Life on the Road

THE CAMELS PLODDED steadily across the Erg de Ténéré, their feet throwing up little puffs of fine white sand. The terrain was flat, featureless, gravel covered with sand, no dunes, and only the occasional boulder for relief. The temperature had been bearable—it seldom climbed past 110°F, except during the midday halt. There had been no wind since the caravan left, and it had made good progress, was even, if the cameleers were to be believed, ahead of schedule.

At every halt, the travelers would chatter among themselves in Tamashek. Sometimes, if they felt in the mood, they would break into French to tell stories of desert life. These were apparently random anecdotes, but they all touched on desert life, and in some way on survival. They included stories about the blind leading the sighted across the desert, and about how sand could grind into the eye and make a man blind. There were many stories about camels: how a camel's health is more important than your own—how many men can carry a sick camel?; how to use fire to cauterize the wounds caused by the rawhide straps of packs; and how to hold down a camel while it is burned for its own good; how to pacify a recalcitrant camel by push-ing a plug of tobacco into its nostrils; how to accumulate your camel's dung to make a small fire for tea later on; how much milk to take from a camel; how to hobble a camel; even how and when to kill one if necessary.

There were other topics too: how to take care of your water—it was here they cautioned about setting a *guerba* on the ground, for its contents would be sucked into the desert through its apparently impermeable skin. How to defecate in the desert without disrobing, a neat trick calling for extraordinary balance. About hunger, and how to overcome it, and about when you must drink, and when you can go without. About women, and their manifold treacheries and their inescapability. About family, and bloodlines, and history and the ancient days. About illness, and about the necessity of charms, despite the hectoring of the *imams*. There were many stories about men getting lost in the desert, of men setting off and never arriving, of whole caravans vanishing, of men led astray by demons. Mostly these last were tales from the past, for these travelers professed not to believe in demons, only in man's incomparable incompetence, but the tense they used was the present, and they never laughed while telling them.

These stories, and the cameleers' evident expertness, were all somehow reassuring, despite their often dire tone. The hazards were clear enough, but so were the lifelines, what the Tuareg called "their necessaries." Necessary water, of course. Necessary forage, which water made possible. The necessary camel. And at the end of the journeys, where the "necessaries" all came together, the desert oasis.

☙

THE CARAVAN, camels in convoy, has always been the char-acteristic mode of Saharan travel, as indeed it still is, albeit in rump form. There is safety in numbers, after all, in an environment in which a sick camel or a broken leg or wild men of the open desert would mean certain death.

Caravans could be small, family affairs, a score of camels, half a

A small caravan. (Akakus)

dozen people, as this one was. Many were made up of a hundred or so camels, and these are still common enough today. In previous centuries some were much larger, such as the trading caravans in which merchants banded together to make the crossing; sometimes these numbered five thousand camels or more. In the earlier days, when the riches of Old Ghana were pouring across the desert to Marrakech and Tripoli, and a parallel stream of slaves from the apparently endless resource of central Africa were stumbling across the desert from Bornu to Tripoli and Fezzan, caravans of twenty thousand and even thirty thousand camels were not unknown. As a consequence, the great market towns of those days, places like Sijilmasa or Murzuq in the north, Timbuktu and Gao in the south, were always thronged with outsiders, visitors, traders. In Timbuktu great warehouses were set up that housed trade goods, contained stables for camels, and, upstairs, had suites of rooms available for merchants and their servants. Some of the larger trading houses kept warehouses of their own at both ends of the major cross-Sahara routes. The population of a town could swell by fifteen thousand people, or even more, in a good year.

In modern times, caravans of five hundred camels still occasionally can be found, but very seldom any larger.

Because of the hazards of the journey, and the time it takes, a caravan's departure was traditionally a matter of some ceremony. Heinrich Barth watched a large caravan setting off from Agadez, his description a typical mix of romanticism and pedantry: The departure was "heralded by drumming, and a wild, enthusiastic cry, raised over the whole extent of the encampment, with great spirit, answered to the beating of the drums. . . . Here was a nation in motion, going on its great errand of supplying the wants of other tribes, and bartering for what they stood in need of themselves. All the drums were beating; and one string of camels after another marched up in martial order, led on by the 'adogu' the most experienced and steadfast among the servants or followers of each chief."[1]

Historically, the greatest caravans were those that crossed the desert on its north-south axis, demanding substantial resources in camels and supplies. The crossing from Morocco to Timbuktu took, tradition has it, fifty-two days, nearly two months of slogging through sand, sere scrub, and stones. Traders and camel-masters were routinely away for six months, a year—it could sometimes take four months just to assemble enough men and beasts to make the return trip, the most profitable one, safe for travel. Gustav Nachtigal cooled his heels in Murzuq, in Libya, for nearly four months waiting for a caravan to depart for Bornu, but it kept being put off as rumors of unrest in the south unsettled the merchants he was to accompany. It would sometimes take a year before a caravan large enough to be considered safe could be assembled. Most of the terminus cities, in the south as well as the north of the desert, had produce and animal markets that depended on these long delays for their profit.

Few camel trains any longer make their way across the desert, their place taken by overladen buses, or by diesel-engined trucks. Nevertheless, caravans can still commonly be seen in the desert, on routes difficult for motor vehicles but also paralleling the occasional paved highway, and on certain routes the camel is still the overwhelming favorite mode for travelers. One of these is the round-trip from Timbuktu to the Taghaza salt mines that lasts, on average, forty days. Another is the Aïr Mountains (or Agadez)-Bilma-Zinder triangle. Bilma is one of the greatest and oldest salt-mining centers of the Sahara, one of the underpinnings of the power of old Kanem-

Bornu and a source of its sultan's riches; Zinder was a trading town with access to the Hausa markets. Bilma's salt still drives the traffic: Caravans set out from Agadez and the Aïr region laden only with money; in Bilma they buy salt to take to Zinder, where they trade it for cash or for millet; the millet they take back to Agadez, to trade for more money. The circle will take the caravan six months, but there is profit to be made; a successful trip will keep a man and his family comfortable for a year.

Almost every week a caravan sets off on the first leg of this venerable triangle, from the Agadez region or the Aïr oases to Bilma. Salt trading is still their main purpose, but along with the traders there are often fellow-travelers heading home to Bilma or Fachi, thence north to Tripoli or south to the Hausa towns. They go along for the company, taking their own camels and their own food. There is no fee for joining such a venture. The caravan is going anyway, and anyone is welcome who is not a burden.

The stages of the route, east from Agadez past the Tree of Ténéré and across the dunes of the Erg of Bilma, were laid down by long custom. Everyone knew where they began and ended, and all the camel-masters knew where the best camping sites were to be found. The modern route differs in no way from the ancient one, nor from the stage-by-stage plan laid out for Heinrich Barth by the Emgedesi Emgeri, a leader of the Aïr Tuareg, in 1840.[2]

On the appointed day the travelers made their way to the spot where the caravan was to assemble. About a week earlier, the baggage for the caravan had begun to accumulate in a U-shaped cut in the Tiguidit cliffs, about thirty miles south of Agadez. The baggage grew in untidy piles, each separated by about a camel's length, each pile the property of a family camel-master who was solely responsible for its safety. A Tuareg or Hausa caravan has no captain, no leader, no overall hierarchy except that of caste and function— camel-masters, baggage-masters, servants—unless of course there is an important personage on the caravan, a sheikh or a rich man or a warrior. Desert celebrities are well known, and generally easy to spot by the busywork of their entourages and their own inbuilt swagger.

The only Saharan caravans that deviate from this ordered chaos are those of the Chaamba, who are otherwise as anarchic a society as it is possible to be. Chaamba caravans, heavily armed and tightly controlled, are unique in desert travel, a long way from the chaotic agglomerations of the Tuareg: The authority of their camel-masters is as absolute as an eighteenth-century European sea captain's, their power wielded with the same brutal efficiency.

In the last few days before departure, a servant was assigned to watch over each pile. In these less perilous days, that is usually enough. In precolonial times, however, armed guards were necessary, for raids and looting were common even before the caravan departed. These days baggage may lie untouched on the desert for days before the men and camels start to arrive. No two parties seemed to have any gear in common, except of course for the ubiquitous water bags.

"How do you decide what to take with you?" a camel-master was asked.

The cameleer looked down pityingly. "What you take depends on what you have," he said. "If you are carrying millet for sale, and you have too much, you add another camel or two. You can always add camels." Sometimes, he explained, you can add camels along the way; there are always a few for sale. "Like this caravan," he said. "We are going to Bilma, but we are carrying nothing, except money for those who need it. Only supplies for ourselves. From Bilma we carry salt, so we need more camels. Is it better to take extra camels now, or to buy them in Fachi along the way, or in Bilma? Each man has his own answer."

"What is yours?"

"We take two camels for each man, and a she-camel for milk. I have family at the last oasis before Bilma. I will get more camels there. Others take many more. Those who come from Timia will also need camels to bear forage, for there is none on their route."

"You buy the salt?"

"You can, that is why people take money, but my family has right-of-possession. The salt is ours."

Bilma used to be the property of the Bornu sultans, but is now theoretically under the suzerainty of the sultan of Agadez, though it is a long way from the Aïr. The salt mines, which have been worked for at least eight hundred years without interruption, are theoretically state property, and the extracted salt is taxed, not directly but through family consortiums, some of them Tuareg, some Tubu, a few Hausa. Like everything else in Niger, the army seems to get its share; tax money is easily diverted for a small "tribute." This is not new: In earlier times, caravans paid for protection too, and tribute was paid to every petty chieftain along the way, for his *droit-de-passage*. Classically the sultan gets his cut, and arbitrates disputes; and although this system has been, at least in theory, superseded by state power, in practice the sultan still acts as a state surrogate and the system is perpetuated.

For about ten miles in the direction of Agadez there was nothing but *reg*, hard stone and gravel, the texture of a good-grade country road. A little farther was an ancient wadi, dry and dusty. The presence of water was betrayed by scraggly acacias scattered with odd regularity across the empty riverbed. Little heaps of sand showed where the wells were. They were shallow, not much more than three or four feet deep. "Seasonal," the camel-master pointed out. "Dry half the year. Last about three months after the rainy season."

This was a surprise. There is a rainy season here?

"Not really. In the Aïr. But water travels."

The Aïr Mountains were on the other side of Agadez. The water must travel forty miles or more under intensely arid and sunbaked terrain through a network of underground watercourses.

The wells are left alone until the last day, when the servants crowd around to fill the *guerbas*. The camels are watered every third day on the road, or whenever there is a well.

The loading of the camels for the small caravan assembled at Tiguidit took less than an hour, and when the caravan actually departed family groups simply plodded away in no discernible order and to no discernible orders. The last to mount were the baggage-masters, having satisfied themselves that the loads were properly stowed and that nothing had been left behind. Then they, too, ambled away into the desert.

ℰℐ

C A R A V A N S have always set off very early in the morning, well before sunup, usually around 4:00, and certainly before 5:00. They camp in the heat of the day, then travel again until well into the night. The sun is clockwork enough, and the Tuareg day is divided into periods organized around inclinations of the sun: *Dengelwak* and *arora* are dawn and early morning respectively, and good for traveling; *agedelchit* and *terut* are forenoon and zenith, when prudent men avoid the sun; *takkes* and *almez* are late afternoon and dusk, both prime traveling times. Journeys are always measured in days, never in fixed distances.[3] In practice, it doesn't seem to matter whether they travel by day or by night; the *caravanniers* never seem to lose their way.

The daily routine is unvarying. The first business is morning prayer. This is followed by the first tea of the day, weak and syrupy, a desert staple without which life would seem insupportable. Breakfast, usually just some *zummita* paste or a small ball of foul-smelling dried fish steeped in camel's milk, follows, though sometimes, if time presses, breakfast will be taken "on the run," after the caravan has set off, youths or the least experienced assigned to trot between camels to deliver it. If breakfast is eaten in camp, the next chore is to round up the camels, which have been left to forage for what they can find—the camp is, if possible, at a place where at least some sparse vegetation grows. This can take several hours, depending on how far the beasts have wandered. If there was no forage, the camels eat what they have carried, and remain hobbled through the night. The loads are then restowed and the caravan moves out, the baggage-masters checking constantly to see everything is properly packed. They mount their own camels only when satisfied nothing is improperly tied. At around noon a halt is called; the camels are unloaded again and left to forage for themselves. After prayers, more tea is brewed and "lunch" served, usually more *zummita* and perhaps a few dates. After a few hours the camels are rounded up again and the caravan plods on until well after dusk. The evening devotions are longer and the evening meal more substantial, usually including at least some camel or goat meat, milk, and more dates. And of course tea. Tents are seldom pitched, unless there are women in the caravan. The *caravanniers* simply wrap themselves in their blankets and sleep on the sand. The "latrine" is the far slope of the closest dune, sometimes distressingly nearby. Hands are washed, but no other ablutions take place until the caravan has reached its destination. Teeth are cleaned by chewing on fibers.

A caravan's passage is oddly silent, muted, even secretive. Camels' feet make no noise on the dunes, and even on the *hamada* or *regs*, their soft feet make a padding sound, and never clatter. So you can hear the creak of leather, the sloshing of the water in the skins, the grumbles and old-man moans and lisping panting of the camels, murmuring conversations and occasionally a melancholy singing. Even when the pace is picked up—perhaps a water hole is nearby, or the sun is beating overhead and shade is within reach, or simply because the drivers suspect some unknown peril, human-caused or natural—the sounds escalate only slightly. There will be a few shouts, the crack of whips, irritated curses. If the need to move more quickly is urgent, camels that won't go faster are encouraged to extra exertion by slicing into their necks with a sword or a dagger, and prodding the fresh wound with a stick.

Occasionally, when the going is obvious—the caravan may be following a wadi, or making for a distant escarpment, or following a pathway made by centuries of travelers—the *caravanniers* dismount and walk together, gossip a little, and perhaps sing, to themselves and their beasts. Their gait closely resembles that of the camels: slightly shambling, loose and long-legged, covering the ground in an astonishingly efficient way.

∾

ON THE THIRD DAY out from Agadez—somewhere in a barren valley after Tin taborak—a lake appeared in the middle distance. Of course, it wasn't really a lake. There wasn't any open water for hundreds of miles, and this "lake" seemed to shimmer in the heat. However, it was not at all like the pools of "water" one sees so often in the middle distance on blacktop highways, shiny patches of superheated air. This really did look like water, with discrete boundaries and what surely were waves.

A few days earlier a Tuareg elder in Agadez had engaged in a somewhat circular discussion about mirages in the desert.

"There is always water," the old man had said, "in mirages."

He was squatting on his heels in a dusty street, his back propped against a wall. He was drawing patterns in the sand with a twig.

"It's just the heat playing tricks, isn't it?"

"There are always tricks in the desert," the old man said, scuffing out his design and starting again.

"But it doesn't mean anything?"

"Oh, but it does. The water is no-water, but a mirage is a seeing, not a no-seeing."

"So can you *use* mirages, in a practical way?"

There is a physical explanation for mirages, or *shrab* as they're called in Tamashek: The shimmering of superheated air on hot days results from disorganized refraction, caused by turbulence, which is caused in turn by layers of air of different temperatures. Cooler air refracts the sun's rays at different angles than the less-dense heated air, and so objects of varying distances seem to coalesce. Sometimes, when mirages are caused at temperature boundaries in the air instead of near the ground, the refracted air acts as a lens, and can magnify distant images. All this is complicated, though, by the appearance of "water" where there really is none—there is no water over the horizon to be reflected. It is the sky that is the object of the mirage, reflected on the ground.

So, the Tuareg elder was asked, what use are mirages? When trees appear in a mirage, are they real trees, somewhere? What of the stories that people have seen ships sailing in a pool of water, whole oases, glorious shrubs and trees, palm trees swaying in the wind? Forests of trees? Even cities?

A mirage shimmering on the horizon. (Academie de Grenoble)

The encyclopedias are carefully ambiguous. "Under unusual conditions," says the *Encyclopaedia Britannica*, without saying what they
are, "more elaborate mirages may appear as cities, forests, oases and
even the images of ships in a nearby body of water plying the sky of
a desert."[4] They may appear as cities, but *are* they cities? In 1897 an
exploring expedition clearly saw what they called a "Silent City."
One of the expedition members wrote, "It required no effort of the
imagination to liken it to a city, but was so distinct that it required,
instead, faith to believe that it was not in reality a city."[5] They could
plainly see houses, streets, trees, building spires. Was this a distant
city refracted to appear near? Or was it something else? Mirages of
this sort are not like internal visions; they are objective reality. You
can photograph them, and the photograph will be just as you remember: What looked like a lake to you will look like a lake in the
photo; if you see a city, a city will appear on film. But the *content* of
the mirage? Is that objective reality too? Was it really a city? What if
the city was only in your head, invisible to others in your party?

The Tuareg elder was no more helpful. "It's like sight, not like a
vision," he said, "but you must interpret what you see in any case,
understand what you see."

What he meant was that mirages are not always false. Sometimes only the sense of distance, the perspective, is false. Because of it, bushes can seem like trees, grasses like a waving forest, rocks like mountains—and sometimes they are seen upside down.

George Lyon reported the effect in 1818. "I have frequently, in riding along, been delighted in observing in the distance a tree which appeared sufficiently large to shade me from the sun and to allow of my reposing under it until the [other] camels came up, and have often quickened my pace in consequence until, on a near approach, it has proved to be nothing more than a bush, which did not throw a shade sufficient even to shelter one of my hands. Sand hills deceived even more, always appearing very distant when the sun is upon them, and it has often happened that I have been startled by seeing a man or camel rise close to me, on the top of one of these apparently distant hills."[6]

Sometimes, though, the seeing isn't what it seems. The Tuareg elder insisted you could learn to distinguish between the two, but sometimes mirages are a product of the internal landscape, and not the distorted refraction of light. They resemble visions, but they are just short-circuits brought on by evaporating moisture deep in the folds of the brain. To the lost and desperate, however, vision and mirage have similar consequences.

Ryszard Kapuscinski, traveling in 1999 through the Mauritanian desert in a truck in the company of some Moors, reported such a vision: "The lifeless still horizon, so crushed by the heat that it seemed nothing could ever issue forth from it, all at once sprang to life and became green. As far as the eye could see stood tall, magnificent palm trees, entire groves of them along the horizon, growing thickly, without interruption. I also saw lakes, yes, enormous blue lakes, with animated undulating surfaces. Gorgeous shrubs grew there, with-spreading branches of a fresh, intense, succulent deep green. All this shimmered continuously, sparkled, pulsated, as if it were wreathed in a light mist, soft-edged and elusive." His companion, who saw no such vision, brought him a *guerba,* and he drank greedily of their dwindling stock of water. As he felt his thirst subsiding "and the madness within me dying down, the green vista began to vanish. Its colors paled, its contours blurred. By the time I had emptied the goatskin, the horizon was once again flat, empty, and lifeless."[7]

The Tuareg elder in Agadez was asked what could be done about the desperate thirst that seemed to produce the most vivid visions.

"Nothing," he replied. "Take water or wait for death."

"And the oases? The forests? The lakes? The water?"

"It is not a vision of Paradise," he said, "if that is what you're asking. It is just the human spirit trying to escape its fate."

&

ON THE FOURTH DAY the little caravan debouched from the sand sea with its rolling dunes onto a gravel plain, and plodded steadily across it at an oblique angle. It was similar to thousands of such plains in the Sahara, gray stone, a few boulders, otherwise utterly featureless. The stages of the route may be laid down by centuries of practice, as the *caravanniers* told everyone who would listen, but there was no sign of a "road" at all, or even a pathway. And in the sand seas, if a breeze was present, the tracks of the camels at the head of the caravan were extinguished by the time the stragglers reached them. Nevertheless, not once did the lead camel hesitate or come close to losing its way. How the guides knew where they were going was a mystery.

A week earlier, traveling this time in a Landcruiser, they had been crossing just such a gravelly plain, a dull mix of gray and dun. It was flat, utterly flat, just gravel and sand, just as this *hamada* was. The last vegetation had been several miles back, tufts of dry grass and a few stunted acacias, nibbled to the thorns by passing camels. The horizon was a blue smudge that might have been hills but never seemed to get any closer. Overhead, the sky was a bitter grayish yellow, the sun baleful and sulfurous. The Landcruiser's passing left no tracks, even on close inspection. There was no sign, indeed, that anyone had ever passed here.

At midmorning, the driver abruptly hauled on the wheel and made a turn—twenty degrees? thirty?—to the right and headed off in a new direction toward no feature, no prominence, no landmark. He was expressionless, a Tuareg in deep-desert gear, his *tagelmoust* loosely draped, exposing his mouth, his thin lips stained blue. He turned. Why? He didn't say. From what landmark? None. Toward what? There was nothing.

After thirty more minutes of grinding travel, a tree appeared ahead. A solitary tree, the only tree for twenty-five miles. It was less than six feet tall, gnarled and almost leafless.

The driver didn't stop but turned left, fifteen, twenty degrees, more or less. After another few minutes the terrain changed. There were ripples in the sand, and small dunes appeared. He threaded his way among the dunes until the gravel plain was lost to sight. There were dunes on all sides, all of them identical, about sixty feet high, slightly blurred from the blowing sand. There was no path. The driver hauled on the wheel, left, right, left left right, right, right, left left, the featureless dunes replicated as monotonously as Pacific swells at mid-ocean.

After a while he stopped, killed the motor, and got out. There was no sound but the pinging of the engine and the wind in the ears.

"Come," he said, "I want to show you something."

He plodded over a small dune. There was nothing different about it, just a dune, like all the others. On the other side was a small wadi, with a rock escarpment on its far side, not much more than six feet in height. At its foot, toppled, were several large tree trunks, fossilized remnants of the forest that had once grown here. The driver slid to the base of the dune and squatted next to a stone trunk. Toward one end, carved into the stone, was a series of small reliefs. The animals depicted looked like bison, but were probably cattle and goats, though not very well executed: The fossilized wood was too brittle and chipped too easily.

The driver pulled a small hammer and a battered screwdriver from his pocket and hacked away at the wood—stone?—behind the drawings, chipping about half of a small bison into his palm and slipping it into a small bag. Then they returned to the vehicle and drove away, threading among the dunes again. Sure enough, after a while the solitary acacia reappeared, and the gravel plain, and the driver hauled on the wheel as before. There were still no signposts, no markers, no landmarks, no trees, no wadis, no hills, nothing.

The desert is a hazardous place, even for the experienced, and travelers will take what signs they may. Wherever possible, small cairns of stones will be placed on a hillock or some prominence visible from a distance, especially where the roads are uncertain. Most travelers passing by feel obliged to maintain these cairns by adding a few stones to the pile. In the High Arctic, the Inuit call such way-guides *inukshuks*. The Tuareg call them *aalum*, or teachers.

And yet, there had been no teachers to be seen this day in the Ténéré. Why didn't he get lost?

&

THIS QUESTION has fascinated Saharan travelers for centuries. The British traveler Nigel Heseltine, passing through the Tibesti in the 1950s, scribbled in his notebook, before he'd even seen a single inhabitant: "We had not yet seen a Tubu . . . but this was their inhabited country, and as soon as I saw the camels' prints I felt their presence. How many secrets did they know of this terrain which the vague lines sketched by the map-makers had not even hinted at? They moved perfectly at home, following landmarks invisible to us, knowing precisely when and where they would come upon a well, needing only the milk of their camels, a few dried dates and a little meal for the weeks they would spend before returning to the high plateaus of the mountains."[8]

René Caillié wrote in his notebook in 1824: "Though without a compass, or any instrument of observation, they possessed so completely the habit of noticing the most intimate things, that they never go astray, though they have no path traced out for them, and though the wind in an instant completely covers with sand and obliterates the tracks of the camels."[9]

What are these "intimate things"? Some of it, of course, has to do with celestial navigation: The Tuareg are as familiar with the stars and the angles of inclination of the sun and moon as any ancient mariner. But the Tuareg seldom travel in straight lines, and outsiders who have tried to keep track with a compass have found the instrument of little use. Any journey is a sinuous series of deviations and side-tracks; the nomads will be diverted by shifting shadows, wind patterns, blown sand, moonlight, the stars, the setting and rising sun, the incidence of scrub grasses, ancient erosion gullies, wadi traces, the now-useless "divides," the silhouettes of hills, mirages— and smell.

European explorers of the nineteenth century discounted the tales as scarcely believable, but early travelers knew about this notion of smell as a navigational aid. Leo Africanus, writing in the early 1500s, described what happened to a caravan of merchants that had become lost in the middle of the Libyan desert: "The caravan had a certain blinde man in their companie which was acquainted with all those regions: This blinde guide riding foremost upon his camell, commanded some sand to be given to him at every mile's end, by the smell whereof he declared the situation of the place: But when they were come within fortie miles of this region, the blinde man, smelling of the sand, affirmed that they were not farre from some place inhabited; which some believed not for they knew that they were distant from Egypt some fower hundred and eightie miles, so they took themselves to be nearer unto Augela [a bedraggled little oasis town on the caravan route from Egypt to Mauritania, known to Herodotus as a place to lay in supplies of dates]. Howbeit within three days they found three castles, the inhabitants thereof wondering at the approach of strangers, and being greatly astonied, presently shut all their gates and would give the merchants no water to quench their extreme thirst. But the merchants by main force entered and having gotten water sufficient, betook themselves againe to their journie."[10]

Not every nomad has this gift of navigation, as they will readily tell you. A caravan today will never set off unless it has at least one such in its party, a guide who is treated with the utmost respect. Desert travelers have often been advised that choosing a guide is much more difficult, and much more important, than choosing companions, trade goods, or even camels. Some claiming to be guides haven't been; others have been bandits who would lead travelers deliberately astray. In latter days, many who claim to be guides seem to know perilously little about camels, being rather more used to the internal combustion engine.

᙮

WIND-MOLDED DUNES are regarded as unreliable guides to navigation; winds are channeled around obstructions like mountains and massifs, so that dunes are affected by different winds on different sides. Lighter winds can blow from several directions, and the dunes, being of fine sand, can be buffeted about in the slightest breeze; nomadic navigators therefore discount them as route indicators. Strong winds and sandstorms, which are the only winds that can move large particles, usually come from one direction, and the undulations of the sand sheets, as opposed to sand dunes, are laid out accordingly, making sand sheets a navigational aid.

The Toyota driver, when asked how he knew where to turn when there was neither dune nor sheet, nor any other marker, answered elliptically.

" I knew where the tree *was*," he explained. "I had the sun on my shoulder, so I steered toward where it *is*."

"You were guided by the sun?"

"The sun and the *knowing*."

In a sandstorm, a few days later, the same man headed out into the swirling mess. Visibility was a few yards. No visual clues were available, certainly not the sun. A check of the compass showed he was heading true north, just as he had said he would. Somehow, he *knew*.

Not all travelers have shared this view of the Saharan nomads as omnicompetent masters of the desert. Archibald Robbins in the early 1800s left a portrait of his captors that makes them out to be wanderers moving erratically across the desert, not always knowing where water was to be found, driven more by whim and caprice than knowledge. Even the grim lifestyle of the deep desert left some room, it seems, for bumblers.

Getting lost, however, is very seldom something that a desert traveler does more than once. Disorientation generally means death. A story often told in the salt-mining town of Bilma concerns a caravan from Zinder whose guide lost the way. A score of men and a hundred camels died because their guide made a mistake, and missed the wells.

❧

AFTER THE *HAMADA*, the little caravan threaded its way once again between rows of dunes of the Erg of Bilma. From aloft, perched on the saddle that somehow wraps itself around the camel's ungainly back, one's perspective on the desert is quite different from the view on foot or from the inside of a Landcruiser. It takes time to get used to the camel's lurching gait, to know when to brace oneself and fit in with the rhythm of the camel's stride, but once this is mastered, the view from a camel's back is surprisingly more expansive, the horizons, when the dunes don't intervene, much more distant than from the ground. A camel's stride doesn't look long, and its gait is unhurried, but it covers ground at a pace much faster than a walking man.

Camels can continue to walk steadily all day if necessary, and the following day too, without any sustenance, either food or water. Indeed, as Archibald Robbins put it, "were it not for the camel, the immense desert called the Zahara must be wholly deserted by human beings."[11] Camels turned the Sahara from a barrier to something approaching a community. The analogy of sailors on the ocean, with islands as oases, is apt. One can sail the seas if one can navigate and has a seaworthy vessel. Camels are eminently desert-worthy, seemingly built for the task.

The camel is not native to the Sahara. It was introduced from Arabia by the Berbers of the northern Sahara, probably around the third century, several centuries before the Arab invasions, but it then swiftly became indispensable. This, in any case, is the truism, accepted virtually everywhere. But what to make, then, of this note, buried in an academic report in 1999: "Professor Rufus Churcher returned to investigate the lake sediment deposits they discovered

Camels in the Sahara. (Arabnet)

last season in the eastern end of the [El-Dakhla] oasis, three separate areas of sediment from the late Pleistocene period, approximately 250,000–12,000 years old. The Teneida Palaeobasin yielded the richest source of animal fossils for Professor Churcher, an extinct camel, a warthog, a hippopotamus, cattle."[12] So perhaps there were camels in the Sahara in prehistoric times. Perhaps they became extinct and had to be re-imported.

Desert crossings were being made long before the third century, but at even greater peril, and only by the shortest possible routes. Horses were occasionally used, even oxen, but neither of these adapts well to desert life. Camels can walk uncomplainingly into a drifting wall of blowing sand, protected by their long-lashed and double-lidded eyes, hairy ear openings, and the ability to close their nostrils against the wind. Their two-toed feet spread on soft sand, bearing their weight without sinking. They can subsist, if necessary, on sparse and thorny grasses. They can store fat in their humps, drawing on these reserves as needed. There are "water cells" in their stomachs that have been used by the Tuareg in dire extremity (if the camel is killed, there are gallons of water stored there, enough to keep a man alive another day). The camels can go for several days without drinking, for they lose moisture only slowly, and can recover it quickly (sometimes regaining lost weight in ten minutes by drinking, at one session, up to twenty-five gallons of water). In summer, a camel can endure up to five days without drinking anything; in winter, they have been known to endure a fortnight or more. Where the pasture is plentiful, they don't need to be watered at all, or so the Tuareg believe; and in such places the Tuareg too subsist entirely without water, for the camels graze and the nomads drink camel's milk. A productive camel can provide for its own calf and still yield a gallon of milk a day. Camels are large beasts—many more than twelve feet high—and of substantial mass. Their large size is a survival mechanism in the desert, for they absorb heat slowly and release it parsimoniously. A camel's body temperature rises steadily during the day; at night the stored heat dissipates. In neither case is much water lost.

Saharan camels are famous for their endurance. When the French brought horses into the Algerian desert in the 1850s the Tuareg planned a race, to see whether the "English" horse or the Arab was superior. The course? "A fortnight's run through the sand." Why not? The camels could do it.[13]

&

IT ALWAYS SURPRISED European explorers and their military escorts, who tended to mistake a lack of technology for backwardness, with what astonishing speed news reverberated around the Sahara. The distances are immense and the population small, but the camel allows the people who inhabit the desert to be highly mobile, in ancient days as at present circulating constantly between the Sahel and the Maghreb, the Atlantic and the Nile, so much so that at times they "gave the desert the atmosphere of a small village."[14]

Leo Africanus, in a learned disquisition on camels, wrote admiringly of a camel called the Raguahill, which "are camels of a slender and low stature, which albeit they are unfit to carry burthens yet do they so excell the other two kindes in swiftness, that in the space of one day they will travell an hundred miles, and will so continue over the deserts for eight or ten daies altogether without provender. When the king of Tombuto [Timbuktu] is desirous to sende any message of importance unto the Numidian merchants with great celeritie, his post or messenger riding upon one of these camels, will run from Tombuto to Darha or Sijilmasa, being nine hundred miles distant, in the space of eight daies at the farthest: But such as travell [thus] must be expert in the way through the deserts, neither will they demaund less than five hundred ducats for every journey." Leo had identified the three types of camels that are still used today: The first were the Huguin, "[which are] grosse, and of a tall stature, and most fit to carry burthens," a thousand pounds of Italian weight in his view. "The second kind of camel is called Becheti, and having a double bunch, are fit both to carry burthens, and to ride upon, and these are bred only in Asia." The third kind were the Raguahill. The African camel, Leo maintained, far excels the two-humped camels of Asia "for travelling fortie or fiftie daies together, without any provender at all."[15]

Leo's catalogue is worth repeating in full because it accurately reflects the types of camels still working in the Sahara, and the uses to which they are generally put. In the last century, raiding parties of Tuareg, and the French military, generally used Leo's "Raguahill," more commonly called *mehari* camels (from which, via Greek and Latin, is derived the word "dromedary"), whose virtue was indeed their great speed. They are still employed when speed is of the essence and burdens are small. The Heguin, a name still in use, are the transport trucks of the desert. An adult Heguin can carry a man, his water, and two slabs of salt weighing 220 pounds each, and carry them apparently forever. A fully laden transport camel can look to the untutored eye grossly top-heavy, its burden piled on its back four, five feet or more, looking as unstable as some of the buses that crawl across the desert, but they seldom topple. The two-humped Bactrian camel, which Leo called Becheti, is seldom found in the Sahara today.

Leo himself twice crossed the desert on the back of a camel, and found them "gentle and domesticall beasts." The desert dwellers, he noted, "esteeme [the camels] to be their principall possessions and riches, so that speaking of the wealth of any of their princes or governors, he hath (they say) so manie thousand camels, and not so manie thousand ducats. Moreover [they] that possesse camels live like lords and potentates in great libertie, because they can remaine with the camels in barren deserts, whither no kings nor princes can bring armies to subdue them."

Which, no doubt, is the reason that for millennia "to own camels, and yet more camels, is the ultimate ambition of every Targui. A man may be rich in donkeys, goats or sheep, or he may have houses, gardens and slaves, but camels are the coveted possessions."[17]

Today, in the mud-built towns of the Western Desert, each family compound has a high-walled stable, in which the camels are kept when they are not being used. The doors to these stables are narrow, and oddly low. They make it difficult for the camels to wander out, or to be easily stolen, for to enter or exit the camel must drop to its knees and shuffle awkwardly through. Since antiquity these doors have been called "needle's eyes," which is why "it is easier for a camel to go through the eye of a needle than for a rich man to enter into the Kingdom of God."[18]

⁓

TWENTY DAYS after setting off from Tiguidit, two days more than Barth took a hundred and fifty years earlier, the little caravan plodded into Bilma. The oasis of Bilma is pleasant enough—hills of golden sand, waving palm trees, the cooing of doves, springs bubbling from the ground, and just outside town a magnificent pool, filled from a spring higher up on a sandy ridge, in which children can usually be found, happily splashing. But the town itself is dreary and salt-soaked, with an air of desperate shabbiness and a pervasive smell of burning garbage, and the outskirts, where the salt is dug, look like the moon, a vast iron-gray landscape heaped with rubble and pocked with pits that look like meteor craters, the drying basins for the salt excavated in the "mines," shafts sometimes thirty feet deep. Salt stalagmites give these pits a weirdly deformed look. This is not one of the enchanted oases of Saharan legend.

But paradise or not, oases remain indispensable for travelers. Oases, after all, are where desert paths meet—they are the crossroads of the Sahara. As islands in the sand sea, they are at once safe havens and victualing stops. They are home to merchants; places for traffic in foodstuffs, livestock, news, and gossip; marketplaces for a bewildering array of races and languages. Like most oases, Bilma also has its specialized activity—Bilma's business is salt, that of other oases trade, or produce, fodder for animals and food for people. But like all oases, Bilma is also a community, with permanent residents and civil codes of conduct. The nomads, for their part, come in for trade, intelligence, and refuge when water is scarce in the hot summer months, and they come to gather dates, or to buy them, the greater part of their annual food supply. In this sense, travelers and residents—the desert and the oases—are two halves of an integrated economic and social structure. Even for nomads who have no wish to be anything else it is the oases that give the Sahara texture, that make collective social and political life in the desert possible. Obviously, the larger the oasis, the larger its population and the larger the number of nomads that depend on it. Mostly, relations between the two communities—resident and nomad—are harmonious. Sometimes, however, there is discord, and squabbles break out over the date harvest or water supply. Oases, like islands in the ocean, are prone to a rancorous politics, and in the Sahara blood and language still cause violence, sometimes in quarrels that are very ancient.

In the old days when the desert was much more animated by camel caravans and the nomads raided from their remote refuges, some oases on the major routes were fortified, in which case they were called *ksars,* built to withstand predators; their dwellings were jammed together on a rocky outcrop, like medieval-European fortified villages, while the gardens and palm groves lay on the flatlands below, sometimes up to five miles away. But the typical oasis town was not an effective fort.

Historically, oasis towns were crowded with life, both pious and raffish, as indeed they still are. Muezzins called the faithful, but down in the squares "courtesans" plied their trade just as diligently, and when a large caravan arrived so did all the other entertainers of Saharan tradition: men with dancing camels, jugglers, date-spitters, itinerant tambour players, vendors of fermented date-palm juice called *laqbi,* and more. This, too, still goes on: In the camel market on the outskirts of Agadez raucous crowds are still occasionally entertained by an elderly man with a virtuoso display of basso profundo farting, playing "tunes" of mind-boggling complexity. Sometimes the mood was—and is—less cheerful: Because travelers have perforce to plod in after weary days on the road and are therefore vulnerable to both blandishment and more forceful forms of persuasion, oases are also the lair of ne'er-do-wells—rip-off artists and cheaters, traffickers in vice and other illicit matters. Things are more orderly now than they were a hundred and fifty years ago, when outsiders of whatever ethnic or religious persuasion were fair game, and Christians were routinely killed and their bodies dumped outside the walls, but muggers and thieves are still pervasive—and outsiders are still targets.

❧

OASES ARE also still very much an idea as much as they are a reality. Oases help preserve the notion that life in the great desert is still possible. The image of an oasis is always parked in the back of a nomad's mind; the Tuareg always seem to speak of oases in the future tense, never the present, as something to be attained, as a purpose for the journey, as a place to find rest, where there will be companionship and peace. This is not very different, after all, from the idea of paradise, only smaller in scale and much more attainable.

In this spirit, of all the memories of the desert, of all the souvenirs of all the stages along the way from Agadez to the salt mines of

Bilma, or from there southward to Zinder, or thence northward to
Agadez again, the most powerful memory is of the little oasis town of
Fachi. As the geologists would have predicted, Fachi is in a small depression and yes, there is now a diesel pump to pull the water from a
deep aquifer, but none of that detracts in the least from its allure:
Fachi was and is in the middle of the Erg of Bilma, surrounded by an
ocean of sand, as solitary and still a place as exists anywhere on this
planet, as hot and arid as any place in the Sahara, made of ruined for-
tifications and tumbledown houses. Yet there they were, palm trees
nearly buried in the golden sand, but alive, and green, and thus entirely magical. Oases give life through shade and water, water and
shade, and of the two, it is hard to know which is better esteemed.
Water is necessary, of course, but shade in the desert is a miracle.

EPILOGUE

❧

The Sahara as Home

IN A NUMBER of ways modernity has intervened in the Sahara, though seldom for the better. Prospectors have found oil and gas in the Libyan and Algerian Deserts, and are combing Mali and Niger and Tunisia and the Egyptian Western Desert for more, ever more. Oil trucks are rumbling across the *hamadas,* and Qaddafi has contained the northern desert with a skein of massive pipelines that is bringing temporary lushness for the first time in ten thousand years. Camels still plod parallel to the pipes, but there are also swaying trucks and buses, each piled high with people and animals and packs bound in nets, the poor of the world on the move. Trucks roar through the oases; the truck stops in Tamanrasset and Tuat and the way stations of the Aïr are polluted with discarded plastic bags and the sand is stained black with leaked crankcase oil. Many oasis towns look as though they have a thin scum of money on a sea of indigence; infrastructure is crumbling, garbage uncollected, town water polluted with slime.

There are other signs of malaise: The Paris-Dakar motor racers (increasingly regarded in the Sahara as symbols of colonialist carelessness

and arrogance) are being pelted with stones by indignant Maurita-
nians as they roar through the oases; the Berbers of the north are beginning once again to stir against the "Arab colonists"; the Polisario
guerrillas, their joints beginning to creak, remain in limbo; Cana-
dian companies stand accused of financing slave labor in Sudan;
Egypt is casting a predatory eye on Sudan's Sudd Marshes, their
only possible supply of new water; and many ancient quarrels survive into modernity, their intensity scarcely mitigated by the long
centuries.

In Tamanrasset plans for an industry of eco-tourism are being
hatched, and Tuareg guides are taking reverent foreigners into the uttermost desert to teach them the ancient ways. But the few tourists
who do come are made wary by the civil war in Algeria, and in any
case quick-fix Westerners seldom have the time for forty-day camel
travel or the patience to study the minutiae of desert lore. In the eastern Sahara, past the formidable Tibesti, caravans of people still make
their way up the Bilma Road, no longer stumbling slaves but refugees
fleeing the collapsing south, under the captaincy of people smugglers,
whose job it is to take them secretly to the Mediterranean coast,
whence they are shipped as contraband into Europe.

But in the desert's essence, very little changes. The *medinas* of
Timbuktu and Agadez still turn out their scholars. Exquisite crafts
still emerge from the workshops, not all of it destined for sale to
tourists, but for the adornment of the elegant Tuareg themselves.
And the nomads are still there, not yet shackled by bureaucratic restraints, in some ways as free as they ever were.

There are still djinn in the dunes, the date palms still give their
shade and yield their fruit, water still trickles from the massifs at the
heart of the desert, the addax still run across the sand, so fleet it
seems they could fly. The salt miners are still at work, and young
boys are still learning to become camel-masters as their fathers did,
and nomads with their camels and goats in the deep gullies of the
Ahaggar can still look up at the end of the world and see the sun
slanting against the jagged red rocks of the Atakor.

The empty desert, the fearful void, is full after all. Full of the tracks of time, of bones both mute and eloquent, of djinn and the whistling wind, of drumming sand and mirages, as rich in story, as the Tuareg say, as a breast is of milk. Full of the grinding weight of history, of soldiers come, blood feuds unexpunged, drum-groups riding to arms, thievery and brigandage. Full of the disappeared and the reappeared. Of open wells and wells fallen in, full of sand and dust, dust and sand. And thirst. Full of fading towns, crumbling oases, mosques in disrepair, in which the faithful still pray on their knees, as they've done for a thousand years and more. Full of heroes and their legendary exploits. Full of men dreaming, of stories still unfolding. Full of rich men, poor men, hard men, free men. Full of horizons not yet explored.

Sometimes there are images of almost hallucinatory power. Such was the sight—in the crumbling sandstone and golden dunes of the Tassili n'Ajjer, a hundred miles from the nearest well or the nearest human settlement and five hundred from the nearest source of electric current—of two men trudging northward, out of the deep desert, bearing on their backs the shiny carcass of an electric refrigerator. The traveling party, who were in the Tassili to see the cave paintings and the last of the living Saharan cypresses, watched them pass, mouths agape at the strangeness of it. No one said anything, or greeted the men as they struggled past.[1]

There was nothing, really, to say.

Modernity may intrude, but time is a dune with many ridges, and there are still immense tracts of Sahara unmarked by the modern, where the growl of the internal combustion engine is never heard, tracts that are tranquil and deadly, just as they always were.

History, in the Tuareg phrase, is a continuity of sorrows. If this is so, the Saharan history is very deep, and penetrates to the human bone. The Sahara is a crucible of raw emotions, as all uncompromising places are. That is part of its magic.

ℰℐℴ

THE THREE TUAREG who loomed out of the yellow, drifting sand at the start of this book, passing through in silence, their *tagelmousts* drawn across their faces, veiled and hidden, riding by without word or salutation, plodding through the superheated air, soundless but for the creaking of saddle leather, leaving no trace of their passing, like ghosts crossing from the long past into the unknown future, disappearing as they came into the shrouding sand of the endless desert—these three desert nomads were not, after all, heading nowhere. They were heading into the endless sand in the direction of nothing very much, but they were neither lost nor purposeless. They were, after all, home.

స

N o t e s

See Bibliography for full citations.

Introduction

The "outsider" quotes on the Sahara come from a wide variety of sources. The first type of source is the traveler yarn, which has a venerable history in Saharan writing, dating back at least to the fourteenth century, if not earlier. Two of the exemplars cited here are *Desert Life*, by "B. Solymos," a most curious small memoir of time spent in Sudan in the nineteenth century, and Nigel Heseltine's *From Libyan Sands*, of all the modern accounts perhaps the most engaging. Douglas Porch's *The Conquest of the Sahara* is a thorough account of the colonial period. Gustav Nachtigal, for his part, was one of the most intrepid of those nineteenth-century European explorers who delivered credible accounts of the deep desert to Western eyes; he was the first outsider to reach and survive the Tibesti, and while not as scholarly as, say, Heinrich Barth, his massive three-volume account of his travels makes riveting reading.

1. Solymos, *Desert Life*, p. vi.
2. Porch, *Conquest of the Sahara*, p. 76.
3. Heseltine, *From Libyan Sands*, p. 64.
4. Nachtigal, leaving Fezzan for Tibesti. *Sahara and Sudan*, vol. 1, p. 57.
5. Heseltine, *From Libyan Sands*, p. 41.
6. "Polisario Guerrillas Fight Aging War," *Toronto Globe & Mail*, June 19, 1999.
7. Christopher, *Ocean of Fire* [Frontispiece].

1. In a Geographer's Eye

Paul Johnson's sweeping *Birth of the Modern World* was the source for the passage on the predations of the Barbary pirates of the Maghreb. Hugh Clapperton was another of the nineteenth-century European explorers—the Denham-Clapperton-Oudney expedition to Lake Chad was successful, but full of acrimony and lurid accusations and counteraccusations (Denham at one point falsely accused Clapperton of buggery, which did their relationship very little good). Thierry Tillet's compilation *Sahara* represents the work of dozens of specialists, and is the result of a symposium on the prehistory of the Sahara held by the Abbey of Salignac, in the Haute-Vienne, France, in 1991. Tillet himself spent fourteen years in the southern Sahara, and is a specialist on the Aterian culture. Two references are sourced to the Web site africana.com, a Louisiana-based black history source that is evenhanded and always reliable. Irma Turtle, whose Arizona-based Turtle Tours has operatives in Mali and Niger particularly, is terrific for those interested in, say, old African ceremonies or in meeting tribal people on their home ground. As for Archibald Robbins—the account of his shipwreck and enslavement was widely disbelieved at the time, but much of what was thought to be the sheerest fiction has proven to be better reportage than many later travelers were able to manage.

1. Johnson, *Birth of the Modern World*, p. 288.
2. Details from Elizabeth Heath, africana.com
3. Robert Baum, Sudan, africana.com
4. Battuta, *The Travels of Ibn Battuta*, vol. 4, p. 947.
5. Hajar, *Concealed Pearls*, vol. 3, p. 480.
6. Africanus, *The History and Description of Africa* (Pory's note to readers).
7. Caillié, Travels through Central America (introduction).
8. Africanus, *The History and Description of Africa*, Book 6, p. 797.
9. Robbins, *Journal*, p. 56.
10. Africanus, *The History and Description of Africa*, Book 6, p. 798.
11. Phrase from Irma Turtle, Arizonan who is well known among the Tuareg of the Aïr.
12. Africanus, *The History and Description of Africa*, Book 6, p. 799.
13. Tillet, *Sahara*, p. 40.
14. Porch, *Conquest of the Sahara*, p. 263.
15. Clapperton, *Difficult and Dangerous Roads*, p. 234.
16. Porch, *Conquest of the Sahara*, p. 33.
17. Africanus, *The History and Description of Africa*, Book 6, p. 800.
18. Solymos, *Desert Life*, p. 46.
19. Bredin, *Pale Abyssinian*, p. 60.

2. From the Distant Past

Two sources should be particularly noted for this chapter. The first is the splendid book titled *Golden Trade of the Moors*, by William Bovill, perhaps the best historical survey yet produced of African trade between the old African empires and the north. The second is a source much underestimated by professional historians but still as thorough, credible, and reliable as ever: the *Encyclopaedia Britannica*. With some exceptions, we have relied on the print version, which we continue to think more user-friendly than its Web-based counterpart.

1. Agence France Presse, June 3, 2001.
2. Heseltine, *From Libyan Sands*, p. 42.
3. Gardi, *Sahara*, p. 136.
4. Kunzig, *Discover* magazine, January 2000, "Exit from Eden."
5. Saint-Exupéry, *Wind, Sand and Stars*, p. 90.
6. *Encyclopaedia Britannica* 5:614.
7. Tillet, *Sahara*, p. 40.
8. Bovill, *Golden Trade of the Moors*, p. 3.
9. Heseltine, *From Libyan Sands*, p. 208, footnote: Cf. Lt. Gralt, *Le Secteur Nord du Cercle de Gouré.*
10. Geophysical Research Letters, July 15, 2000.
11. Kunzig, *Discover* magazine, January 2000, "Exit from Eden."
12. Washington and Meehl, "Historical and future trends of the Sahara desert," *2001 Geophysical Research Letters*, 228 (July 15):2683.
13. Kutzbach, Bonan, and Harrison, "Vegetation and soil feedbacks on the response of the African monsoon to orbital forcing in the early to middle Holocene," *Nature*, 1996, 384:623–26, and Harrison, Kutzbach, Prentice, Behling, Sykes, "The response of northern hemisphere extratropical climate and vegetation to orbitally-induced changes in isolation during the last interglaciation," *Quaternary Research*, 1995, 43:174–84.
14. UNEP Bulletin, July 2001.
15. *Science*, #281, p. 633, 1998.
16. Ahmed Mokhtar Brere, University of Tennessee, 1979.
17. G. Drouhin, *Reviews of Research on Arid Zone Hydrology* (UNESCO, 1953).
18. Heseltine, *From Libyan Sands*, p. 43.

3 . The Sand Seas

Many explications of the physics of moving sand exist (a great number, given the more or less relaxed research involved, done as doctoral theses not on deserts but on beaches, and posted on the Web), but the best jargon-free survey is still that of the *Britannica*. David Mountfield's riotous *African Exploration* is a first-rate popular account of Europe's long-standing fascination with the African interior, and his profiles of the Saharan explorers such as Heinrich Barth, George Lyon, and Mungo Park can hardly be bettered. H. T. Norris's *Saharan Myth and Saga* is a fascinating account of the legends that have accreted to the Sahara since Carthaginian times.

1. Mountfield, *African Exploration*, p. 88.
2. Aebi, *Seasons of Sand*. p.—.
3. Ibid., p.—.
4. *New York Times*, January 14/00.
5. Norris, *Saharan Myth and Saga*, p. 27.
6. Ibid., p. 54.
7. Herodotus, *Histories*, Book 3, p. 26.
8. Solymos, *Desert Life*, p. 46.
9. *Encyclopaedia Britannica* 5:613.
10. *Encyclopaedia Britannica* 16:209.

11. Several passages adapted from the *Encyclopaedia Britannica*.
12. Heseltine, *From Libyan Sands*, p. 51.

4 . T h e   W i n d s

George Lyon made only one trip into the Sahara, in 1818, reaching almost to the Tibesti Mountains before he turned back. The narrative of his travels was a sensation when he published it a few years later. His accounts of native life in the Saharan towns were meticulously observed, and his descriptions of the slave trade were influential in notching up British indignation against the practice. Owen Watkins (*With Kitchener's Army*) was a literary-minded surgeon whose journal, published in 1900, recorded colorful anecdotes of desert life. His book was particularly popular at the time for his wonderfully jingoistic account of Kitchener's thrashing of the Mahdist forces in Egypt. Kitchener was busy doing the same to the Boers at the other end of the African continent when Watkins's book came out.

1. Wren, *Beau Geste*, p. 4.
2. *Toronto Star*, 21 March 99; also Cloudsley-Thompson, *Man and the Biology*, p. 8.
3. Dale W. Griffin, in the June 2001 issue of the journal *Aerobiologia*.
4. *Limnology and Oceanography Journal*, September 2001.
5. Lyon, *Narrative of Travels*, p. 94.
6. Solymos, *Desert Life*, p. 15.
7. Nachtigal, *Sahara and Sudan*, vol. 1, p. 127.
8. Watkins, *With Kitchener's Army*, p. 263.
9. Solymos, *Desert Life*, p. 41.
10. *Encyclopaedia Britannica* 16:149.

5 .   T h e   S u r p r i s i n g   M a t t e r   o f   W a t e r

The National Geographic Society's *The Desert Realm* is a survey of all the world's great deserts and is accompanied, as might be expected, by splendid photographs. The Sahara chapter was contributed by Tor Eigeland, who is particularly good on the region around the Ahaggar and Tassili. The *Tirailleurs* (full title: *Les Tirailleurs Algeriens dans Le Sahara: Récits faits par trois survivants de la Mission Flatters et recueillis par F. Patorni, interprète militaire*) is a curiosity: accounts collected by the French military from the few survivors after the majority of a disastrous exploration expedition had been massacred by Tuareg nomads. *Chiefs and Cities of Central Africa* is another curiosity: Olive MacLeod traveled in the Lake Chad area in the early years of the twentieth century, one of a number of intrepid Englishwomen to explore Africa at the time (the most famous perhaps being Mary Kingsley, who wandered alone through the Congo, despite knowing none of the local languages). Her book included a number of rather far-fetched but colorful legends. And the third curious source is Henry Morton Stanley, the peripatetic American explorer who became famous for "discovering" Livingstone in the African interior. His views on the Africans (and therefore his books) are regarded as somewhat disreputable in these more politically correct days, but he was, nonetheless, indefatigable in collecting legends, some of which are recounted here. Mungo Park's achievements are noted in the text.

1. Study by Farouk Al-Baz of Boston University and other scientists.
2. *Encyclopaedia Britannica* (on-line version), *The Hydrosphere: Distribution and Quantity of the Earth's Waters.*
3. *Encyclopaedia Britannica* (on-line version), *Groundwater* and *The Earth Sciences: Hydrologic Sciences: Study of the Waters Close to the Land Surface: Evaluation of the Catchment Water Basin: Groundwater.*
4. Eigeland, *Desert Realm*, p. 120.
5. Ibid.
6. Porch, *Conquest of the Sahara*, p. 116.
7. Djerima, *Tirailleurs*, p. 102.
8. *National Geographic*, March 1999, pp. 30–31.
9. Heseltine, *From Libyan Sands*, p. 163.
10. Lonely Planet, *North Africa*, p. 764.
11. Clapperton, *Difficult and Dangerous Roads*, p. 230.
12. Heseltine, *From Libyan Sands*, pp. 118–119.
13. Ibid., p. 124.
14. Mountfield, *African Exploration*, p. 74.
15. MacLeod, *Chiefs and Cities*, p. 205.
16. Ibid.
17. Lyon, *Narrative of Travels*, p. 128.
18. Heseltine, *From Libyan Sands*, p. 203.
19. Barth, *Travels and Discoveries in North and Central Africa*, vol. 1, p. 267.
20. Nachtigal, *Sahara and Sudan*, vol. 1, p. 65.
21. Porch, *Conquest of the Sahara*, p. 63.
22. Cloudsley-Thompson, *Sahara Desert*, p. 311.
23. *Encyclopaedia Britannica* 13:103.
24. Stanley, *In Darkest Africa*, p. 488.
25. Frazer, *Native Races of Africa*, p. 520.
26. Stanley, *In Darkest Africa*, p. 487.
27. Watkins, *With Kitchener's Army*, p. 23.
28. Herodotus, *Histories*, Book 2, pp. 30–33.
29. Park, *Travels*, p. LXXIV.
30. Pliny, *Natural History*, vol. 5.
31. Solymos, *Desert Life*, p. 55.
32. Porch, *Conquest of the Sahara*, p. 237.
33. Barth, *Travels and Discoveries in North and Central Africa*, vol. 1, p. 341.
34. Lyon, *Narrative of Travels*, p. 93.
35. Nachtigal, *Sahara and Sudan*, vol. 1, p. 233, n.

6. The Massifs

Dozens of encyclopedias and reference books have material on the Ahaggar and the geology of the Saharan desert. We have drawn from a number of them, including the *Encyclopedia of the Orient*, edited on the Web by Tore Kjeilen. Some of the geographic and geological material is from UNESCO's very detailed description of the Tassili National Park and the Tassili region. Much of the rest of the chapter is from personal observation and conversations with other Saharan travelers. Heinrich Barth is cited in this chapter and several times in subsequent ones; his achievements have been noted in the text, and so have those of Gustav Nachtigal.

1. UNESCO.
2. Barth, *Travels and Discoveries,* vol. 1, p. 242.
3. Tounsy, *Voyage to Dartur.*
4. Africanus, *The History and Description of Africa,* vol. 3, p. 799.
5. Nachtigal, *Sahara and Sudan,* vol. 1, p. 235.
6. Sahara and Sudan.

7. The Tenacity of Life

Jean-Marc Durou's *Le Grand Rêve Saharien* is a romance, a quirky mix of reportage, elegant photography, and elegiac essays about the great dream of the greatest desert.

1. *Revue Bois et Forets des Tropiques,* No. 153, January/February 1974.
2. Heseltine, *From Libyan Sands,* p. 189.
3. UNESCO citation of Tassili as World Heritage Site.
4. Durou, *Grand Réve Saharien,* p. 72.
5. Solymos, *Desert Life,* p. 101.
6. Panafrican News Agency (Dakar), February 5, 2001.
7. Mauny, *Textes et documents,* p. 40, n. 5.
8. Lyon, *Narrative of Travels,* p. 184.
9. Watkins, *With Kitchener's Army,* p. 130.
10. Solymos, *Desert Life,* p. 116.
11. Battuta, *The Travels of Ibn Battuta,* vol. 4, p. 949.

8. First Peoples

When it first came out in 1995, James Newman's *The Peopling of Africa* made several inspired guesses, based on scanty linguistic and other clues, about the origins of populations in Africa, almost all of which have been amply borne out by later research.

1. Newman, *The Peopling of Africa,* p. 3.
2. *Encyclopaedia Britannica* 16:148.
3. *National Geographic Magazine,* March 1999, p. 25.
4. Barth, *Travels and Discoveries,* vol. 2, p. 180.
5. Fred Wendorf, Southern Methodist University, quoted in *Boston Globe,* May 19, 2001.
6. Barth, *Travels and Discoveries,* vol. 2, p. 179.
7. Nachtigal, *Sahara and Sudan,* vol. 1, p. 285.
8. Heseltine, *From Libyan Sands,* p. 165.
9. Lhote, *A la découverte des fresques de Tassili.*
10. Farouk El Baz, of Boston University, in *Boston Globe,* May 19, 2001.
11. Newman, *Peopling of Africa,* p. 55.
12. Ibid., p. 57.

13. Mufuka, *Dzimbahwe, Life and Politics in the Golden Age*, p. 13.
14. *Boston Globe*, May 19, 2001.

9. Empires of the Sun

The best sources for the ancient empires of Old Africa are Bovill's *Golden Trade* and the multivolume UNESCO-funded *General History of Africa*, especially volume 3, *Africa from the Seventh to the Eleventh Century*, edited by the Czech historian of Islam, Professor I. Hrbek. Unlike many worthy international projects, the *General History* has avoided or evaded the traps of political probity and has achieved an astonishingly rigorous academic independence. It includes data still unpublished elsewhere. The most intriguing source is Ahmed Baba's history of the Sahel. This no longer exists, but Heinrich Barth, when he was in Timbuktu, was allowed access to the great man's library, and made extensive copies.

1. Reuters report, May 2001, quoting Zahi Hawass, director of the Giza Plateau.
2. Reuters report, Bahariya, May 24, 2000, later withdrawn, said the archaeologists had discovered the tomb "booby trapped with a two foot deep layer of yellow powder that sickened the team," another score, however temporary, for the curse of the mummy. The mysterious powder turned out to be hematite, an iron ore, and it didn't sicken anyone.
3. *National Geographic*, October 1999, p. 79.
4. Barkindo Bawuro Mubi, *Sultanate of Mandara*, p. 71.
5. Pliny, *Natural History*, Book IV, p. 36.
6. Africanus, *The History and Description of Africa*, vol. 3, p. 797.
7. Adapted from Newman, *Peopling of Africa*, pp. 49–51 (our conclusions).
8. Hrbek, *General History of Africa*, vol. 3, p. 59.
9. Bovill, *Golden Trade*, p. 5.
10. Cloudsley-Thompson, *Sahara Desert*, p. 313.
11. Norris, *Saharan Myth and Saga*, p. 224.
12. *Encyclopaedia Britannica* "Ghana, History of."
13. Bovill, *Golden Trade*, p. 68.
14. David P. Johnson, Jr., africana.coma
15. Bovill, *Golden Trade*, p. 72.
16. Hrbek, *General History of Africa*, vol. 3, p. 179.
17. Bovill, *Golden Trade*, p. 73.
18. Bovill, *Golden Trade*, p. 75.
19. Frobenius, *The Voice of Africa*, p. 450.
20. From the histories of Ahmed Baba, as copied by Heinrich Barth, vol. 3, p. 662.
21. Ibid.
22. Barth, *Travels and Discoveries*, vol. 3, p. 283.
23. Ahmed Baba, quoted in ibid., vol. 3, p. 665.
24. Ibid.
25. Barth, *Travels and Discoveries*, vol. 3, p. 294.
26. Ibid.
27. Ibid., p. 292.

28. Ibid., p. 296.
29. Still, maybe they weren't always so. A hundred years ago Olive MacLeod recounted how "in the afternoon the *jeggara* [sultan] came to pay us a visit of state, the first time he had left the palace for many weeks. He is enormously tall, 6 feet and 5 inches, as is characteristic of his race; for his people are descended from giants" (*Chiefs & Cities*, p. 196).
30. Ibn Khaldum, quoted in Bovill, *Golden Trade*, p. 223.
31. Today the Fulani number maybe ten million or more, spread thinly all the way across the southern fringes of the desert and down into Cameroon near Lake Chad, into Nigeria, and in the west, into Senegal and Guinea. They are a tall, haughty, aquiline people a creamy milk chocolate in color, but there are notable curiosities about their ethnic makeup. For example, the infants of some Fulani, notably the Wodaabe in Niger, are curiously white when born, turning darker a few weeks later, which has set off endless speculation among race-conscious ethnographers over the centuries about their "true origins"—they were Berbers, perhaps, or Nubians, or Judeo-Syrians, or Jews, or Indians. They call themselves Pullo in the singular and Fulbe in the plural; even more confusingly, they are often referred to by the name of their language, Peul, or sometimes Pular, or Foulah, or Fellata. They themselves are peculiarly insistent on their own racial purity, tracing their origins to Old Ghana, descendants of the cattle herders who roamed in the southwestern fringes of the desert in the third and second millennia before the Christian era. They are probably cousins to the Sereer and Wolof of Senegal. They have close ethnic links with the Tukulor people of the far west, who had some hand in the founding of ancient Tekrur; the Tukulor were Islamicized very early by desert standards, during the days of the Almoravid ascendancy. The Fulbe and Tukulor languages are virtually identical. Beckwith and Fisher, *African Ceremonies*, p. 21, and Heseltine, *From Libyan Sands*, p. 111.
32. Barth, *Travel and Discoveries*, vol. 1, pp. 475.
33. Ibid.
34. Ibid., p. 493.
35. Clapperton, *African Exploration*, p. 1.
36. Barth, *Travels and Discoveries*, vol. 3, p. 298.
37. Adapted from *Encyclopaedia Britannica* 19:773–774.

10. Route Maps

Bovill, again, is an indispensable source for information on the trans-Saharan traffic, and so is Douglas Porch's *Conquest of the Sahara*. Among the curiosities cited here is an excerpt from the Parisian journal *Le Tour du Monde*, a sort of early French version of the *National Geographic*, only prephotography (the editors used some splendid steel engravings, however, as illustrative matter). The journal published many a memoir from colonial servants who wandered around the far-flung places of the French empire.

1. Between the *darb al arbain* and the massif of Tibesti far to the west, the oases were in ancient times too few for productive commerce, although there is a modern route along the Bahr-el-Ghazal that leads to Siwa. This one starts at the northwest corner of Lake Chad and heads northeastward up the Bahr-el-Ghazal

to the nondescript oasis of Faya. Skirting the Tibesti to the east, the route heads across bleak countryside to the Al-Kufrah oasis, which *caravanniers*, mindful of its remoteness, were wont to call The Last Outpost, a magical ring of mauve hills that captivated those few travelers who reached it. Thence it leads northward to Siwa, a junction point for several other desert highways. This bleak road has in recent years become a favorite of people smugglers, and cramped truckloads of refugees can frequently be seen lumbering across the desert, heading for the Mediterranean coast.

2. Bovill, *Golden Trade*, p. 145.
3. Battuta, *The Travels of Ibn Battuta*, vol. 4, p. 946.
4. Some details from *Encyclopaedia Britannica* 7:631.
5. Commandant V. Colomieu, "Travels in the Algerian Sahara, from Géryville to Ouargla," *Le Tour du Monde*, 1863.
6. Ibid.
7. Porch, *Conquest of the Sahara*, p. 104.
8. Al-Bakri in eleventh century.
9. Africanus, *The History and Description of Africa*, vol. 3, p. 824ff.
10. Barth, *Travels and Discoveries*, vol. 3, p. 298.
11. Ibid., vol. 1, p. 299.
12. Ibid., vol. 1, p. 319.
13. Mountfield, *African Exploration*, p. 75.

11. White Gold, Yellow Gold, Black Gold

Ibn Battuta's contributions have been acknowledged in the text. The paper from *Ghana Notes* is a meticulous examination of the modern gold-mining industry in West Africa and its techniques. Lloyd Cabot Briggs's *Tribes of the Sahara* is more than forty years old now, but still an indispensable source for those interested in the origins of the nomadic peoples of the desert.

1. Into Africa. The conversation with the salt dealer in Mopti, as well as certain details of conversations with Mohammed Ali in Timbuktu in Chapter 12, were first recorded in *Into Africa* by Marq de Villiers and Sheila Hirtle, Key Porter Books, Toronto, 1998.
2. Battuta, *The Travels of Ibn Battuta*, vol. 4, p. 946.
3. Ibid., vol. 4, p. 947.
4. Barth, *Travels and Discoveries*, vol. 1, p. 392.
5. Bovill, *Golden Trade*, pp. 68–69.
6. Quoted in ibid., p. 121.
7. Herodotus, in his *Histories*, details several versions of this practice, see vol. 4, pp. 195ff.
8. Hrbek, *General History*, vol. 3, pp. 200ff.
9. Ibid., p. 196.
10. J. J. Scarisbrick and P. L. Carter, Ghana Notes & Queries #1, 1961, Accra.
11. Philebert, *Ingenieur au Corps*, p. 54.
12. Lyon, *Narrative of Travels*, p. 249.
13. Hrbek, *General History*, vol. 3, p. 342.

14. Ibid.
15. Porch, *Conquest of the Sahara*, p. 60.
16. Briggs, *Tribes of the Sahara*, p. 185.
17. Porch, *Conquest of the Sahara*, p. 61.
18. Heseltine, *From Libyan Sands*, p. 192.

12. Adepts of the Uttermost Desert

One citation is from Angela Fisher's book *Africa Adorned*, beautiful photographs of an Africa rapidly vanishing. Fisher has worked with several collaborators and has produced a number of other splendid photographic records of Africa, including her spectacular *African Ceremonies*, produced with Carol Beckwith.

1. *Tribes of the Sahara*, p. 191.
2. The reconquest, which took several centuries, was completed in 1492 by the Catholic monarchs Isabel and Fernando when they conquered Granada in January, taking advantage of the rivalry of the last Muslim governors of Spain. The discovery of America, of course, took place that same year, in October.
3. Norris, *Shinqiti*, p. 22.
4. Abadie, *Colonie du Niger*, 174n.
5. Heseltine, *From Libyan Sands*, p. 39.
6. Briggs, *Tribes of the Sahara*, p. 172.
7. Ibid., pp. 172–73.
8. Porch, *Conquest of the Sahara*, p. 263.
9. Bovill, *Golden Trade*, p. 92; Niane, *General History*, vol 4, p. 170 and Hrbek, p. 251, vol. 3, p. 158.
10. Porch, *Conquest of the Sahara*, p. 66.
11. Ibid., p. 67.
12. Rodd, *People of the Veil*, p. 350.
13. Norris, *Saharan Myth and Saga*, p. 40.
14. The Moors of the western Sahara have a rather different view. Their women are always veiled in the presence of strangers, but not always the men. A Moor will sometimes remove his veil if asked, if, for example, an interlocutor wishes to "put a face" to the man he is talking to. A Tuareg, on the other hand, would refuse and would be offended.
15. Called Inaden by the Tuareg and Mallem by the Moors, they themselves claim to be "the sons of Our Lord David."
16. Fisher, *Africa Adorned*, p. 194.
17. At the time the conqueror Sonni Ali took over Songhai in 1464 and overran Mali, the Tuareg of what is now Mali and eastern Mauritania were governed by a queen called Bikun Kabi. Clearly, this notion of great queens is suspect, but it speaks to the Tuareg's peculiar matrilineal improvisations on classic Arab Muslim traditions.
18. From *Islamic Digest*, www.islamicdigest.org/focus2.htm
19. Porch, *Conquest of the Sahara*, p. 74.
20. Ibid., p. 65.
21. *National Geographic*, February 1905, p. 76.
22. Porch, *Conquest of the Sahara*, p. 266.

23. Barth, *Travels and Discoveries*, vol. 3, p. 278.
24. Ibid., vol. 1, p. 497.
25. Porch, *Conquest of the Sahara*, pp. 67–72.
26. Barth, *Travels and Discoveries*, vol. 3, p. 305.
27. Lyon, *Narrative of Travels*, p. 67.
28. Ibid., p. 313. James Richardson, on whose expedition Barth traveled, was fascinated by the Tuareg notions of malevolent spirits. Richardson was himself a missionizing Christian, and the intent of his travels was partly to convert the heathen; his somewhat florid notebooks are filled with details of Tuareg lore. "We were now fairly in the region of the Genii, the land of mystery and disembodied spirits, and the whole country is intersected and bounded on every side with the battlemental ranges of black, gloomy and fantastically-shaped mountains distinguishing the country of the Ghat Touaricks, where their friends and confederates, the Jenoun or Genii, deal with them in the most harmonious friendship. There exists a compact between the Genii and the Touaricks. The Touarick fathers solemnly vowed, alone of mortals, eternal friendship to the Genii, and they would never molest them in the various palaces which they, the Genii, had erected in the Touarick country, nor use any means, either through Mohamet, or the Holy Koran, to injure them or dislodge them from the black turret-shaped hills; and for this devotion on their part, the Genii promised to afford them protection at all times against their enemies, more particularly during the night, giving them vision and tact, and surprise their enemy during the dream hour or darkness. So the Touaricks are reckoned very devils at night, and usually attack their enemy at this time, and hack him to pieces with their broadswords." See Richardson, *Travels*, vol. 1, p. 436.
29. Ibid.
30. Fisher, *Africa Adorned*, p. 192.
31. Porch, *Conquest of the Sahara*, p. 79.
32. Nachtigal, *Sahara and Sudan*, vol. 1, p. 139.
33. Ibid., p. 46.
34. Clapperton, *Different and Dangerous Roads*, p. 84.
35. Porch, *Conquest of the Sahara*, pp. 31–32.
36. Robbins, *Journal*, p. 97.
37. Lyon, *Narrative of Travel*, p. 241.
38. Ibid., p. 197.
39. Nachtigal, *Sahara and Sudan*, vol. 1, p. 225.

13. Life on the Road

For details on the life of the Tuareg, you can't do better than the two-volume *The Pastoral Tuareg*, by the anthropologist team of Johannes and Ida Nicolaisen, who spent more than three years traveling with Tuareg families and studying their ways. It is beautifully illustrated and very thorough, with many oddities, such as a long and rather solemn chapter on Tuareg joking. The report of the Dakhleh Oasis project was a loan from one of the researchers there, Alan Hollett.

1. Barth, *Travels and Discoveries*, vol. 1, p. 392.
2. The stages are given in detail in ibid., p. 601.

3. Nicolaisen and Nicolaisen, *The Pastoral Tuareg,* vol. 2, p. 786.
4. *Encyclopaedia Britannica* 9:240.
5. Thornton, www.unmuseum.org
6. Lyon, *Narrative of Travels,* p. 348.
7. *The New Yorker,* 23 August 1999.
8. Heseltine, *From Libyan Sands,* p. 62.
9. Porch, *Conquest of the Sahara,* p. 53.
10. Africanus, *The History and Description of Africa,* p. 801.
11. Robbins, *A Journal,* p. 127.
12. Dakhleh Oasis Project 1996–97, p. 2.
13. Solymos, *Desert Life,* p. 294.
14. Porch, *Conquest of the Sahara,* p. 53.
15. Africanus, *The History and Description of Africa,* vol. 3, pp. 940–41.
16. Africanus, *The History and Description of Africa,* vol. 3, p. 939.
17. Porch, *Conquest of the Sahara,* p. 75.
18. Solymos, *Desert Life,* p. 273.

Epilogue: The Sahara as Home

1. Story recounted by Jack Bausmann, former senior Associated Press foreign correspondent.

e✃ℌ

Bibliography

Abadie, Maurice. *La Colonie du Niger*. Paris: Societé de Editions, 1927.

Aebi, Ernst. *Seasons of Sand: One Man's Quest to Save a Dying Sahara Village*. New York: Simon & Schuster, 1993.

Africanus, Leo (al-Hassan ibn-Mohammed al-Wezaz al-Fasi). *The History and Description of Africa and the Notable Things Therein Contained*. 3 vols. Translated by John Pory. London: Hakluyt Society, 1896.

Agatharchides of Cnidus. *On the Erythraean Sea*. London: Hakluyt Society, 1989.

Ajayi, J. F. *A Thousand Years of West African History*. Ibadan, 1965.

Allin, Michael. *Zarafa: A Giraffe's True Story, from Deep in Africa to the Heart of Paris*. New York: Walker & Co., 1998.

Bancel, Nicolas, et al. *Images d'empire: Trente Ans de Photographies Officielles sur l'Afrique Française*. Paris: Éditions de la Martinière & La Documentation française, 1997.

Barkindo Bawuro Mubi. *The Sultanate of Mandara to 1902*. Stuttgart: F. Steiner, 1977.

Barth, Heinrich. *Travels and Discoveries in North and Central Africa, 1849–55*. 3 vols. New York: Drallop Publishing Company, 1857–1859.

Battuta (Ibn Battuta). *The Travels of Ibn Battuta 1325–1354*. Translated by H. A. R. Gibb & C. F. Beckingham. 5 vols. London: Hakluyt Society, 1962.

Beckwith, Carol, and Fisher, Angela. *African Ceremonies*. 2 vols. New York: Harry N. Abrams, 1999.

Boahen, A. Adu. *Britain, the Sahara and the Western Sudan 1788–1861*. London: Oxford University Press, 1964.

Bovill, E. W. *Caravans of the Old Sahara, An Introduction to the History of the Western Sudan*. London: Oxford University Press, 1933.

————. *The Golden Trade of the Moors: West African Kingdoms in the Fourteenth Century*. Princeton: Markus Wiener Publishers, 1995.

Boyer, G. *Un Peuple de l'Ouest Soudanais, Mémoires de l'Institute Français d'Afrique Noire*. Dakar: IFAN, 1953.

Bredin, Miles. *The Pale Abyssinian*. London: Flamingo, 2001.

Brett, Michael, and Fentress, Elizabeth. *The Berbers*. Cambridge: Blackwell Publishers Inc., 1996.

Briggs, Lloyd Cabot. *Tribes of the Sahara*. Cambridge: Harvard University Press, 1960.

Caillié, Réné, *Travels through Central Africa to Timbuktoo and across the Great Desert to Morocco, Performed in the Years 1824–28*. 2 vols., London: Henry Colburn, 1830. (Reprinted in a facsimile edition, London: Darf Publishers, 1992.)

Cambridge Modern History, Vols I–XII. London: Cambridge University Press, 1912.

Christopher, Robert. *Oceans of Fire*. New York: Rand McNally & Co., 1956.

Clapperton, Hugh. *Difficult and Dangerous Roads: Hugh Clapperton's Travels in Sahara and Fezzan 1822–1825*. Edited by Jamie Bruce-Lockhart and John Wright. London: Sickle Moon Books, 2000.

Close, Angela E., ed. *Prehistory of Arid North Africa: Essays in Honor of Fred Wendorf*. Seattle: Southern Methodist University Press, n.d.

Cloudsley-Thompson, J. L. *Man and the Biology of Arid Zones*. London: Edward Arnold, 1977.

————, et al. *Sahara Desert*. London & Oxford: Pergamon Press, 1984.

Cooley, William Desborough. *The Negroland of the Arabs Examined and Explained*. London: J. Arrowsmith, 1841.

Davidson, Basil. *Africa in History*. New York: Macmillan, 1966.

Defrasne, Col. Jean. "Les Forces Armées Françaises devant la Crise de Fachoda," *Revue Historique des Armée 149* (1982): 96–107; 150 (1983): 102–113.

de Joos, Louis. *Through the Sahara to the Congo*. London: Blackie and Son Ltd., 1961.

Deng, Francis Mading. *Dinka Cosmology*. London: Ithaca Press, 1980.

Djata, Sundiata A. *The Bamana Empire by the Niger: Kingdom, Jihad and Colonization 1712–1920*. Princeton: Markus Wiener Publishers, 1997.

Djerima, Messaoud ben, et al. *Les Tirailleurs algeriens dans le Sahara: Récits faits par trois survivants de la Mission Flatters et recueillis par F. Patorni, interprète militaire*. Paris: Constantine, 1884.

Drouhin, G. *Reviews of Research on Arid Zone Hydrology*. UNESCO, 1953.

Durou, Jean-Marc. *Le Grand Rêve Saharien*. Arles: Actes Sud, 1997.

Eigeland, Tor, et al. *The Desert Realm: Lands of Majesty and Mystery*. Washington, D.C.: National Geographic Society, 1982.

Encyclopaedia Britannica and Britannica Online. 15th edition (print version), 1998; and on-line version, 2001.

El-Tounsy, Muhammad Ibn Omar. *Voyage to Darfur*. Paris: Daprat, 1851.

Evans-Pritchard, E. E. *The Nuer*. Oxford: Oxford University Press, 1940.

Fisher, Allan G. B., and Fisher, Humphrey J. *Slavery and Muslim Society in Africa*. New York: Doubleday and Co., 1970.

Fisher, Angela. *Africa Adorned*. New York: Harry N. Abrams, 1994.

Fox, Robin Lane. *Alexander the Great*. London: Penguin Books, 1973.

Frazer, J. G. *Native Races of Africa & Madagascar*. London: Percy Lund Humphreys & Co., 1938.

Frobenius, Leo. *The Voice of Africa*. New York: Benjamin Blom, 1968.

Gardi, René. *Sahara: Monograph about a Great Desert*. Berne: Kümmerly and Frey, 1970.

Gladstone, Penelope. *Travels of Alexine: Alexine Tinné, 1835–1869*. London: John Murray 1970.

Graves, Robert. "Introduction." *New Larousse Encyclopedia of Mythology*. London: Paul Hamlyn, 1959.

Guerzoni, Stefano, and Chester, R., eds., *The Impact of African Dust across the Mediterranean*. Environmental Science and Technology Library, V. 11, 1997.

Hajar of Ascalon (Ibn Hajar al-Asqal). *The Concealed Pearls*. Beirut: Alam al-Kutub, 1987.

Halliburton, Warren J., *Nomads of the Sahara*, edited by Kathilyn Solomon Probosz. New York: Maxwell Macmillan, 1992.

Harpur, James, and Westwood, Jennifer. *The Atlas of Legendary Places*. New York: Weidenfeld & Nicolson, 1989.

Herodotus. *Histories books 1–6*. Cambridge: Harvard University Press, 1921.

Herold, J. Christopher, et al. *The Age of Napoleon*. New York: American Heritage Publishing Co., 1963.

Heseltine, Nigel. *From Libyan Sands to Chad*. London: Museum Press Ltd., 1995.

Hourani, Albert. *A History of the Arab Peoples*. Cambridge: Belknap Press, 1991.

Hrbek, I., ed. *General History of Africa Vol. 3: Africa from the Seventh to the Eleventh Century*. Berkeley: University of California Press, and Paris: UNESCO, 1992.

Huntingford, G. W. B. trans. *The Periplus of the Erythraean Sea*. London: Hakluyt Society, 1980.

Huré, Gen. R., et al. *Armée Française en Afrique 1830–1962, l'*. Paris: Charles-Lavauzelle, 1977.

Johnson, Paul. *The Birth of the Modern World Society 1815–1830*. London: Phoenix, 1992.

Julien, Charles André. *Histoire de l'Afrique du Nord de la conquête arabe à 1830*. Paris, 1956.

Kapuscinski, Ryszard. *The Shadow of the Sun*. New York: Knopf, 2001.

Lhote, Henri. *Peintures Prehistoriques du Sahara*. Paris: Palais du Louvre, 1957.

———. *Les Touaregs du Hoggar*. Paris: A. Colin, 1984.

———. *A la découverte des fresques du Tassili*. Paris: Arctaud, 1973.

Lonely Planet. *Egypt, North Africa & West Africa editions*. Hawthorn, Australia: Lonely Planet Publications, 1995.

Lyon, Captain G. F. *A Narrative of Travels in Northern Africa in the Years 1818–1820*. Facsimile of 1821 edition, London: Darf Publishers, 1985.

MacLeod, Olive. *Chiefs and Cities of Central Africa*. London: William Blackwood and Sons, 1912.

Marozzi, Justin. *South from Barbary: Along the Slave Routes of the Libyan Sahara*. London: HarperCollins, 2001.

Maugham, Robin. *Journey to Siwa*. London: Chapman and Hall, 1950.

———. *The Slaves of Timbuktu*. London: Longmans, Green and Co., 1961.

Mauny, R., et al. *Textes et Documents Relatifs a l'histoire de l'Afrique: Extraits des Voyages d'Ibn Battuta*. Dakar: Université de Dakar, Faculté des Lettres et Sciences Humaines, 1966.

Moore, Randy, and Vodopich, Darrell S. *The Living Desert*. Aldershot: Enslow Publishers Inc., 1991.

Moorhouse, Geoffrey. *The Fearful Void*. New York: J. B. Lippincott Co., 1974.

Mountfield, David. *A History of African Exploration*. London: Hamlyn, 1976.

Mufuka, Ken, et al. *Dzimbahwe, Life and Politics in the Golden Age*. Harare Publishing House.

Nachtigal, Gustav. *Sahara and Sudan*. 3 vols. Translated by Allan G. B. Fisher and Humphrey J. Fisher. Vol. 1, *Fezzan and Tibesti*, published by Barnes & Noble, New York, 1974; Vol. 2, *Kawar, Bornu, Kanem, Borku, Ennedi*, published by C. Hurst and Co., London, 1980; Vol. 3, *The Chad Basin and Bagirmi*, published by C. Hurst & Co., London, and Humanities Press Intl. Inc., Atlantic Highlands, N.J., 1987.

Newman, James L. *The Peopling of Africa*. New Haven: Yale University Press, 1995.

Niane, D. T., ed. *General History of Africa*, vol. 4, *Africa from the Twelfth to the Sixteenth Century*, Paris: UNESCO, 1984.

Nicolaisen, Johannes, and Nicolaisen, Ida. *The Pastoral Tuareg*. 2 vols. London: Thames & Hudson, 1997.

Norris, H. T. *Saharan Myth and Saga*. London: Oxford University Press, 1972.

————. *Folk Literature and Song*. London: Oxford University Press, 1968.

Norwich, John Julius. *Sahara*. London: Longmans, 1968.

O'Connor, David. *Ancient Nubia, Egypt's Rival in Africa*. Philadelphia: The University Museum of Archaeology and Anthropology, University of Pennsylvania, 1993.

Oliver, Caroline. *Western Women in Colonial Africa*. Westport, Connecticut: Greenwood Press, 1982.

Oliver, Roland, ed. *The Dawn of African History*. Oxford: Oxford University Press, 1961.

Pakenham, Thomas. *The Scramble for Africa*. New York: Random House, 1991.

Park, Mungo. *Travels in the Interior Districts of Africa Performed under the Direction and Patronage of the African Association in the Years 1795, 1796, and 1797*. Printed by W. Bulmer and Co., London, for the author, 1799.

Petrides, George A. *A Field Guide to Trees and Shrubs*. Boston: Houghton Mifflin Co., Peterson Field Guide Series. 1986.

Philebert, le General, and Rolland, Georges. *Ingénieur au Corps des Mines, La France en Afrique et le Transsaharien*. Paris: Librairie Algérienne et Coloniale, 1890.

Pliny. *The History of the World Commonly Called the Natural History*. Translated by Philemon Holland. London: Adam Philip, 1603.

Porch, Douglas. *The Conquest of the Sahara*. New York: Fromm International, 1986.

Richardson, James. *Travels in the Great Desert of Sahara in the Years of 1845 & 1846; Containing a Narrative of Personal Adventures during a Tour of Nine Months through the Desert amongst the Touaricks and Other Tribes of Saharan People; Including a Description of the Cases and Cities Of Ghat, Ghadames and Mourzuk*. (2 vols.) London: F. Cass, 1970.

Robbins, Archibald. *A Journal Comprising an Account of the Loss of the Brig Commerce, of Hartford, (Con.) James Riley, Master, Upon the Western Coast of Africa, August 28th, 1815; Also of the Slavery and Sufferings of the Author and the Rest of the Crew, upon the Desert of Zahara in the Years 1815, 1816, 1817; With Accounts of the Manners, Customs, and Habits of the Wandering Arabs; Also, A Brief Historical and Geographical View of the Continent of Africa*. Hartford, Conn.: Silas Andrus, 1818.

Roberts, Paul William. *River in the Desert: Modern Travels in Ancient Egypt*. New York: Random House, 1993.

Rodd, Francis Rennell. *People of the Veil*. London: Macmillan & Co., 1926.

Rouch, Jean. *Contribution a l'Histoire des Songhay, part 2, Mémoires de l'Institute Français d'Afrique Noire*. Dakar: IFAN, 1953.

Saint-Exupéry, Antoine de. *The Little Prince*. New York: Harvest/Harcourt Brace & Co, 1943/1971.

————. *Wind, Sand and Stars*. London: Heinemann, 1939.

Schon, James Frederick. *Journals of the Rev. James Frederick Schon and Mr. Samuel Crowt*. Edited by Robert Rotberg. London: Frank Cass and Co., 1970.

Solymos, B. (B. E. Falkonberg). *Desert Life: Recollections of an Expedition in the Soudan*. London: W. H. Allen & Co., 1880.

Speke, John Hanning. *Journal of the Discovery of the Source of the Nile*. New York: Dover, 1996 (facsimile of 1863 edition).

Spitz, Lt. Joseph. *Histoire du 2e Régiment de Zouaves*. 2 tomes. Angers, Lachèse et Cie, 1898.

Stanley, Henry M. *In Darkest Africa*. New York: Scribner's, 1890.

Swift, Jeremy, and Boulat, Pierre. *The Sahara*. Amsterdam: Time-Life International, 1975.

Tillet, Thierry, ed. *Sahara: Paléomilieux et Peuplement Préhistorique au pléistocène supérieur*. Paris: L'Harmattan, 1997.

Tremearne, A. J. N. *The Niger and the West Sudan: The West African's Note Book*. London: Hodder & Stoughton and Arthur H. Wheeler & Co., 1900.

Tristram, H. B. *The Great Sahara, Wanderings South of the Atlas Mountains*. London: John Murray, 1860.

Tounsy, Omar el-. *Voyage to Darfur*. Paris: Daprat, 1851.

Toussaint-Samat, Maguelonne. *History of Food*. Maiden, Mass.: Blackwell Publishers Inc., 1994.

Vieuchange, Michel. *Smara, The Forbidden City*. New York: Ecco Press, 1987.

Watkins, Owen S. *With Kitchener's Army*. London: S. W. Partridge & Co., 1900.

Weiss, Col. Pierre. *Le Secret du Sud*. Paris: Editions Berger-Levrault, 1937.

Willcox, A. R. *The Rock Art of Africa*. London: Croom Helm, 1984.

Wolff, H., and Blachére, A. *Les Régiments de Dromadaires: Lt Col Flatters et ses Héroïques Compagnons*. Paris: Librairie Algérienne et Coloniale, 1884.

Wren, Percival Christopher. *Beau Geste*. Washington, D.C.: Gateway Editions, Regnery Publishing Inc., 1998.

Ziegler, Christiane. *The Louvre's Egyptian Antiquities*. Paris: Editions Scala/Réunion des Musées Nationaux, 1997.

Research Papers

Dakhleh Oasis Project: An Archaeological Study. Field Expedition Reports: 1992–93; 1993–94; 1996–97; and 1998–99. Anthony J. Mills, dir., Padstow, Cornwall, UK

THE TEMPLE AT DEIR EL-HAGGAR: The Conservation Project
A. J. Mills and A. K. Zielinski
Padstow, Cornwall, UK

∞

Index

Europe/Europeans *(continued)*
  merchants of, 13
  Muslim invasion of, 15
  Renaissance, 21, 192, 218
  and/on Tuareg, 253, 254
  and water supply, 115–16
  water table, 96

Fachi, 268, 269, 288
Fada, 100, 140, 165
Farafra, 35, 173, 221
Fatimids, 175, 208
Fez, 186, 187, 188, 203
  trade routes, 205, 207, 215
Fezzan, 31, 32, 64, 80, 107, 136, 137,
    176, 192, 243
  caravans crossing, 193
  Garamantes in, 175
  groundwater, 96
  settled Arabs of, 263
  slave trade, 234
  trade, 203
  trade routes, 204, 205, 266
Flatters, Paul-Xavier, 99, 133
Flatters expedition, 209–10, 252
Foucauld, Charles-Eugéne, 128
France/French, 15, 17, 78, 127, 162,
    211, 251
  in Algeria, 14, 115
  and camels, 284
  colonial era, 13, 16, 18
  conquest of Sahara, 241
  in Ennedi, 141
  fighting Tuareg, 252–53
  hold on Ouargla, 209
  protectorates, 16
  in Timbuktu, 213
  and Tubu, 245
  in Tunisia, 16
Franco-Spanish occupation of Morocco,
    14
Fulani (tribe), 192, 200–201, 240
  sacked Timbuktu, 213
  theocracies, 194–200
  written language, 218
Funj kingdom, 17

Gao, 29, 176, 187, 188, 189, 203
  caravans to, 266
  dunes, 60, 64
  in gold trade, 231
  markets, 223, 224
  Niger River in, 112, 113
  road to, 222
  sacked, 191
  trade routes, 204–5, 206, 210,
    214–17, 218, 220
Gaou (village), 192, 193
Garama, 176, 177–78
Garamantes, 168, 175–78, 243, 244
Garamantians, 205
Gazabi, 32
Germa, 177, 178, 190
Gezira, 17
Ghabbour, S. I., 39
Ghadamès, 31, 115, 176, 205
  merchants from, 213
  slave trade, 232
  trade routes, 207
Ghana
  modern, 40, 113, 182, 187, 229
  see also Old Ghana
Ghardaia, 146, 208, 209, 240
al-Gharnati, Abu l'Hasan Ali Ibn Said,
    19
Ghat, 23, 31, 107, 133, 144–45, 163,
    205
Ghib'an, 72–75
Giza, pyramids of, 171
Gobir, 195, 196, 200
Gogdem, 30–31
Granada, 15, 17, 20
Grand Dune, 65
Grand Erg Occidental, 29
Grand Erg Oriental, 29
Great Desert, 19, 175
Great Emptiness, 203, 214
Great Ergs of Algeria, 30, 65, 130
Great Lakes, 40
Great Man-Made River, 98
Great Rift, 128
Great Western Erg, 45
Greco-Roman period, 173, 174

Tuareg, 2, 3–4, 11, 16, 29, 30, 42, 43,
63–64, 99, 100, 107, 128, 139,
143, 164, 188, 200, 246–63, 290,
291–92
adapting to Islam, 256
and animals, 148, 149–50
bands of, 217
and camels, 283, 284
caravan(s), 268, 269
Chaambu enemies of, 241
consider themselves superior, 240
controlling, 189
copper mine, 229
"cousins" of Tubu, 243, 244
day of, 271–72
on desert travel, 72
destroyed Sijilmasa, 208
drum groups, 247–48
eating habits, 262–63
family salt consortiums, 270
ferocious, unruly, 22, 133, 162, 216,
247, 252–55
finding water, 116–17
goats and gardens, 135, 256
herdsmen, 166, 201
individualism, 194
intermarriage, 240
Islam, 181, 194–95
legends, 142
and massifs, 124–25, 131, 134
and Moors, 242
navigation through desert, 276–81
and oases, 287
in Ouargla, 209
overran Timbuktu, 190
photographs, 219
preying on caravans, 114
raiding, 136, 192, 284
rebellions, 51, 59, 155, 248
ritualized greetings, 121–22
"rock paintings," 165
rock salt trade, 224
rulers in Ahaggar, 218
salt use, 227
and sand, 67
and scorpions, 151, 152
in Senussi revolt, 15

slaves, 235–37
stories about addax, 153–54
subdivisions and definitions of
desert-ness, 62–63
tagelmousts, 221, 248–49, 260
"their necessaries," 265
Tifinagh script, 169
and Timbuktu, 213, 214
war with Fulani, 198
and winds, 77, 81
women, 70, 249, 256, 257, 258–61
Tuat, 213, 222, 289
Tubu (Toubou, Tibou, *Tubu Reshade*,
"the People of the Rock," the
Teda), 3–4, 16, 81, 151, 163, 176,
238–39, 240, 243–46, 263, 278
in Ennedi, 140
family salt consortiums, 270
individualism, 194
intermarriage, 240
and Islam, 181, 256
language, 162
raids by, 103, 136
ritualized greetings, 121
in Tibesti, 136–39, 140
Tukulor tribe, 185, 199, 239
Tummo Mountains, 205, 263
Tunis, 187, 193, 205, 215
Tunisia, 11, 12, 15–16, 28, 208
desertification, 51
earthworms, 40
French occupied, 14
independence, 18
limestones, 41
natural gas, 41
oases, 159
oil in, 41, 289
waterfall in, 124
Turkey/Turks, 13, 177, 209, 245

Uigh-es-Serir, 43, 54
Ukrainian steppe, 94
Umayyads, 207, 208
UNESCO, 131, 132, 155, 214
United Nations, 50
United States
water table, 96